Requirements for Certification

Requirements for Certification

of Teachers, Counselors, Librarians, Administrators

for Elementary and Secondary Schools

Seventy-ninth Edition, 2014–2015

Edited by
Elizabeth A. Kaye

The University of Chicago Press
Chicago and London

The University of Chicago Press, Chicago 60637
© 2014 by The University of Chicago
All Rights Reserved
Seventy-ninth edition 2014
Published annually since 1935
International Standard Book Number-13: 978-0-226-13945-6 (cloth)
International Standard Book Number-13: 978-0-226-13959-3 (e-book)
DOI: 10.7208/Chicago/9780226139593.001.0001
International Standard Series Number: 1047-7071
Library of Congress Catalog Card Number: A43-1905

Contents

Introduction to the Seventy-ninth Edition
2014–2015

Why do we need a book of requirements for educator certification in our electronic age? This volume provides a concise, accessible summary of relevant information that is simply not consistently available on the websites of individual state certification offices. The goal of our compilation is to provide a "balcony view" of state certification regulations that enables readers to access and compare information either about different positions within a single state or about a single position in one or more states.

Interestingly, states present the material on their certification websites in a variety of formats and levels of accessibility. While some are carefully designed to be user-friendly and intuitively clear to navigate, others are the electronic version of a procedures manual for staff. With an array of online application forms, automated certification systems, and literally hundreds of pages of state legislative regulations reproduced verbatim, it can be a significant challenge to unearth a clear, consistent overview of the field one is exploring, along with suggestions on where to dive in more deeply when full detail is required. We aim to provide exactly that service.

What we present in *Requirements for Certification* is that much-needed survey of current information on certification requirements for all fifty states and the District of Columbia. Updated annually and presented in a clear, concise outline format, the book provides a fresh overview of certification information for teachers, counselors, librarians, and administrators, as well as those who aspire to join their ranks. For this seventy-ninth edition, forty-four states have changed their requirements since last year, in degrees ranging from minor to extensive. As this volume moves into its seventy-ninth year of continuous publication, it provides an essential service to both the public and to the professionals who consult it.

Requirements for Certification had its inception in the Board of Vocational Guidance and Placement (now Career and Placement Services) at the University of Chicago. The original study was made by Robert C. Woellner, professor of education and head of the Board, and M. Aurilla Wood, placement counselor. The digest continued under the direction of Elizabeth H. Woellner until her retirement in 1983. Produced only in mimeograph form its first year, the digest was published and made available for sale by the University of Chicago Press in 1935 and has appeared in annual editions since that time.

We continue to express our profound gratitude to the state certification officers for their interest and cooperation under extreme duress. This book simply could not be as current, as accurate, and as helpful as it is without their collaboration. We trust that these efforts, by helping to make the requirements for educator certification as widely available as possible throughout the United States and its possessions and territories, will bear fruit both for the certification professionals and for those who seek access to their knowledge.

Alabama

Stages and Titles of Teaching Certificates

I. Class B Professional Educator Certificate (valid 5 years)
   A. Issued on basis of a bachelor's degree and completion of all other requirements for issuance
II. Class A Professional Educator Certificate (valid 5 years)
   A. Issued on basis of a master's degree and completion of all other requirements for issuance
III. Class AA Professional Educator Certificate (valid 5 years)
   A. Issued on basis of completion of an approved, planned sixth-year program of at least 30 semester hours of postmaster's graduate credit, which may result in an education specialist degree, and completion of all other requirements for issuance
IV. Class A Professional Leadership Certificate (valid 5 years)
   A. Issued on basis of a master's degree and completion of all other requirements for issuance
V. Class AA Professional Leadership Certificate (valid 5 years)
   A. Issued on basis of completion of an approved, planned sixth-year program of at least 30 semester hours of postmaster's graduate credit, which may result in an education specialist degree, and all other requirements for issuance

Requirements for Teaching Certificates

I. Teaching certificates available include:
   A. Early childhood education (P–3)
   B. Early childhood special education (P–3)
   C. Elementary education (K–6)
   D. Collaborative special education teacher (K–6)
   E. Middle level (4–8)
   F. High school (6–12)
   G. Collaborative special education teacher (6–12)
   H. Elementary-secondary (P–12)
   I. Special education (P–12 for hearing impairment, speech or language impairment, visual impairment, or gifted. Speech or language impairment is available only for the Class A and Class AA Professional Educator Certificates.)
II. Certificates are endorsed in specific teaching field(s).
III. The Teacher Certification Chapter of the Alabama Administrative Code adopted December 9, 2010, contains all current information applicable to earning a certificate in Alabama and is accessible via the following links: www.alsde.edu/CertificationsForms
   or

If the link does not work, go to www.alsde.edu and click on Offices: Office of Teaching and Leading: Teacher Certification: Documents: Alabama Administrative Code.

IV.   Specific Teaching Certificates and Their Requirements

   A.   Class B Professional Educator Certificate

     1.   Earn a bachelor's degree from a regionally accredited senior institution, *and*

     2.   Meet academic requirements in teaching field in which certification is sought through 1 of the following options:

       a.   Alabama State Board of Education–approved program, *or*

       b.   Valid professional educator certificate issued by another state, U.S. Territory, the District of Columbia, or the Department of Defense Education Activity (DoDEA) at the bachelor's degree level, *or*

       c.   Educator preparation program in another country, *or*

       d.   Valid certification by the National Board for Professional Teaching Standards (NBPTS) in a teaching field in which Alabama offers comparable certification; see page 212 of document accessible via link at III, directly above

   B.   Class A Professional Educator Certificate

     1.   Earn a master's degree from a regionally accredited senior institution, *and*

     2.   Meet academic requirements in teaching field for which certification is sought through 1 of the following options:

       a.   Alabama State Board of Education–approved program, *or*

       b.   Valid professional educator certificate issued by another state, U.S. Territory, the District of Columbia, or DoDEA at the master's degree level, *or*

       c.   Educator preparation program in another country, *or*

       d.   Valid NBPTS certification in a teaching field in which Alabama offers comparable certification; see page 212 of document accessible via link at III, directly above *or*

       e.   Valid speech-language pathology license issued by any state's board of examiners in speech pathology and audiology; see page 211 of document accessible via link at III directly above.

   C.   Class A Professional Educator Certificate: Alternative Class A Approved Program

     1.   Meet Alabama State Board of Education–approved program requirements specified on pages 374–379 of the Teacher Education Chapter of the Alabama Administrative Code at this link http://www.alsde.edu/home/Sections/SubsectionDocuments.aspx?SectionID=66&Subsection=47

If the link does not work, go to www.alsde.edu and click on Offices: Office of Teaching and Leading: Teacher Education: Documents: Alabama Administrative Code-Current Teacher Education Chapter

D. Class AA Professional Educator Certificate
   1. Complete an approved, planned sixth-year program of at least 30 semester hours of postmaster's graduate credit with a regionally accredited senior institution *and*
   2. Meet academic requirements in teaching field for which certification is sought through one of the following options:
      a. Alabama State Board of Education–approved program, *or*
      b. Valid professional educator certificate issued by another state, U.S. Territory, the District of Columbia, or DoDEA at the sixth-year level, *or*
      c. Educator preparation program in another country, *or*
      d. Valid NBPTS certification in a teaching field in which Alabama offers comparable certification; see page 212 of document accessible via link at III, directly above

Administrative/Supervisory Certificates and Their Requirements

I. Class A Professional Leadership Certificate
   A. Earn a master's degree from a regionally accredited senior institution, *and*
   B. Meet requirements in administration through 1 of the following options:
      1. Alabama State Board of Education–approved program in Instructional Leadership (note: prior to admission to the program, the applicant must have had at least 3 full years of full-time, acceptable professional educational experience in a P–12 setting, to include at least one full year of full-time P–12 teaching experience) (Instructional Leadership certification allows one to serve as an administrator and/or supervisor), *or*
      2. Valid professional educator certificate in administration issued by another state, U.S. Territory, the District of Columbia, or DoDEA at the master's degree level and 3 full years of full-time administrative experience in a P–12 school system(s).
   C. Meet requirements in supervision through a valid professional educator certificate in supervision issued by another state, U.S. Territory, the District of Columbia, or Department of Defense Education Activity (DoDEA) at the master's degree level and 3 full years of full-time supervisory experience in a P–12 school system(s).
II. Class AA Professional Leadership Certificate
   A. Complete an approved, planned sixth-year program of at least 30 semester hours of postmaster's graduate credit with a regionally accredited senior institution,

and

B. Meet requirements in administration through 1 of the following options:
1. Alabama State Board of Education–approved program in Instructional Leadership (Instructional Leadership certification allows one to serve as an administrator and/or supervisor),
    or
2. Valid professional educator certificate in administration issued by another state, U.S. Territory, the District of Columbia, or DoDEA at the sixth-year level and 3 full years of full-time administrative experience in a P–12 school system(s).

C. Meet requirements in supervision through a valid professional educator certificate in supervision issued by another state, U.S. Territory, the District of Columbia, or DoDEA at the sixth year level and 3 full years of full-time supervisory experience in a P–2 school system(s).

Support Services Certificates and Their Requirements

I. Class A Certificate for Library-Media, School Counselor, School Psychometrist, or Sport Manager
A. Earn a master's degree from a regionally accredited senior institution,
    and
B. Meet academic requirements in support area in which certification is sought through 1 of the following options:
1. Alabama State Board of Education–approved program,
    or
2. Valid professional educator certificate issued by another state, U.S. Territory, the District of Columbia, or DoDEA at the master's degree level,
    or
3. Educator preparation program in another country,
    or
4. Valid certification by the NBPTS in the support area
    a. See page 212 of document accessible via link at Requirements for Teaching Certificates, III, above
        or
5. For school counseling, verification of compliance with the Council for Accreditation of Counseling and Related Education Programs (CACREP) approach.
    a. See page 214 of document accessible via link at Requirements for Teaching Certificates, III, above,
        and

C. Two full years of full-time educational experience in a P–12 school system. Applicants through the CACREP approach do not have to meet this requirement.

II. Class AA Certificate for Library-Media or School Counselor
A. Complete an approved, planned sixth-year level program of at least 30 semester hours of postmaster's graduate credit from a regionally accredited senior institution,
    and

B. Meet academic requirements in support area in which certification is sought through 1 of the following options:
   1. Alabama State Board of Education–approved program,
      or
   2. Valid professional educator certificate issued by another state, U.S. Territory, the District of Columbia, or DoDEA at the sixth-year level,
      or
   3. Educator preparation program in another country,
      or
   4. Valid certification by the NBPTS in the support area
      a. See page 212 of document accessible via link at Requirements for Teaching Certificates, III, above
         and
C. Two full years of full-time educational experience in a P–12 school system.

III. Class AA Certificate for School Psychologist
   A. Complete an approved, planned sixth-year level program of at least 30 semester hours of postmaster's graduate credit from a regionally accredited senior institution,
      and
   B. Meet academic requirements in school psychology through 1 of the following options:
      1. Alabama State Board of Education–approved program,
         or
      2. Valid school psychologist professional educator certificate issued by another state, U.S. Territory, the District of Columbia, or DoDEA at the sixth-year level,
         or
      3. Educator preparation program in another country,
         or
      4. Verification of compliance with the Nationally Certified School Psychologist (NCSP) approach.
         a. See page 215 of document accessible via link at Requirements for Teaching Certificates, III, above,
            and
   C. Two full years of full-time educational experience in a P–12 school system. Applicants through the NCSP approach do not have to meet this requirement.

Alabama Educator Certification Testing Program

I. Applicants for an Alabama professional educator certificate, professional leadership certificate, or alternative approach certificate must meet the requirements of the Alabama Educator Certification Testing Program (AECTP) as a precondition for certification.
   A. AECTP consists of basic skills assessments (measuring fundamental skills in applied mathematics, reading for information, and writing) and subject area assessments.
      1. Basic skills assessments are administered as part of the ACT WorkKeys System.
      2. Subject area assessments consist of Alabama State Board of Education-

approved tests from the Praxis II: Subject Assessment series, administered by the Educational Testing Service (ETS).

Out-of-State Reciprocity

I. Professional educator certification in Alabama is not offered reciprocally on the basis of educator preparation programs completed outside of Alabama.

II. Alabama professional educator certification is only considered reciprocally on the basis of holding a valid professional educator certificate issued by another state, a U.S. Territory, the District of Columbia, or the Department of Defense Education Activity (DoDEA) and if Alabama offers comparable certification.

Alaska

Initial Teacher Certificates

I. Initial/Two-Year Teacher Certificate (valid 2 years; may be reissued once with 1-year extension)
    A. Requirements—Candidate:
        1. Has passing scores on an approved basic competency exam (BCE); for details, consult http://www.eed.state.ak.us/TeacherCertification/praxis.html;
        2. Has completed an approved teacher-preparation program as verified by an Institutional Recommendation (IR) and the corresponding transcripts, or a State Recommendation (SR);
            and
        3. Has never held an Initial or Provisional Alaska teacher certificate, and is not eligible for reinstatement of a Professional or Master teacher certificate.
        4. For the 1-year extension, official transcripts—showing the completion of 3 semester hours of approved Alaska studies (AK) course work and the completion of 3 semester hours of approved Alaska (MC) multicultural course work—must be received by the Teacher Certification office prior to the expiration date of the Initial certificate.
            a. An applicant who has satisfied the Alaska studies and Alaska multicultural course work requirements at the time of application will be issued an Initial/Three-Year teacher certificate.
II. Initial/Out-of-State Teacher Certificate (valid 1 year; may be reissued twice for a total of 2 one-year extensions)
    A. Requirements—Candidate:
        1. Has never held an Alaska teacher certificate;
            and
        2. Holds a current, valid out-of-state teacher certificate at the time the applicant's contract for instructional services begins in an Alaska public school district.
            a. Out-of-country certificates will not be accepted.
        3. For the first 1-year extension, the following items must be received by the Teacher Certification office prior to the expiration of the Initial/Out-of-State certificate:
            a. Official passing scores on an approved basic competency exam (see Initial Teacher Certificates I, A, 1, above);
                and
            b. Institutional Recommendation, State Recommendation, or Program Enrollment Form.
        4. For the second 1-year extension, official transcripts must be received by the Teacher Certification office prior to the expiration date of the Initial/Out-

of-State certificate showing the completion of 3 semester hours of approved Alaska studies course work and the completion of 3 semester hours of approved Alaska multicultural course work.

     5. Endorsements placed on an Initial/Out-of-State teacher certificate will reflect the endorsements on the applicant's out-of-state certificate.

         a. If an applicant holds more than one valid out-of-state certificate, the applicant must choose which out-of-state certificate to submit with the Initial application.

III. Initial/Program Enrollment Teacher Certificate (valid 1 year; may be reissued twice for a total of 2 one-year extensions)

    A. Requirements—Candidate:

      1. Has never held an Alaska teacher certificate;

      2. Has passing scores on an approved basic competency exam (see Initial Teacher Certificates I, A, 1, above);
and

      3. Is currently enrolled in an approved teacher preparation program as verified by a Proof of Program Enrollment form and official transcripts.

         a. Program must be completed within 2 years of the issuance of the Initial certificate.

         b. Program enrollment cannot be used for individuals enrolled in special education programs; rather, they must complete their program prior to applying for the Initial certificate.

      4. For the first 1-year extension, the certificate holder must submit the following items to the Teacher Certification office prior to expiration date of the Initial/Program Enrollment certificate:

         a. Updated official transcripts;
and

         b. Updated Proof of Program Enrollment form or an Institutional Recommendation or a State Recommendation.

      5. For the second one-year extension, the certificate holder must submit all of the following items to the Teacher Certification office prior to expiration of the Initial certificate:

         a. Official transcripts showing 3 semester hours of approved Alaska studies course work; 3 semester hours of approved Alaska multicultural course work; and completion of a state-approved teacher preparation program;
and

         b. Institutional Recommendation or State Recommendation.

      6. Endorsements placed on an Initial/Program Enrollment teacher certificate will reflect the teacher-preparation program described on the Proof of Program Enrollment form.

IV. Initial/Reemployment Teacher Certificate (valid 1 year; nonrenewable)

    A. Requirements—Candidate:

      1. Has never held a Reemployment teacher certificate in Alaska;

and

2. Has held an Alaska teacher certificate that was valid for at least 2 years.
3. The most recent Alaska teacher certificate held by candidate must have expired more than 1 year prior to the date of application.
4. Endorsements placed on an Initial/Reemployment certificate will reflect the endorsements on the applicant's previous Alaska teacher certificate.
   a. During the life of the Reemployment certificate, no endorsements may be added or removed.
5. An applicant who has held a Reemployment teacher certificate is no longer eligible for another Initial certificate, but must apply for a Professional teacher certificate to continue teaching.

B. Additional Requirements
1. Special Education—applicants who wish to teach special education to children with disabilities must, in addition to meeting other requirements for teacher certification, secure an endorsement based upon completion of an approved teacher-training program in special education.
   a. Preschool Special Education—those who wish to teach preschool children with special needs and who are not eligible for an endorsement in preschool special education must have completed at least 6 semester hours in early childhood special education in addition to holding a teaching certificate with a special education endorsement. This does not constitute an endorsement in Early Childhood Special Education.
2. Gifted—applicants who wish to teach gifted children must, in addition to meeting requirements for teacher certification, have completed at least 6 semester hours in gifted education.
   a. This does not constitute an endorsement.
3. Vocational Education—applicants who wish to teach vocational trades must have an endorsement in vocational education or a Type M Limited Certificate.

V. Second Initial Teacher Certificate (valid 3 years: nonrenewable)
A. Requirements—Candidate:
1. Has held an Initial or Provisional teacher certificate;
2. Has passing scores on an approved basic competency exam (see Initial Teacher Certificates I, A, 1, above);
3. Has completed a teacher-preparation program as verified by an Institutional Recommendation and transcripts, or by a State Recommendation;
4. Presents official transcripts showing 3 semester hours of approved Alaska studies course work; 3 semester hours of approved Alaska multicultural course work; and 6 semester hours of course work completed in the 5 years prior to application (recency credit);
   and
5. Has never held a Reemployment teacher certificate in Alaska.
6. If the applicant has held a Professional or regular Type A teacher certificate, the certificate must have expired more than 1 year prior to the date of application.

Professional and Master Teacher Certificates

I. Professional Teacher Certificate (valid 5 years; renewable)
    A. Requirements—Candidate:
        1. Has 2 years of teaching experience while holding a valid teacher certificate (see I, A, 8, immediately below)
            or
            Holds a current Initial teacher certificate that was valid on September 16, 2011;
        2. Has passing scores on an approved basic competency exam (see Initial Teacher Certificates I, A, 1, above);
        3. Has passing scores on a content area exam, e.g., Praxis II (see I, A, 8, immediately below);
        4. Has completed a teacher-preparation program as verified by an Institutional recommendation and transcripts, or by a state recommendation;
        5. Presents official transcripts showing 3 semester hours of approved Alaska studies course work; 3 semester hours of approved Alaska multicultural course work; and 6 semester hours of course work completed in the 5 years prior to application (recency credit);
        6. Presents verification of current employment in an Alaska public school district in a position requiring a certificate or a fingerprint card submitted with application;
            and
        7. Completes application and fees; fees are nonrefundable.
        8. If all of the requirements for a Professional certificate, with the exception of the 2 years of teaching experience and the content area exam have been met, the applicant may apply for a Second Initial certificate.
    B. Renewal requirements: Prior to the expiration date of the certificate, applicant must:
        1. Earn 6 semester hours of renewal credit taken during the life of the certificate being renewed, of which, a minimum of 3 semester hours must be upper-division or graduate credit;
        2. Present verification of current employment in an Alaska public school district in a position requiring a certificate;
            a. If an applicant is not employed in this capacity at the time of renewal, a fingerprint card will be required.
            and
        3. Complete application and pay all fees; fees are nonrefundable.
        4. For certificates issued on September 2, 2011, and beyond, the 6 renewal credits earned must be:
            a. Related to the certificated person's employment at the time of renewal, if that employment requires a certificate;
            b. Related to the certificated person's endorsements,
                or
            c. A required element of a program that will lead to an endorsement under 4 AAC 12.395 that the certificated person seeks to acquire.
    C. Additional Requirements—See Initial Teacher Certificates, IV, B, 1–3, above.

II. Master Teacher Certificate (valid 10 years; renewable)
- A. Requirements—Candidate must:
  1. Meet all requirements for the Professional certificate;
  2. Hold a current Initial or Professional certificate;
  3. Hold current National Board certification issued by National Board for Professional Teaching Standards (NBPTS), and
  4. Complete application and pay all fees; fees are nonrefundable.
- B. Renewal requirements—Candidate has:
  1. Current, renewed National Board certification;
  2. Six semester hours of renewal credit taken during the life of the Master certificate being renewed, of which a minimum of 3 semester hours must be upper-division or graduate credit;
  3. Verification of employment in an Alaska public school district in a position requiring a certificate;
     - a. If an applicant is not employed in this capacity at the time of renewal, fingerprint cards will be required.

     and
  4. Complete application and pay all fees; fees are nonrefundable.
  5. For certificates issued on September 2, 2011, and beyond, the 6 renewal credits earned must be:
     - a. Related to the certificated person's employment at the time of renewal, if that employment requires a certificate;
     - b. Related to the certificated person's endorsements,
       or
     - c. A required element of a program that will lead to an endorsement under 4 AAC 12.395 that the certificated person seeks to acquire.
  6. If the requirements to renew a Master certificate have not been met, an applicant must meet all current renewal requirements for the Professional certificate.
- B. Additional Requirements—See Initial Teacher Certificates, IV, B, 1–3, above.

Administrative Certificates

I. Type B Administrative Certificate (valid 5 years; renewable)
- A. Requirements—Candidate has:
  1. At least 3 years of experience as a certificated teacher or special service provider;
  2. Completed an approved teacher-education program in school administration;
  3. Master's or higher degree from a regionally accredited institution;
  4. Recommendation of the preparing institution;
  5. Six semester hours or 9 quarter hours of credit earned during the 5-year period preceding the date of application;
     - a. See Provisional Type B Administrator certificate, directly below
  6. Three semester hours of approved Alaska studies and 3 semester hours of approved multicultural education/crosscultural communications; and
     - a. See Provisional Type B Administrator certificate, directly below

7. Completed application packet, which includes a signed and notarized application, the institutional recommendation form, official transcripts, 2 sets of completed fingerprint cards, and processing fees, all of which are nonrefundable.

B. Renewal Requirements: Prior to the expiration date of the certificate, applicant must have:

1. Six semester hours of renewal credit taken during the life of the certificate being renewed, of which a minimum of 3 semester hours must be upper-division or graduate credit;

2. Verification of current employment in an Alaska public school district in a position requiring a certificate; and

   a. If an applicant is not employed in this capacity at the time of renewal, a fingerprint card will be required.

3. Completed application and paid all fees; fees are nonrefundable.

4. For certificates issued on September 2, 2011, and beyond, the 6 renewal credits earned must be:

   a. Related to the certificated person's employment at the time of renewal, if that employment requires a certificate;

   b. Related to the certificated person's endorsements;
      or

   c. A required element of a program that will lead to an endorsement under 4 AAC 12.395 that the certificated person seeks to acquire.

II. Provisional Type B Administrator Certificate (valid 2 years; nonrenewable)

A. This certificate is for applicants meeting all other requirements for certification, but who lack 6 semester hours of credit earned during the 5-year period preceding the date of application, or who lack 3 semester hours of credit in Alaska studies and/or 3 semester hours of credit in multicultural education or crosscultural communications.

B. In order to avoid a lapse in certification, the Provisional Type B Administrator certificate holder must submit official transcripts to the Teacher Certification office showing the completion of 3 semester hours of approved Alaska studies course work and the completion of 3 semester hours of approved Alaska multicultural course work prior to the expiration date of the Provisional certificate.

1. In addition, prior to the expiration date of their certificate, the Provisional certificate holder must apply for the 5-year regular Type B Administrative certificate.

III. Superintendent Endorsement

A. Requirements—Candidate has:

1. Completed Institutional Recommendation showing completion of an approved superintendency program from a regionally accredited university;
   and

2. Verification of at least 5 years of employment as a classroom teacher or administrator.

   a. At least 3 years must have been satisfactory employment as a teacher with a teaching certificate or comparable certificate issued by another state; and at least 1 year must have been satisfactory employment as an administrator with a Type B certificate or comparable certificate from another state.

IV. Special Education Administrator Endorsement
  A. Requirements—Candidate has:
  1. Completed Institutional Recommendation showing completion of an approved special education administrative program from a regionally accredited university;
  and
  2. Verification of at least 3 years of employment as a certified special education teacher or school psychologist, with a teaching or special services certificate or comparable certificate issued by another state.

V. Director of Special Education
  A. Requirements for applicants who wish to be employed solely as the administrator or director of special education and are not eligible for a special education administrator endorsement:
  1. Possess both a Type B certificate and a teaching certificate endorsed for special education or for a related services specialty. (This does not constitute an endorsement.)
     a. To be assigned as a classroom teacher in Alaska, applicant must have a valid teacher certificate (Initial, Professional, or Master), since the Type B certificate does not allow the holder to be a classroom teacher.
     b. Applicants who currently hold a valid Alaska teaching certificate and are applying for a Type B certificate are considered an initial applicant for the Type B.

VI. Type C Special Services Certificate (valid 5 years; renewable)
  A. Requirements—Candidate has:
  1. Completed a program in a special service area;
  2. Bachelor's or higher degree;
  3. Recommendation of the preparing institution;
  4. Six semester hours or 9 quarter hours of credit taken within the past 5 years;
  5. Three semester hours of approved Alaska studies and 3 semester hours of multicultural education/crosscultural communications;
  and
  6. Completed application packet, which includes a signed and notarized application, an institutional recommendation form, official transcripts, two sets of completed fingerprint cards, and fees, all of which are nonrefundable.
  B. Renewal Requirements: Prior to the expiration date of the certificate, applicant has:
  1. Six semester hours of renewal credit taken during the life of the certificate being renewed, of which a minimum of 3 semester hours must be upper division or graduate credit;
  2. Verification of current employment in an Alaska public school district in a position requiring a certificate;
     a. If an applicant is not employed in this capacity at the time of renewal, a fingerprint card will be required.
  and

3. Completed application and paid all fees; fees are nonrefundable.
4. For certificates issued on September 2, 2011, and beyond, the 6 renewal credits earned must be:
   a. Related to the certificated person's employment at the time of renewal, if that employment requires a certificate;
   b. Related to the certificated person's endorsements;
      or
   c. A required element of a program that will lead to an endorsement under 4 AAC 12.395 that the certificated person seeks to acquire.

VII. Provisional Type C Special Services Certificate (valid 2 years)
   A. This certificate is for applicants meeting all other requirements for certification, but who lack 6 semester hours of credit earned during the 5-year period preceding the date of application; or who lack 3 semester hours of credit in Alaska studies and/or 3 semester hours of credit in multicultural education or crosscultural communications.
   B. In order to avoid a lapse in certification, the Provisional Type C Special Services certificate holder must submit official transcripts to the Teacher Certification office showing the completion of 3 semester hours of approved Alaska studies course work and the completion of 3 semester hours of approved Alaska multicultural course work prior to the expiration date of the Provisional certificate.
      1. In addition, prior to the expiration date of their certificate, the Provisional certificate holder must apply for the 5-year regular Type C Special Services certificate.

VIII. Type C Endorsements
   A. Endorsements under a Type C certificate include audiology, occupational therapy, physical therapy, school nursing, school psychology, school psychometry, school social work, speech pathology, school counselor, and library science-media.
      1. School Psychology Endorsement Requirements
         a. Candidate must also hold a master's or higher degree in school psychology; be recommended by an institution whose school psychology program has been approved by the National Association of School Psychologists (NCATE) or the American Psychological Association; and have completed a 1200 hour internship (with 600 of the hours in a school setting);
            or
            Be certified under the certification system of the National Association of School Psychologists.
      2. Speech, Language, or Hearing Endorsement Requirements
         a. Candidate must hold either a master's or higher degree with a major emphasis in speech-language pathology, audiology, or speech-language and hearing science;
            or
            Possess certification of clinical competence from the American Speech-Language-Hearing Association.
         b. Candidate must also be recommended for endorsement by an institution with a program approved by NCATE or the American Speech-Language-Hearing Association.

3. Other Special Service Endorsement Requirements
   a. Candidates who wish to be employed to provide such services as speech or language pathology, school psychology, school counseling, orientation and mobility, psychometry, library and/or media services, or school nursing, must have a Type C Special Services Certificate endorsed in the field of employment.
   b. A Type C certificate does not qualify the holder for assignment as a classroom teacher or school administrator.

IX. Reemployment Certificate—Type B and C (valid 1 year, effective the date the complete application packet is received in the office of Teacher Education and Certification; nonrenewable)
   A. Applicants who held a certificate that has been expired for over 12 months may be eligible for the Reemployment Certificate. During the year of validity, the applicant must complete all current requirements for the Regular 5-year certificate and submit an application.
      1. See Administrative Certificates, I, Type B Administrative Certificate; and VI, Type C Special Services Certificate, above, for details
   B. After holding a Reemployment certificate, applicants are only eligible to apply for the Regular 5-year certificate, and will not qualify for Provisional certification.
   C. The endorsements on the Reemployment certificate will be the same as those on the applicant's expired administrative or special services certificate.
   D. During the life of the Reemployment certificate no endorsements may be added or removed.

Other Certificates

For details, consult http://www.eed.state.ak.us/teachercertification/Certification.html
   I. Retired (Lifetime) Certificate
   II. Type E Early Childhood Certificate
   III. Type M Limited Certificate
   IV. Vocational / Technical

Arizona

Elementary Certificates (K–8)

I. Provisional Elementary Education Certificate (valid 3 years; not renewable, but extendable once for 3 years)
   A. Completed application for certification; appropriate fee; and photocopy of valid Arizona IVP fingerprint card issued on or after January 1, 2008, or photocopy of valid Arizona fingerprint clearance card issued prior to January 1, 2008
   B. Bachelor's or more advanced degree from an accredited institution, verified by official transcript(s)
   C. One of the following options:
      1. Completion of a teacher preparation program in elementary education from an accredited institution or a Board-approved teacher preparation program, *or*
      2. Forty-five semester hours of education courses from an accredited institution, including at least 8 semester hours of practicum in grades K–8,
         a. Two years of verified full-time teaching experience in grades PreK–8 may be substituted for the 8 semester hours of practicum.
         b. Courses which teach the knowledge and skills described in the professional teaching standards, such as learning theory, classroom management, methods, and assessment, are acceptable, *or*
      3. A valid elementary education certificate from another state.
   D. Professional Knowledge Elementary Exam—one of the following:
      1. A passing score on the Professional Knowledge Elementary (91) portion of the Arizona Educator Proficiency Assessment (AEPA),
      2. A passing score on a comparable Professional Knowledge Elementary examination from another state or agency,
      3. A valid comparable certificate from the National Board for Professional Teaching Standards, *or*
      4. Three years of full-time teaching elementary education, K–8.
   E. Subject Knowledge Elementary Education Exam—one of the following:
      1. A passing score on the Subject Knowledge Elementary Education (01) portion of the AEPA,
      2. A passing score on a comparable Subject Knowledge Elementary Education examination from another state or agency, *or*
      3. A valid comparable certificate from the National Board for Professional Teaching Standards.

F. Verification of state-approved Structured English Immersion (SEI) training or comparable state-approved SEI training from another state to qualify for the Provisional SEI endorsement (valid for 3 years; additional 3 semester hours of state-approved SEI training required to qualify for full SEI endorsement)
   1. If certified before August 31, 2006: verification of 1 semester hour or 15 clock hours of state-approved SEI training
   2. If certified on or after August 31, 2006: verification of 3 semester hours or 45 clock hours of state-approved SEI training
   3. Individuals who hold an Arizona Full Bilingual or Full English as a Second Language (ESL) endorsement are exempt from the SEI endorsement requirement.
   4. The requirement for a Provisional SEI endorsement may be waived for a period not to exceed 1 year for individuals who graduate from administrator or teacher preparation programs that are not approved by the Arizona State Board of Education and meet all other applicable certification requirements.
G. Arizona Constitution (a college course or the appropriate examination)
H. U.S. Constitution (a college course or the appropriate examination).
   1. If applicant otherwise qualifies for the certificate but is deficient in Arizona and/or U.S. Constitution, applicant will have 3 years under a valid teaching certificate to fulfill the requirement, except that those teaching an academic course on History, Government, Social Studies, Citizenship, Law, or Civics have 1 year to fulfill the requirement(s).

II. Standard Elementary Education certificate (valid 6 years; renewable)
A. Qualify for and hold the Provisional Elementary Education certificate for 2 years
B. Two years of verified full-time teaching experience during the valid period of the Provisional certificate may be used to convert the Provisional certificate to a Standard certificate
C. Three semester hours or 45 clock hours of instruction in research-based systematic phonics from an accredited institution or other provider
D. Verification of 3 semester hours or 45 clock hours of state-approved SEI training or comparable state-approved SEI training from another state to qualify for the Full SEI endorsement
   1. Individuals who hold a Full Bilingual or Full ESL endorsement are exempt from the SEI endorsement requirement.
E. A photocopy of valid Arizona IVP fingerprint card issued on or after January 1, 2008, or a photocopy of valid Arizona fingerprint clearance card issued prior to January 1, 2008.

Secondary Certificates (7–12)

I. Provisional Secondary Education Certificate (valid 3 years; nonrenewable but extendable once for 3 years). Requirements include:
A. See Elementary Certificates I, A and B, above
B. One of the following options:
   1. Completion of a teacher preparation program in secondary education from

an accredited institution or from a Board-approved teacher preparation program,

or

2. Thirty semester hours of education courses, including at least 8 semester practicum in grades 7–12,

   a. Two years of verified full-time teaching experience in grades 7–Postsecondary may substitute for the 8 semester hours of practicum.

   b. Courses which teach the knowledge and skills described in the professional teaching standards, such as learning theory, classroom management, methods, and assessment, are acceptable.

   or

3. A valid secondary education certificate from another state.

C. Professional Knowledge Secondary Exam—one of the following:

   1. A passing score on the Professional Knowledge Secondary (92) portion of the AEPA,

   2. A passing score on a comparable Professional Knowledge Secondary examination from another state or agency,

   3. A valid comparable certificate from the National Board for Professional Teaching Standards,

   or

   4. Three years of full-time teaching secondary education, 7–12.

D. Subject Knowledge Secondary Education Exam—one of the following:

   1. A passing score on the Subject Knowledge Secondary Education portion of the AEPA

      a. Subject Knowledge assessments offered for the following: art, biology, business, chemistry, economics, English, French, geography, German, health, history, mathematics, music, physics, political science/American government, social studies, and Spanish

      b. If a proficiency assessment is not offered in a subject area, an approved area shall consist of 24 semester hours of subject-related courses from an accredited institution.

      c. An approved area in general science comprises 12 semester hours of life science courses and 12 semester hours of physical science courses.

      d. If a language assessment is not offered through the AEPA, a passing score of Advanced Low on the American Council on the Teaching of Foreign Languages (ACTFL) may demonstrate proficiency of that foreign language in lieu of the 24 semester hours of courses in that subject;

   2. A passing score on a comparable Subject Knowledge Secondary Education examination from another state or agency;

   3. A valid comparable certificate from the National Board for Professional Teaching Standards;

      or

   4. Master's degree from an accredited institution in the appropriate subject area.

E. See Elementary Certificates, I, F, 1–4, above

F. See Elementary Certificates, I, G and H, above.

II.   Standard Secondary Education Certificate (valid 6 years; renewable)
    A.   See Elementary Certificates, II, A–D, above, except for secondary level

Early Childhood Education Certificate, Birth through Age 8 or through Grade 3

Note: All teachers serving children Birth through Kindergarten must have either an Early Childhood Education certificate or Early Childhood endorsement. Also, an individual who holds the Early Childhood Education teaching certificate or the Early Childhood endorsement in combination with an Arizona Cross-Categorical, Emotional Disability, Learning Disability, Mental Retardation, Orthopedic/Other Health Impairment or Severely and Profoundly Disabled Special Education teaching certificate is not required to hold the Early Childhood Special Education certificate.

I.   Provisional Early Childhood Education Certificate (valid 3 years; nonrenewable but extendable once for 3 years)
    A.   See Elementary Certificates, I, A and B, above
    B.   One of the following 3 options:
        1.   Completion of a teacher preparation program in early childhood education from an accredited institution or a Board-approved teacher preparation program;
            or
        2.   Thirty-seven semester hours of early childhood education courses from an accredited institution, to include all of the following areas of study and a minimum of 8 semester hours of practicum;
            a.   Foundations of early childhood education; child guidance and classroom management; characteristics and quality practices for typical and atypical behaviors of young children; child growth and development, including health, safety and nutrition; child, family, cultural and community relationships; developmentally appropriate instructional methodologies for teaching language, math, science, social studies and the arts; early language and literacy development; and assessing, monitoring and reporting progress of young children
            b.   Practicum must include a minimum of 4 semester hours in supervised field experience, practicum, internship, or student teaching setting serving children birth through preschool,
                or
                One year of full-time verified teaching experience birth through preschool
            c.   One year of verified full-time teaching experience with children in kindergarten through grade 3 in an accredited school may substitute for 4 semester hours in a supervised student teaching setting serving children in kindergarten through grade 3.
                or
        3.   A valid early childhood education certificate from another state.
    C.   Professional Knowledge Early Childhood Exam—one of the following:
        1.   A passing score on the Professional Knowledge Early Childhood (#93) portion of the AEPA,

2. A passing score on a comparable Professional Knowledge Early Childhood examination from another state or agency,
3. A valid comparable certificate from the National Board for Professional Teaching Standards,
    or
4. Three years of full-time teaching early childhood education, birth through grade 3.

D. Subject Knowledge Early Childhood Education Exam—one of the following:
    1. A passing score on the Subject Knowledge Early Childhood Education (#36) portion of the AEPA,
    2. A passing score on a comparable Subject Knowledge Early Childhood examination from another state or agency,
        or
    3. A valid comparable certificate from the National Board for Professional Teaching Standards

E. Master's degree in Early Childhood Education from an accredited institution
F. See Elementary Certificates, I, F, 1–4 above
G. See Elementary Education, I, G and H, above

II. Standard Early Childhood Education Certificate, Birth through Age 8 or through Grade 3 (valid 6 years; renewable)
A. Qualify for the Provisional Early Childhood certificate; and acquire 2 years of verified full-time teaching experience during the valid period of the Provisional certificate to convert the Provisional certificate to a Standard certificate,
    or
B. Hold current National Board Certification in Early Childhood.
C. See Elementary Certificates, II, D and E, above

III. Other Special Education Certificates
A. Consult http://www.azed.gov/certification for complete descriptions of requirements for the following special education certificates: Early Childhood (Birth–5 years); Cross-Categorical (K–12) Learning Disability (K–12); Hearing Impaired (Birth–Grade 12); Emotional Disability (K–12); Visually Impaired (Birth–Grade 12); Orthopedic Impairments or Other Health Impairments (K–12), Mental Retardation (K–12); Severely and Profoundly Disabled (K–12)

IV. For specific information on other certificates offered, consult http://www.azed.gov/educator-certification. Certificates include:
A. Arts education (art, dance, dramatic arts, music), PreK–12; adult education; athletic coaching, 7–12; foreign language teacher; junior officer reserve training corps (JROTC), 9–12; Native American Language Certificate, PreK–12; substitute, K–12; and teaching intern

Endorsements

I. Endorsements are attachments to teaching certificates and indicate areas of specialization. They cover K–12 unless otherwise indicated. Once issued, endorsements are automatically renewed with the teaching certificate. Consult http://www.azed.gov/certification for details.

A. Endorsements are issued in following areas: art, bilingual education, computer science, cooperative education, dance, dramatic arts, driver's education, early childhood (Birth–Age 8 or Grade 3), English as a second language (ESL), gifted education, library-media specialist, mathematics specialist (K–8), middle grade (5–9), music, physical education, reading endorsements, and structured English immersion

Administrative Certificates

I. Supervisor Certificate, PreK–12 (valid 6 years; renewable)

A. Required for all personnel whose primary responsibility is administering instructional programs, supervising certified personnel, or similar administrative duties, except for individuals who hold a valid Arizona Principal or Superintendent Certificate

B. Requirements for the Supervisor Certificate
1. See Elementary Certificates, I, A, above
2. A valid Arizona Early Childhood, Elementary, Secondary, Special Education, Career and Technical Education certificate or other professional certificate issued by the Arizona Department of Education
3. Master's or higher degree from an accredited institution
4. Three years of verified full-time teaching experience or related education services experience in a PreK–12 setting
5. Completion of a program in educational administration which shall consist of a minimum of 18 graduate semester hours of educational administration courses which teach the knowledge and skills described in the Professional Administrative Standards (R7-2-603)
    a. Courses to include 3 credit hours in school law and 3 credit hours in school finance
6. A practicum in educational administration or 2 years of verified educational administrative experience in grades PreK–12
7. A passing score on the supervisor, principal, or superintendent administrator portion of the AEPA
8. See Elementary Certificates, F, 1–4, above
9. See Elementary Certificates, G and H, above.

II. Principal Certificate, PreK–12 (valid 6 years; renewable)

A. Required for all personnel who hold the title of, or perform the duties of, Principal or Assistant Principal as delineated in Title 15 of the Arizona Revised Statutes, except for individuals who hold a valid Arizona Superintendent Certificate and have completed 3 years of verified full-time teaching experience

B. Requirements include:
1. See Elementary Certificates, I, A, above
2. Master's or higher degree from an accredited institution

3. Three years of verified full-time teaching experience in grades PreK–12
4. Completion of a program in educational administration for principals, including at least 30 graduate semester hours of educational administration courses teaching the knowledge and skills described in the Professional Administrative Standards (R7-2-603)
    a. Courses to include 3 credit hours in school law and 3 credit hours in school finance
5. A practicum as a principal or 2 years of verified experience as a principal or assistant principal under the supervision of a certified principal in grades PreK–12
6. A passing score on either the Principal or Superintendent portion of the AEPA
7. See Elementary Certificates, F, 1–4, above
8. See Elementary Certificates, G and H, above.

III. Superintendent Certificates, PreK–12 (valid 6 years; renewable)
A. Individuals who hold the title of Superintendent, Assistant Superintendent, or Associate Superintendent and who perform duties directly relevant to curriculum, instruction, certified employee evaluations, and instructional supervision may obtain a Superintendent Certificate.
B. Requirements include:
1. See Elementary Education Certificates, I, A, above
2. Master's or higher degree, including at least 60 graduate semester hours from an accredited institution
3. Completion of a program in educational administration for superintendents, including at least 36 graduate semester hours of educational administrative courses teaching the knowledge and skills described in the Professional Administrative Standards (R7-2-603)
    a. Courses to include 3 credit hours in school law and 3 credit hours in school finance
4. Three years of verified full-time teaching experience or related education services experience in PreK–12 setting
5. A practicum as a superintendent or 2 years of verified experience as a superintendent, assistant superintendent, or associate superintendent in grades PreK–12
6. A passing score on the superintendent administrator portion of the AEPA
7. See Elementary Certificates, F, 1–4, above
8. See Elementary Certificates, G and H, above.

IV. Other administrative certificates offered include: interim supervisor, interim principal, and interim superintendent, all PreK–12. For specific requirements for each, consult http://www.azed.gov/educator-certification

Professional Non-Teaching Certificate, (PreK–12)

I. School Psychologist Certificate, PreK–12 (valid 6 years; renewable)
A. Master's or higher advanced degree from an accredited institution

B.   One of the following 5 options:
1.   Completion of a graduate program in school psychology, consisting of at least 60 graduate semester hours,
or
2.   Completion of a doctoral program in psychology and completion of a retraining program in school psychology from an accredited institution or Board-approved program with a letter of institutional endorsement from the head of the school psychology program,
or
3.   Five years experience within the last 10 years working full time in the capacity of a school psychologist in a school setting serving any portion of grades kindergarten through 12, verified by the school district superintendent or human resources department,
or
4.   A Nationally Certified School Psychologist Credential,
or
5.   Diploma in school psychology from the American Board of School Psychology.
C.   A supervised internship of at least 1,200 clock hours with a minimum of 600 of those hours in a school setting
1.   Three years experience as a certified school psychologist within the last 10 years may be substituted for the internship requirement.
D.   See Elementary Certificates, I, A, above.
II.   School Psychologist Interim Certificate, PreK–12 (valid 2 years; nonrenewable)
A.   See Elementary Education certificates, I, A, above
B.   Master's or higher degree in psychology from an accredited institution
C.   Verification of current enrollment in an accredited school psychology program or a Board-approved school psychology program signed by the dean of a college of education or the administrator of a Board-approved school psychology preparation program
D.   Verification that the holder of the interim certificate shall be under the direct supervision of college and certified school personnel, including a school or school district–based certified school psychologist who holds a valid Arizona School Psychologist Certificate.
III.   Guidance Counselor Certificate (PreK–12) (valid 6 years; renewable)
A.   Master's or higher degree from an accredited institution
B.   Completion of a graduate program in guidance and counseling from an accredited institution, or a valid guidance counselor certificate from another state
C.   Photocopy of valid Arizona IVP fingerprint card issued on or after January 1, 2008, or photocopy of valid Arizona fingerprint clearance card issued prior to January 1, 2008
D.   One of the following 3 options:
1.   Completion of a supervised counseling practicum in school counseling,
2.   Two years of verified full-time experience as a school guidance counselor,
or
3.   Three years of verified full-time teaching experience.

IV.   Speech-Language Pathologist, PreK–12 and Speech-Language Technician, Pre-K–12
      For details, consult teacher certification website (see Appendix 1)

Career and Technical Education Certificates

CTE certificates all span grades K–12 and include: agriculture, business and marketing; education and training; family and consumer sciences; health careers; and industrial and emerging technologies. For details, consult http://www.azed.gov/educator-certification

Reciprocity

For information on fingerprint reciprocity; comparable out-of-state exams; and reciprocal certificates for the following areas, consult www.azed.gov/educator-certification: provisional elementary education, K–8; provisional secondary education, 7–12; provisional early childhood education, Birth–Age 8 or Grade 3; provisional arts education, PreK–12, provisional special education; reciprocal principal, Pre-K–12; reciprocal superintendent, PreK–12, and reciprocal supervisor, PreK–12.

Arkansas

Types of Licenses

I.   Standard License (valid 5 years; renewable)
     A. Prerequisites
         1. Hold a bachelor's or higher degree from an accredited institution
         2. Successfully complete the following tests:
             a. Praxis Core Academic Skills for Educators (Core) Tests
             b. Praxis II: Content test for all parts required, *and*
             c. Praxis II: Principles of Learning and Teaching
         3. Criminal background check by the Arkansas State Police and the FBI
         4. Child Maltreatment Central Registry Check
         5. Novice teachers must successfully complete induction program
         6. Pass Praxis III: Professional Assessment
     B. Renewal Requirements
         1. Accrue 60 professional development hours during each year of the 5-year renewal cycle
             a. A 3-hour college credit course may count as 15 hours of professional development, but no more than half of the required 60 hours may be met through college credit hours.
II. Non-Traditional Licensure
     A. To give talented and highly motivated applicants with college degrees in fields other than education an opportunity to obtain the proper credentials and become teachers in an Arkansas public school. Contact the Office of Educator Effectiveness (see Appendix 1) for full details.
         1. Prerequisites: See Standard License, I, A, 1 and 2, a and b, above
         2. Complete application and supporting documents
         3. Successful personal interview

Levels and Areas of Licensure

I.   Levels of Licensure are defined as the grade-age-level parameters of the teaching license. They include the following:
     A. Birth–Kindergarten: Integrated
     B. Kindergarten/Young Adulthood: Grades K–12
     C. Elementary (K–6)
     D. Middle Childhood/Early Adolescence: Grades 4–8
     E. Adolescence/Young Adulthood: Grades 7–12
     F. Postsecondary: Above grade 12
II. Teacher Licensure Competency Areas are defined as the particular content field(s) of the teaching license.

A. Areas include adult education; agriculture sciences technology (7–12); art (K–12); business technology (4–12); coaching education (K–12); drama/speech (K–12); early childhood instructional specialist (birth–8); educational examiner (K–12); English-language arts/social studies (4–8); English-language arts (7–12); ESL education (K–12); family and consumer sciences (K–12); foreign language (K–12); gifted and talented education (K–12); industrial technology (K–12); library media specialist (K–12); life science (7–12); marketing technology (7–12); mathematics/science (4–8); mathematics (7–12); music-instrumental (K–12); music-vocal (K–12); physical science (7–12); physical education/health (K–12); reading education (K–12); speech-language pathologist (K–12); school counseling (K–12); school psychology specialist (K–12); social studies (7–12); special education (K–12); teachers of hearing-impaired students; teachers of visually impaired students (K–12).

B. Exception areas include special education; added endorsements; educational leadership and supervision; ancillary student services; and professional and technical

   1. Applicants cannot test out of exception areas but must complete the program of study and the required Praxis assessment.

III. Adding Areas of Licensure

Note: Questions about adding additional licensure areas may be directed to the Office of Educator Licensure (see Appendix 1). Speak only with a supervisor who works with adding areas of licensure. Be sure to document with whom you spoke and what was said.

A. Prerequisites

   1. Hold a valid Standard Arkansas teaching license. See Types of Licenses, I, A and B, above.

B. To add non-exception teaching areas within the same level of licensure, applicant must pass the State Board–required specialty area assessment(s).

C. To add exception areas within the same level of licensure:

   1. Complete an approved performance-based program of study, *and*

   2. Pass the State Board–required assessment(s).

D. Teachers may test out of licensure areas within their level of licensure and one level above or below their initial level of licensure.

E. To add an area of licensure or endorsement for which there is not a State Board–required specialty area assessment:

   1. Successfully complete an approved performanced-based program of study, *and*

   2. Complete the State Board–required pedagogical assessment.

F. Special Situations

   1. The non-instruction student services areas of school psychology specialist and speech language pathology shall have completed a master's degree and the State Board–required assessment to be licensed.

   2. Teachers or administrators adding elementary (K–6), all middle school areas, or secondary social studies to their valid standard license shall have completed

a 3-credit-hour course in Arkansas history and 6 hours of language arts to be identified.

3. Additional areas/levels of licensure or endorsement shall be added to a valid standard license upon receiving documentation that all requirements have been met and upon receiving an application requesting the additional licensure area or endorsement.

Administrative Licensure

I. Levels of Licensure
   A. Building Level Administrator—Principal, assistant principal, or vice principal (P–12)
   B. Curriculum/Program Administrator—A school leader responsible for program development and administration, and/or employment evaluation decisions. Each Curriculum/Program Administrator License is limited to one of the following areas:
      1. Special Education (P–12)
      2. Gifted and Talented Education (P–12)
      3. Career and Technical Education (grade levels P–12)
      4. Content Area Specialist (P–12)
      5. Curriculum Specialist (P–12)
      6. Adult Education (Post-secondary)
   C. District Level Administrator—Superintendent, assistant superintendent, or deputy superintendent (P–12)

II. Types of Licensure
   A. Standard License
      1. Have 4 years of experience in classroom teaching, in counseling, or in library media
      2. Hold a graduate degree that includes a program of study with an internship
         a. For candidates holding a graduate degree in an area other than educational leadership, the Arkansas institution of higher education will review his/her credentials to determine his/her individual needs.
      3. Participate in a mentoring experience upon first employment
         a. The mentor provided should have relevant experience sought by the new administrator, at least 3 years of administrator experience, hold a standard teaching license, and have completed the mentorship training.
         b. Districts shall submit their administrator mentoring plans to the Arkansas State Department of Education for approval.
      4. Successfully complete the School Leaders Licensure Assessment (SLLA) with a minimum cut-score of 163
         a. Candidates should practice actual administrative experience during their induction year(s) before attempting the SLLA.
   B. District Administrator License
      1. Hold a standard teaching license

2. Have 4 years of classroom teaching experience and be licensed as a Building-Level Administrator or Curriculum/Program Administrator
3. Hold an advanced degree or complete an advanced program of study based on individual needs inclusive of an internship and portfolio development based on the Standards for Administrator licensure
4. Successfully complete the School Superintendent Assessment (SSA) with a score of 156

Reciprocity

I. Eligibility to apply:
   A. Hold a valid or expired teaching license from another state,
     or
   B. Degree must be from an institution that holds regional or national accreditation recognized by the United States Department of Education (USDOE). The education program must also hold national accreditation recognized by the USDOE or be state-approved.
II. A 3-hour Arkansas history course will be required for Arkansas licensure when the licensure area is elementary, any middle school area, or secondary social studies.
III. For full details on exceptions to eligibility requirements as well as information on candidates from other countries, contact the Office of Professional Licensure (see Appendix 1).

California

All multiple and single subject professional teacher preparation programs require candidates to pass an assessment of teaching performance in order to earn a teaching credential. For full details about the Teaching Performance Assessment (TPA), consult the website (see Appendix 1).

Teaching Credentials

I. Multiple Subject Teaching Credential—Commonly used in elementary school service
II. Single Subject Teaching Credential—Commonly used in secondary school service
III. Education Specialist Instruction Credential—Commonly used in special education settings
IV. Five-Year Preliminary Multiple Subject and Single Subject Teaching Credential (nonrenewable)
    A. Requirements for California-Trained Teachers
        1. Bachelor's or higher degree from regionally accredited college or university, except in professional education
        2. Teacher preparation program, including student teaching, completed with grade of C or higher on a 5-point scale at California college or university with a Commission-accredited program
        3. California basic skills requirement*
        4. U.S. Constitution (course or examination)
        5. Subject-matter competence by obtaining passing score on appropriate subject-matter examination or obtaining letter from California college or university with approved subject-matter program (subject-matter letter is not an option for Multiple Subject credential applicants)
        6. Completion of course in developing English language skills, including reading
        7. Completion of course in foundational uses of computers in educational settings
        8. Multiple Subject Teaching Credential only: all California-prepared applicants must pass Reading Instruction Competence Assessment (RICA), unless exempt
    B. Requirements for Teachers Trained in Other States or U.S. Territories
        1. Bachelor's or higher degree from regionally accredited college or university
        2. Possession of comparable teaching credential (does not have to be valid at time of application)
        3. Prior to or within first year of issuance of credential, candidate must satisfy California's basic skills requirement.
            a. Unless the basic skills requirement is satisfied within 1 year of issuance date of credential, credential will not be valid for employment in California's public schools until requirement is met.
        4. There are 3 different routes under which an out-of-state-trained teacher may qualify for certification, and each route has specific renewal requirements.
            a. Route 1: Less than 2 years of out-of-state, full-time teaching experience
            b. Route 2:

        i.   Two or more years of full-time teaching experience in a public or regionally accredited private school, *and*

        ii.   Photocopies of performance evaluations from 2 separate years of the verified out-of-state teaching experience on which the candidate received ratings of "satisfactory" or better.

    c.   Route 3: Possess National Board for Professional Teaching Standards (NBPTS) Certificate (results in issuance of clear credential)

C.   Requirements for Teachers Trained Outside of the United States

    1.   The equivalent of a bachelor's or higher degree from a regionally accredited college or university located in the United States

    2.   Completion of a comparable teacher preparation program, including student teaching, that is equivalent to a teacher preparation program from a regionally accredited college or university located in the United States

    3.   Possession of, or eligibility for, a comparable teaching credential issued by the country in which the program was completed

    4.   Prior to or within first year of issuance of credential, candidate must satisfy California's basic skills requirement

        a.   See B, 3, a, above

    5.   Individuals trained outside the United States must have their foreign transcripts evaluated by a Commission-approved agency prior to submission of their application packet.

V.   Five-Year Clear Multiple Subject and Single Subject Teaching Credential (renewable every 5 years)

    A.   Requirements for California-Trained Teachers

        1.   See IV, A, 1–8, above

        2.   Completion of Commission-approved induction program with verification by induction program director

    B.   Requirements for Teachers Trained in Other States or U.S. Territories

        1.   See IV, B, 1–4, above, with the addition to IV, B, 4, b, i, that the 2 or more years of full-time teaching experience in a public or regionally accredited private school must be in special education

        2.   Complete renewal requirements associated with route under which preliminary teaching credential was issued

        a.   Route 1:

            i.   Complete Commission-approved induction program with verification by induction program director

            ii.   Earn a California English learner authorization

        b.   Route 2:

            i.   Earn a master's degree (or the equivalent in semester units) from a regionally accredited college or university, *or* Complete 150 clock hours of professional activities under the California Standards for the Teaching Profession (CSTP).

            ii.   Earn a California English learner authorization

        c.   Route 3: Individuals who qualify based on National Board (NBPTS) Certification are issued clear credentials.

    C.   Requirements for Teachers Trained Outside the United States

        1.   See IV, C, 1–5, above

        2.   Completion of a course in developing English language skills, including reading (or passage of RICA for holders of Multiple Subject credentials only)

        3.   U.S. Constitution course or examination

        4.   Subject-matter competence by obtaining a passing score on appropriate subject-matter examination or obtaining letter from California college or university with approved subject-matter program

        5.   Commission-approved induction program with verification by induction program director

        6.   CPR training for adults, infants, and children

    D.   Clear credentials are renewed every 5 years via the Commission's online renewal system.

VI.   Authorization for Service for Multiple Subject and Single Subject Teaching Credential

    A.   Teacher authorized for multiple-subject instruction may be assigned to teach in any self-contained classroom in preschool and grades K–12 and in classes organized primarily for adults

    B.   Teacher authorized for single-subject instruction may be assigned to teach any subject in authorized fields in any grade level: preschool, grades K–12 and in classes organized primarily for adults

        1.   Statutory subjects available: agriculture, art, business, English, foundational-level general science, foundational-level mathematics, health science, home economics, industrial and technology education, language other than English, mathematics, music, physical education, science (in one of these areas: biological sciences, chemistry, geosciences, or physics), specialized science (in one of the 4 science areas immediately prior), and social science

VII.   Five-Year Clear Specialist Instruction Credential—Covers specialist areas requiring advanced professional preparation or special competencies, including agriculture, bilingual education, early childhood education, gifted education, mathematics, and reading and language arts

    A.   Requirements

        1.   Hold valid California teaching credential that required bachelor's degree and professional preparation program, including student teaching

        2.   Post-baccalaureate professional preparation program in specialist area

        3.   Recommendation of California college or university with specific, Commission-accredited specialist program

            a.   Applicants trained outside of California who meet requirements in VII, A, 1 and 2, directly above, may still be certified. Student teaching or field work must have been completed with a grade of C on a 5-point scale and applicant must provide photocopy of out-of-state credential listing a comparable authorization.

            b.   Applicants for Bilingual Education and Reading Instructional Leadership Specialist Credentials who trained out of state must apply through and

> be recommended by California college or university with Commission-accredited program.
> B. Authorization for Service
>> 1. Credential authorizes holder to teach in area of specialization in preschool, grades K–12, and in classes organized primarily for adults

VIII. Education Specialist Instruction Credential—Available in following specialization areas: mild/moderate disabilities, moderate/severe disabilities, deaf and hard-of-hearing, visual impairments, physical and health impairments, early childhood special education, and language and academic development
    A. Requirements for California-Trained Teachers
        1. Bachelor's or higher degree from regionally accredited college or university
        2. Professional preparation program in education specialist category completed at California college or university with Commission-accredited program
        3. California basic skills requirement*
        4. U.S. Constitution course or examination
        5. Completion of course in developing English-language skills, including reading
        6. Passage of the Reading Instruction Competence Assessment (RICA)
           a. RICA passage is not required for category of early childhood special education.
        7. Verification of subject-matter competence (see IV, A, 5, above)
           a. Verification of subject-matter competence is not required for category of early childhood special education.
        8. Formal recommendation of California college or university with Commission-accredited program
    B. Requirements for Teachers Trained in Other States, U.S. Territories, or outside the United States
        1. See IV, B and C, above, with the addition to IV, B, 4, b, i, that the 2 or more years of full-time teaching experience in a public or regionally accredited private school must be in special education
    C. Contact Commission on Teacher Credentialing (see Appendix 1) for full information on Clear or Level II Education Specialist Instruction Credential requirements.

IX. Authorization of Service for Education Specialist Instruction Credential
    A. Authorizes holder to teach in area of specialization and at level listed on credential in following settings: special day classes, special schools, home/hospital settings, correctional facilities, nonpublic schools and agencies, and resource rooms

Services Credentials

I. Five-Year Preliminary Administrative Services Credential (nonrenewable)
    A. Requirements for Teachers Prepared in California
        1. Possession of valid Clear California credential, which may be in teaching; designated-subjects teaching; pupil personnel services; librarian; health

services school nurse; clinical or rehabilitative services; or speech-language pathology

2. Five years of successful, full-time experience in public or private schools of equivalent status in any of areas listed directly above in A, 1

3. Approved program of specialized and professional preparation in administrative services,

   or

   Passing score on the California Preliminary Administrative Credential Examination (CPACE) or School Leaders Licensure Assessment (SLLA). Since the final administration of the SLLA #1010 was February 26, 2011, individuals who passed the SLLA on or before that date must apply and qualify for the Administrative Services Credential within 5 years from the date the exam was passed;

   or

   Approved administrative internship program from California college or university

4. California basic skills requirement*

5. Recommendation of California college or university with Commission-accredited administrative services program.

6. California-trained applicants must have offer of employment in administrative position from California school district, nonpublic school or agency, or county office of education,

   or

   May apply for Certificate of Eligibility.

B. Requirements for Teachers Prepared in Other States or U.S. Territories

1. Verify completion of bachelor's or higher degree from regionally accredited college or university

2. Satisfy California's basic skills requirement (BSR)

   a. The 1-year nonrenewable credential is available to an administrator who prepared out of state if all requirements except BSR are complete.

3. Complete teacher preparation program and equivalent elementary, secondary, or special education credential based on that program,

   and

4. Complete administrative preparation program in which candidate was issued, or qualified for, administrative services credential based upon that program,

   or

   Achieve passing score on the California Preliminary Administrative Credential Examination (CPACE) or School Leaders Licensure Assessment (SLLA). Since the final administration of the SLLA #1010 was February 26, 2011, individuals who passed the SLLA on or before that date must apply and qualify for the Administrative Services Credential within 5 years from the date the exam was passed.

5. Administrators prepared out of state with pupil personnel, health, speech-language pathology, or clinical or rehabilitative services program will need to obtain prerequisite credential.

II. Five-Year Clear Administrative Services Credential
   A. Requirements
      1. Preliminary credential (see I, A, 1–6, above)
      2. Two years of successful full-time experience in position requiring preliminary credential
      3. Complete one of the following:
         a. Obtain the recommendation of a Commission-approved program verifying completion of an individualized program of advanced preparation designed in cooperation with employer and the program sponsor
         b. State Board of Education–approved AB 430 Principal Training Program (completion of Modules 1, 2, and 3 must be submitted with the individual's direct application to the Commission). Information on the Principal Training Program, including approved programs and providers, may be accessed through the California Department of Education's website at www.cde.ca.gov
         c. Meet Mastery of Fieldwork Performance Standards through a Commission-approved program (streamlined assessment option to allow candidates to forego the course work component of the program and allow them to demonstrate their knowledge, skills, and abilities through the assessment component of the program)
         d. Commission-approved alternative program based on Commission-adopted guidelines resulting in a formal recommendation from the program sponsor.
         e. Commission-approved performance assessment, when available
      4. Candidates prepared outside of California may earn clear credential without first holding preliminary credential by
         a. Verifying completion of bachelor's or higher degree from regionally accredited college or university,
         b. Satisfying California's basic skills requirement (BSR)
         c. Completing teacher preparation program and earning equivalent elementary, secondary, or special education credential based on that program,
         d. Completing 3 years of elementary, secondary, or special education teaching experience,
         e. Completing administrative preparation program in which candidate was issued, or qualified for, administrative services credential based upon that program,
            or
            Achieving passing score on the California Preliminary Administrative Credential Examination (CPACE) or SLLA. Since the final administration of the SLLA #1010 was February 26, 2011, individuals who passed the SLLA on or before that date must apply and qualify for the Administrative Services Credential within 5 years from the date the exam was passed.
            and
         f. Completing 3 years of out-of-state public school administrative experience and submitting 2 rigorous performance evaluations.

> 5. Administrators prepared out of state with pupil personnel, health, speech-language pathology or clinical or rehabilitative services program will need to obtain prerequisite credential. The 1-year nonrenewable credential is available to administrators who prepared out of state if all requirements except BSR* are complete.
>
> B. Authorization for Service
>> 1. Administrative Services Credentials authorize holder to provide various duties that may allow holder to serve in a number of positions, including superintendent, associate superintendent, deputy superintendent, principal, assistant principal, dean, supervisor, consultant, coordinator, or in equivalent or intermediate-level administrative positions.

III. Clear Teacher Librarian Services Credential

A. Requirements
>1. Bachelor's degree from regionally accredited college or university
>2. Valid prerequisite California teaching credential that required program of professional preparation, including student teaching
>3. Completion of:
>> a. Commission-accredited teacher librarian services program and recommendation of California college or university where program was completed,
>> *or*
>> b. Out-of-state teacher librarian services program consisting of 30 graduate semester units approved by appropriate state agency in state where program was completed
>4. California basic skills requirement (BSR)*
>> a. The 1-year nonrenewable credential is available to an individual who prepared out of state if all requirements except BSR are complete
>5. Possession of an English learner authorization issued by the Commission (excludes English learner authorizations on teaching permits).

B. Authorization for Service
>1. Teacher Librarian Services Credential authorizes holder to assist and instruct pupils in choice and use of library materials; to plan and coordinate school library programs with instructional programs of school district; to select materials for school and district libraries; to conduct planned course of instruction for those pupils who assist in operation of school libraries; to supervise classified personnel assigned to school library duties; and to develop procedures for and management of school and district libraries.
>2. The Special Class Authorization authorizes the holder to provide departmentalized instruction in information literacy, digital literacy, and digital citizenship to students in grades 12 and below, including preschool and in classes organized primarily for adults. Individuals must satisfy all of the following requirements:
>> a. Hold a valid prerequisite California teaching credential as follows:
>>> i. A valid 1-year nonrenewable, Clear, or life Teacher Librarian or Library Media Services Credential

    ii. Library Services Credential

    iii. Standard Elementary, Secondary, Early Childhood Education, or Junior College Teaching Credential with a specialized preparation minor in Librarianship

    iv. General Credential in Librarianship

   b. Completion of a Commission-approved Special Class Authorization program of professional preparation, based on the Teacher Librarian Services Credential and Special Class Authorization in Information and Digital Literacy Program Standards (rev. 2011)

   c. Recommendation from a Commission-approved Teacher Librarian Services program, including the appropriate completed application form and current processing fee

IV. Pupil Personnel Services Credential

 A. Authorization for Services

  1. Credential available in 4 different areas: school counseling, school social work, school psychology, and child welfare and attendance services

 B. Requirements for School Counseling Authorization

  1. Post-baccalaureate study consisting of 48 semester units (30 semester units for out-of-state prepared) specializing in school counseling, including a supervised field experience

  2. California's basic skills requirement (BSR)*

   a. The 1-year nonrenewable credential is available to an individual who prepared out of state if all requirements except BSR are complete

  3. Recommendation of a California college or university with a Commission-accredited School Counseling program

   a. Individuals who trained out of state must:

    i. Verify possession of, or eligibility for, the equivalent authorization in the state where the program was completed, *and*

    ii. Provide written verification from the college or university where the program was completed that the program included supervised field experience with school-age children in school counseling.

 C. Requirements for School Social Work Authorization

  1. Post-baccalaureate study consisting of 45 semester units specializing in school social work, including a supervised field experience

  2. See B, 2, directly above

  3. Recommendation of a California college or university with a Commission-accredited School Social Work program

   a. Individuals who trained out of state must:

    i. Verify possession of, or eligibility for, the equivalent authorization in the state where the program was completed, *and*

    ii. Provide written verification from the college or university where the program was completed that program included supervised field experience with school-age children in school social work.

D. Requirements for School Psychology Authorization
1. Post-baccalaureate study consisting of 60 semester units specializing in school social work, including a practicum and supervised field experience
2. California's basic skills requirement (BSR)*
   a. The 1-year nonrenewable credential is available to an individual who prepared out of state if all requirements except BSR are complete
3. Recommendation of a California college or university with a Commission-accredited School Psychology program
   a. Individuals who trained out of state must:
      i. Verify possession of, or eligibility for, the equivalent authorization in the state where the program was completed,
      and
      ii. Provide written verification from the college or university where the program was completed that the program included a supervised field experience with school-age children in school psychology.
E. Child Welfare and Attendance Authorization. Contact the Commission (see Appendix 1) for full information

V. For detailed information on credentials in speech-language pathology and clinical or rehabilitative services, consult the website (see Appendix 1).

* Unless otherwise noted, for initial issuance all applicants must satisfy California's basic skills requirement (BSR). This requirement does not apply to applicants who are having their credentials renewed, reissued, or upgraded. Out-of-state applicants may be issued a 1-year, nonrenewable credential pending satisfaction of the basic skills requirement (BSR) if a California public school employer cannot find a fully credentialed person to fill the position and offers employment to the credential applicant.

Colorado

The submission process for the Colorado Department of Education (CDE) fingerprint requirement is that the applicant use a fingerprint card provided by a local law enforcement agency; CDE no longer provides the card. Applicants complete the fingerprint card with the assistance of a qualified law enforcement agency, then submit the completed card, with processing fee, to the Colorado Bureau of Investigation.

Teacher Licenses and Authorizations

I. Interim Authorization (valid 1 year; renewable once)
    A. Issued to out-of-state applicant who has not completely fulfilled licensing requirements or does not have documented evidence of 3 years of full-time successful teaching experience
        1. Basic Requirements
            a. Bachelor's or higher degree from a regionally accredited institution of higher education (IHE),
            b. Holds or is eligible for a valid educator certificate or license as a teacher, principal, or administrator in another state,
            c. Institutional recommendation verifying satisfactory completion of an approved program of preparation that confirms grade level or development level(s), subject area(s), or service specialization(s) completed by the applicant,
                and
            d. Has not successfully passed the Colorado State Board of Education–approved assessment(s) required for obtaining a Colorado Initial Educator License.
        2. Renewal Requirements
            a. Submission of a Renewal of Interim Authorization application and evaluation fee
II. Initial License (valid 3 years; renewable). Note: Applicants begin licensing process by using the Initial License application, regardless of experience or previous out-of-state license held.
    A. Issued to Colorado graduates who have:
        1. Passed the required content area exam,
            or
        2. Have 24 semester hours of credit in specified areas.
    B. Issued to out-of-state applicants who:
        1. Have met Colorado's testing requirement(s),
            or
        2. Have 3 years of out-of-state full-time K–12 experience.

C. Basic Requirements
1. Bachelor's or higher degree from an accepted IHE
2. Completed an approved teacher preparation program at an accepted IHE
3. Institutional recommendation verifying satisfactory completion of an approved program of preparation that confirms grade level or development level(s), subject area(s), or service specialization(s) completed by the applicant
   a. Verifies successful completion of student teaching, internship, or practicum and the grade/developmental level(s)/and endorsement/specialization areas of the experience;
   b. Certifies that the applicant has demonstrated thorough knowledge of the subject matter to be taught and has the competencies essential for educational service; and
   c. Has submitted the application for a license, including the official transcripts, the fees, and other supporting data.
4. Obtained a passing score on the Program for Licensing Assessments for Colorado Educators (PLACE) or an approved Praxis II assessment in an applicable content area
D. Renewal Requirements
1. Submission of renewal application and evaluation fees
III. Professional License (valid 5 years; renewable)
A. Issued to applicants who have completed a CDE-approved induction program or to out-of-state applicants who have 3 years of out-of-state, full-time, continuous K–12 work experience in their endorsement area.
B. Requirements
1. See Initial License requirements II, A–C, directly above
2. Completion of a CDE-approved induction program
C. Renewal Requirements
1. Submission of renewal application, evaluation fee, and evidence of 6 semester hours or 90 clock hours of professional development activities throughout the 5-year validity of the license
   a. Activities may include credits derived from college or university courses, in-services and workshops, educational travel, involvement in school reform (curriculum development), internships, and other approved ongoing professional development and training experiences.
IV. Master Certificate (valid 7 years; renewable)
A. Issued to teacher who has successfully completed the National Board for Professional Teaching Standards (NBPTS) voluntary program
B. Held in conjunction with the Professional License, the Master Certificate will be renewed when the Professional License is renewed.
1. Must hold current NBPTS certificate to renew
V. Alternative Teacher License (valid 1 or 2 years; nonrenewable)
A. Issued to applicants accepted to participate in an approved alternative teacher program who hold a bachelor's degree from a fully accredited IHE, show evidence of passing the applicable PLACE or Praxis II assessment in the relevant content area, or meet subject matter requirements.

    B.   Upon successful completion of program and recommendation of approved alternative teacher program, holder is eligible for Initial Teacher License.

VI.   Principal and Administrator Licenses (renewable). Principal License is valid for all administrative or supervisory positions except chief officer of school district; Administrator License is valid for all administrative or supervisory positions except building principal and director of special education.

    A.   Principal Requirements

       1.   Bachelor's or higher degree from a regionally accredited IHE

       2.   Institutional recommendation verifying satisfactory completion of the approved graduate program of preparation for the school principalship, including a practicum

       3.   Three or more years as a licensed educator in an elementary or secondary school

       4.   Evidence of passing the PLACE assessment in content area

    B.   Professional Principal License Requirements

       1.   Master's degree

       2.   See A, 1–4, directly above

    C.   Administrator

       1.   Approved administrator program

       2.   See A, 1, 2, and 4, directly above

    D.   Director of Special Education

       1.   Master's or higher degree in education, special education, or in a related field of special services, from a regionally accredited IHE

       2.   Completion of an approved program for the preparation of special education directors

       3.   Have a minimum of 2 years of full-time experience working with students with disabilities

VII.   Special Services License

    A.   Bachelor's or higher degree from a regionally accredited IHE

    B.   Successful completion of a state-approved special services preparation program at a regionally accredited IHE, and additional requirements as follows:

       1.   School Audiology

          a.   Doctor of Audiology or Ph.D. in School Audiology, *and*

          b.   Praxis II Audiology exam #10340.

       2.   School Counselor

          a.   Master's degree in School Counseling

          b.   State-approved school counseling program

          c.   Practicum, *and*

          d.   PLACE School Counselor exam.

       3.   School Nurse (option 1)

          a.   Bachelor of Science in Nursing, *and*

          b.   Valid Colorado Registered Nurse License.

4. School Nurse (option 2)
    a. Bachelor's degree,
    b. Current national certification in school nursing,
        and
    c. Three years of experience in school nursing.
5. School Occupational Therapist
    a. Bachelor's degree
    b. American Occupational Therapy Association (AOTA) accredited occupational therapy program,
    c. Internship or supervised field experience,
        and
    d. National exam through North Carolina Board of Occupational Therapy (NCBOT).
6. School Orientation & Mobility Specialist
    a. Bachelor's degree,
    b. Approved preparation program for school orientation and mobility specialists,
    c. Practicum,
    d. Academy for Certification of Vision Rehabilitation and Education Professionals (ACVREP) exam,
        and
    e. ACVREP orientation and mobility certificate.
7. School Physical Therapist
    a. Bachelor's degree,
    b. American Physical Therapy Association (APTA) accredited physical therapy program,
    c. Practicum,
        and
    d. Valid Colorado Physical Therapist License issued by the Colorado Department of Regulatory Agencies.
8. School Psychologist
    a. State-approved sixth-year specialist program (60 graduate semester hours) or doctoral program for school psychologist, serving children birth 0–21,
    b. Internship,
        and
    c. Praxis II School Psychologist Exam #10401 or Nationally Certified School Psychologist (NCSP) certification (Prior to September 13, 2008, test code #10400).
9. School Social Worker
    a. Master of Social Work (MSW) degree, including course work in school and special education law,
    b. Practicum including one placement w/ school aged children,
        and
    c. Association of Social Work Boards (ASWB) master's exam, PLACE School Social Worker exam, or Colorado Licensed Clinical Social

Worker (LCSW) issued by the Colorado Department of Regulatory Agencies.

10. School Speech-Language Pathologist
    a. Master's degree in communication disorders or speech-language pathology,
    b. Speech-language pathology program accredited by the Council on Academic Accreditation (CAA) in audiology and speech-language pathology of the American Speech-Language-Hearing Association (ASHA),
    c. Practicum,
       and
    d. ASHA certification or Praxis II Speech-Language Pathology Exam #20330.

Endorsements

I. Endorsements on licenses and authorizations indicate the grade level(s), subject area(s), or other areas of specialization that are appropriate to the applicant's preparation, training, and experience.

II. One of the following 2 requirements must be met to qualify for the added endorsement being sought:
   A. Academic credit: verification of 24 semester hours with a minimum GPA of 2.6 from an accepted IHE or the equivalent as determined by the Department of Education through transcript review;
      or
   B. Assessment: applicants must pass a PLACE exam or Praxis II approved exam in the endorsement area being sought. The PLACE exam has been approved by the Colorado State Board of Education (CSBE) for all endorsement areas.
      1. Early childhood education (0–8)
      2. Elementary Education (K–6)
      3. Secondary endorsement areas (7–12) include: Agriculture and Renewable Natural Resources; Art; Business Education (K–12); Drama; English Language Arts; Family and Consumer Studies; Foreign Languages(s); Health (K–12); Instructional Technology Teacher (K–12); Linguistically Diverse (K–12); Linguistically Diverse Bilingual Specialist (K–12); Marketing; Mathematics; Music; Physical Education (K–12); School Librarian (K–12); Science (K–12); Social Studies; Speech; Teacher Librarian; Technology Education (Industrial Arts) (K–12); and Trade and Industry Education
      4. Special education endorsements include: Early Childhood Special Education; Early Childhood Special Education Specialist; Gifted and Talented Specialist; Special Education Generalist; Special Education Specialist; Special Education Specialist: Deaf and Hard of Hearing; Special Education Specialist: Blind/Visually Impaired
      5. Graduate endorsements include: Instructional Technology Specialist; Reading Specialist; Reading Teacher; Teacher Librarian
      6. Special services provider endorsement area (0–21) includes: Audiologist;

Occupational Therapist; Orientation and Mobility (Peripatology); Physical Therapist; School Nurse; School Psychology; School Social Worker; School Counselor; and School Speech/Language Pathologist

7. Administrative Endorsements include: Principal; Superintendent; Director of Special Education

Connecticut

On or after July 1, 2016, a master's degree in an appropriate subject matter area, as determined by the State Board of Education, related to the certification endorsement area held, will be required to advance teaching certificates to the professional level. Undergraduate course work will no longer be accepted. For more information, go to www.ct.gov/sde/cert and click on "Maintaining Connecticut Educator Certification."

General Requirements

I. In addition to the specific requirements noted below, individuals seeking certification in Connecticut must fulfill the following teacher assessment requirements:
   A. Demonstrate essential skills in mathematics, reading, and writing by passing the Praxis I Academic Skills Assessments or by receiving a waiver
   B. Demonstrate subject matter competence by receiving a satisfactory evaluation on the Praxis II, American Council on the Teaching of Foreign Languages (ACTFL), or the Foundations of Reading tests as required for certification in specific endorsement areas (including elementary, middle grades, secondary, special subjects, and administration)
   C. For teachers advancing from the initial to the provisional certificate, based on appropriate, authorized Connecticut public school experience, successfully complete the Teacher Education And Mentoring (TEAM) program for beginning educators that includes mentorship, professional development, and up to 5 professional growth modules in the following domains of the Common Core of Teaching (CCT): classroom environment; planning; instruction; assessment; and professional responsibility.
      1. At the culmination of each module, beginning teachers will submit a written reflection paper to a district or regional review committee.
II. Connecticut requires each candidate for certification to present either the recommendation of the preparing institution for the certification sought, or verification of 2 years of successful experience appropriate to the specific endorsement requested. Experience in an approved private or out-of-state public school under valid authorization may be acceptable.

Integrated Early Childhood Special Education (Birth–K or Nursery–Grade 3)

I. Initial Educator Certificate for Birth–K and N–3
   A. Bachelor's degree from an approved institution
   B. General education, including study in 5 out of 6 of the following areas, as well as a survey course in U.S. history, semester hours 39
      1. English
      2. Science
      3. Mathematics

  4. Social studies

  5. Fine arts

  6. Foreign language

 C. Human growth and development, including typical and atypical development, psychology of learning, and family studies (may be part of a subject area major or general academic courses), semester hours 15

 D. Completion of a major awarded by an approved institution in any 1 subject area (a major or courses in professional education may not be counted),

   or

  Completion of an interdisciplinary major consisting of 39 semester hours with a concentration of at least 18 semester hours in human growth and development, including typical and atypical development, psychology of learning, and family studies, with the remainder distributed among no more than 3 additional subjects related to human growth and development (a major or course work in professional education may not be counted)

 E. Professional education in early childhood education in each of the following areas, semester hours 36

  1. Foundations of education

  2. Curriculum and methods of teaching

   a. Required courses differ for Birth–K and N–3 endorsements; contact the Bureau of Educator Preparation and Certification (Bureau) for details (see Appendix 1).

  3. Supervised student teaching at the level of the endorsement, semester hours 6–12

   a. Contact the Bureau for additional details (see Appendix 1).

II. Provisional Educator Certificate

 A. Evidence of meeting the general conditions and requirements for an initial certificate

 B. Completion of beginning educator program (Teacher Education and Mentoring [TEAM] program) as may be available from the Department of Education and 10 school months of successful service under the interim or initial certificates or durational shortage area permit,

   or

  Thirty school months of successful teaching in the same area for which the provisional educator certificate is being sought, in a school approved by the appropriate governing body in another state, within 10 years prior to application

III. Professional Educator Certificate

 A. Thirty school months of successful teaching under the provisional educator certificate

 B. Course work beyond bachelor's degree, semester hours 30

  To include:

  1. A planned program at an approved institution of higher education, related directly to the subject areas or grade levels of the endorsement or in an area or areas related to the teacher's ability to provide instruction effectively or to meet locally determined goals or objectives,

or

2. An individual program that is mutually determined or approved by the teacher and the employing board of education and is designed to increase the ability of the teacher to improve student learning

C. On and after July 1, 2016, a master's degree in an appropriate subject matter area, as determined by the State Board of Education, related to the teacher's certification area

Elementary Education (1–6)

I. Initial Educator Certificate
   A. See Integrated Early Childhood Special Education, I, A, above
      1. General education, including study in 5 out of 6 of the following areas, as well as a survey course in U.S. history, semester hours 39
         English, science, mathematics, social studies,
         and either
         Fine arts,
         or
         Foreign language
      2. Must include 6 semester hours in child and/or human growth and development
   B. Completion of a major awarded by an approved institution in any 1 subject area (a major or courses in professional education may not be counted),
      or
      Completion of an interdisciplinary major consisting of 39 semester hours, with a concentration of at least 18 semester hours in any 1 subject area and the remainder distributed among no more than 3 subjects related to the concentration (a major or courses in professional education may not be counted)
   C. Professional education in each of the following areas, semester hours 30
      1. Foundations of education
      2. Educational psychology
      3. Curriculum and methods of teaching
         a. Must include 6 semester hours in language arts
      4. Supervised observation, participation, and full-time, responsible student teaching, semester hours 6–12
      5. Course of study in special education of at least 36 clock hours covering specific areas (contact the Bureau for additional details; see Appendix 1).
II. Provisional Educator Certificate
   A. See Integrated Early Childhood Special Education, II, A and B, above
III. Professional Educator Certificate
   A. See Integrated Early Childhood Special Education, III, A–C, above

Middle Grades (4–8)

Note: The middle grades subject-specific certificate or a secondary academic certificate authorizes the teaching of specific subjects in grades 4–8. Middle grades certificates shall be endorsed for the subject in accordance with the recommendation of the preparing institution or teaching experience appropriate to the endorsement sought.

I. Initial Educator Certificate
    A. See Integrated Early Childhood Special Education, I, A and B, above
    B. Completion of any 1 of the following
        1. A subject area major in any of the following areas: English, mathematics, biology, physics, chemistry, earth science, general science, social science, history, political science, economics, geography, anthropology, sociology,
           or
        2. An interdisciplinary major in humanities, history/social science, or integrated science,
           or
        3. Twenty-four semester hours of study in 1 of the subjects (except general science) listed directly above in B, 1,
           and either
           a. Fifteen semester hours in a second subject of those listed directly above in B, 1 (except general science), which will result in endorsements in 2 subject areas,
              or
           b. Fifteen semester hours in an all-level endorsement area that will not qualify for an additional teaching endorsement
    C. See Elementary Education, I, C, 1, 2, 4 and 5, above
        1. Curriculum and methods of teaching (6 credits minimum) to include
           a. Reading and writing across middle grades curriculum,
              and
           b. Methods for teaching at the middle grades level
    D. For middle grades endorsement in English, history or social science, mathematics, humanities, and integrated science, special courses are required. Contact the Bureau for additional information (see Appendix 1).
II. Provisional Educator Certificate
    A. See Integrated Early Childhood Special Education, II, A and B, above
III. Professional Educator Certificate
    A. See Integrated Early Childhood Special Education, III, A–C, above

Secondary Academic (7–12)

I. Initial Educator Certificate
    A. Bachelor's degree from an approved institution
    B. General education, including a survey course in U.S. history and including study in 5 of the 6 following areas, semester hours 39
        1. English
        2. Natural sciences
        3. Mathematics

   4. Social studies
   5. Arts
   6. Foreign languages
C. Completion of a subject area major awarded by an approved institution in the subject for which endorsement is sought (professional education majors may not be used to fulfill this requirement),
or
Completion of at least 30 semester hours in the subject for which certification is sought and a minimum of 9 semester hours in a subject or subjects directly related to the subject for which certification is sought (professional education majors or courses may not be used to fulfill this requirement or to fulfill the requirements for the specific endorsements listed below)
   1. General science endorsement—Major may be met by completion of at least 39 semester hours in science, including study in biology, chemistry, physics, and earth science.
   2. History and social studies endorsement—Requirements may be met by completion of a major in 1 of the following areas:
       a. History (including 18 semester hours in social studies)
       b. Political science, economics, geography, or anthropology/sociology (including at least 18 semester hours in history)
       c. An interdisciplinary major of at least 39 semester hours in subjects covered by the endorsement, with at least 18 semester hours in history, including U.S. history, western civilization or European history, and nonwestern history; and with at least 1 course each in political science, economics, geography, anthropology, sociology, and psychology
   3. Business endorsement—Major awarded by an approved institution in business or in any 1 of the subjects covered by the endorsement or an interdisciplinary major consisting of 39 semester hours of credit in subjects covered by the endorsement
   4. Foreign language endorsement—24 semester hours in the foreign language in which endorsement is sought
D. Completion of a planned program of study and experience in professional education, including study in the following areas, semester hours 18
   1. Foundations of education
   2. Educational psychology
   3. Curriculum and methods of teaching
   4. Supervised observation, participation, and full-time responsible student teaching, semester hours 6–12
   5. Course of study in special education of at least 36 clock hours covering specific areas
II. Provisional Certificate
   A. See Integrated Early Childhood Special Education, II, A and B, above
III. Professional Certificate
   A. See Integrated Early Childhood Special Education, III, A–C, above

Special Subjects

Special subject endorsements, taught at the elementary and secondary levels, are agriculture, art, health, home economics, technology education, music, and physical education.

I.   Initial Educator Certificate
    A.   Bachelor's degree from an approved institution
    B.   General education, semester hours 39
       1.   See Secondary Academic, I, B, above
    C.   Completion of a subject area major awarded by an approved institution in the subject for which endorsement is sought (professional education majors, except those in physical education and technology education, may not be used to fulfill this requirement),
       or
       Completion of at least 30 semester hours in the special subject or field for which certification is sought and a minimum of 9 semester hours in a subject or subjects directly related to the subject for which certification is sought (professional education majors or courses, except those in physical education and technology education, may not be used to fulfill this requirement)
    D.   Professional education, semester hours 18
       1.   See Secondary Academic, I, D, above
II.   Provisional Certificate
    A.   See Integrated Early Childhood Special Education, II, A and B, above
III.   Professional Certificate
    A.   See Integrated Early Childhood Special Education, III, A–C, above

School Counselor

I.   Initial Educator Certificate
    A.   Holds a Professional Educator Certificate,
       or
       Holds or is eligible for an Initial Educator Certificate with 3 years of successful teaching experience, or completion of a 1-year, full-time supervised school internship as school counselor
    B.   Master's degree
    C.   Study in an approved institution, to include 30 semester hours in a planned program in school counseling
    D.   Recommendation by preparing institution based on knowledge, skills, and understanding in the following areas: principles and philosophy of developmental guidance and counseling; psychological and sociological theory as related to children, youth, and family; career development theory and practice; individual and group counseling procedures; organizational patterns and relationship of pupil services to total school and community programs; pupil appraisal and evaluation techniques; and school-based consultation theory and practice

E.   Evidence of progression of supervised experience in counseling and guidance through laboratory and practicum

F.   Course of study covering specific areas in special education of at least 36 clock hours

II.   Provisional Educator Certificate

A.   See Integrated Early Childhood Special Education II, A and B, above, except that successful service must be in a school counseling capacity

III.   Professional Educator Certificate

A.   Thirty school months of successful service under the provisional educator certificate, interim educator certificate, or provisional teaching certificate

B.   Completion of at least 45 semester hours of graduate credit at an approved institution in counseling and related courses

Intermediate Administration or Supervision

I.   Initial Educator Certificate for Intermediate Administration or Supervision (deputy or assistant superintendent, principal or assistant principal, etc.)

A.   Eighteen semester hours of graduate credit in addition to a master's degree from an approved institution

B.   Fifty school months of successful teaching or administrative service in public schools or approved nonpublic schools, or as a professional or managerial staff member in a state education agency

C.   Recommendation of an approved institution where the applicant has completed a planned program of preparation for school administrative and supervisory personnel

D.   See Superintendent of Schools, I, E, 1–5, below, except in a program for intermediate administrators

E.   See Superintendent of Schools, I, F, below.

II.   Provisional Educator Certificate for Intermediate Administration or Supervision

A.   Same as Integrated Early Childhood Special Education, II, A and B, above, except that successful service must be in an administrative capacity

III.   Professional Educator Certificate for Intermediate Administration or Supervision

A.   Thirty school months of successful service under the provisional educator certificate, interim educator certificate, or provisional teaching certificate

B.   Completion of at least 30 semester hours of graduate credit at an approved institution, in addition to the master's degree

Superintendent of Schools

I.   Initial Educator Certificate (superintendent of schools or executive director of a regional educational service center)

A.   Master's degree from an approved institution, as well as 30 semester hours of graduate credit beyond the master's degree

B.   Completion of 80 school months of successful teaching or service, at least 50 of which shall have been in public schools or approved nonpublic schools, or as a professional or managerial staff member in a state education agency. This total may include the 30 school months of required administrative experience (see I, C, directly below).

C. Thirty school months of full-time administrative or supervisory experience in public schools or approved nonpublic schools, or as a managerial staff member in a state education agency in position(s) that would have required certification had the service been in Connecticut public schools. On specific recommendation of the preparing institution, consideration may be given to applicants who have completed a substantial period of internship in general school administration as part of a supervised, planned program of preparation for the superintendency.

D. Recommendation of an approved institution where the applicant has completed an approved program specifically in preparation for the position of superintendent of schools. The program shall be no less than 30 graduate semester hours, at least 15 of which have been completed at that institution and the remainder approved by it.

E. Graduate study in each of the following areas:
1. Psychological and pedagogical foundations of learning
2. Curriculum development and program monitoring
3. School administration
4. Personnel evaluation and supervision
5. Contemporary educational problems and solutions from a policy-making perspective

F. Course of study covering specific areas in special education of at least 36 clock hours

II. Provisional Educator Certificate
A. See Integrated Early Childhood Special Education, II, A and B, above

III. Professional Educator Certificate
A. Present evidence of having served successfully under the provisional educator or interim provisional educator certificates for a period of at least 30 school months

Other Certificates

I. Teaching Certificates
A. Comprehensive special education (K–12)
B. Teaching English to speakers of other languages
C. Bilingual education
D. Remedial reading and remedial language arts (1–12)
E. Occupational subjects in vocational-technical schools
F. Applied curriculum and technology subjects
G. Adult education
H. School library media specialist
I. School nurse–teacher
J. School dental hygienist–teacher

II. Special Service Certificates
A. Speech and language pathology,
B. School psychology,
C. School social work.
D. School marriage and family therapist

III. Administrative Certificates
A. Reading and language arts consultant,
B. Department chairperson,
C. School business administrator.

Please contact the Bureau (see Appendix 1) for the requirements for these certificates.

Delaware

Effective July 1, 2014, evidence of successful completion of Praxis Series Core Academic Skills for Educators must be submitted before an Initial License can be issued.

Licensure

I. Initial License (valid 3 years; nonrenewable but extendable upon proof of exigent circumstances or up to 3-year leave of absence)
   A. In-State Requirements
      1. Bachelor's degree from regionally accredited college or university
      2. Complete approved student teaching program,
         or
         Enrollment in the Alternative Routes to Teacher Licensure and Certification Program,
         or
         Complete 91 days "in lieu of student teaching" in 1 assignment in a Delaware public/charter school within the last year before application for license, with supporting evidence of satisfactory performance from evaluations,
         and
         Meet or exceed cut-off scores on Praxis Series Core Academic Skills for Educators: Reading 156, Writing 162, Math 150.
   B. Out-of-State or Lapsed Requirements
      1. Department of Education may issue an initial license/certificate to applicant licensed as an educator in another jurisdiction if applicant has less than 3 years of teaching experience, or to an applicant who previously held a valid Delaware Standard Professional Status certificate who has been out the profession for more than 3 years
   C. In addition to an Initial License, applicants must also apply for a standard certificate in the appropriate area; see standard certificate below.
   D. Preparations for Continuing License Application
      Before expiration of Initial License, applicant must:
      1. Complete professional development and mentoring activities
      2. Receive 2 out of 3 satisfactory evaluations
      3. Disclose any criminal conviction history
II. Continuing License (valid 5 years; renewable and extendable upon proof of exigent circumstances or up to 3-year leave of absence)
   A. General Requirements
      1. Successfully complete requirements for Initial License (see I, A–C, directly above),
         and

Receive no more than 1 unsatisfactory annual evaluation, as defined by the Delaware Performance Appraisal System, during period of Initial License.
2. Hold current and valid educator license in another jurisdiction with evidence of completing 3 or more years of successful teaching experience
B. Requirements for Licensed Educators Returning to Work
1. Continuing license issued upon employment for current holders of standard or professional status license
2. Holders of expired licenses out of the profession for less than 3 years may apply with evidence of Delaware certification and will receive an Initial License.
3. Holders of expired licenses out of the profession for more than 3 years must also, within first year of employment, successfully complete district-sponsored mentoring program.
C. An educator holding a current or expired Professional Status or Standard Certificate who is assigned to work outside the area covered by that credential will be issued a Continuing License, with an Emergency Certificate for the new area, for a period of 1 year to enable the educator to fulfill the new area's Standard Certificate requirements.
D. Continuing License Renewal (valid 5 years; renewable)
1. Fulfill 90-clock-hour requirement for professional development
a. At least 45 hours every 5 years must be in activities related to educator's work with students or staff
b. Professional development hours must take place during term of continuing license
c. See Department of Education (Appendix1) for detailed options
d. Disclose any criminal conviction history
III. Advanced Licensure (valid 10 years; renewable)
A. Requirements
1. Application by holder of National Board of Professional Teaching Standards certification or equivalent program approved by Professional Standards Board
B. Renewal
1. Renewable for additional 10-year term provided that educator maintains proficiency under program for which license was first issued
2. If holder does not renew the Advanced License, a Continuing License will be issued upon expiration of the Advanced License.

Alternative Routes to Teacher Licensure and Certification Program

I. Candidates seeking participation in the Alternative Routes to Teacher Licensure and Certification Program shall be issued an Initial License of no more than 3 years' duration.
II. Requirements:
A. Hold a bachelor's degree from a regionally accredited college or university, with a major appropriate to the instructional field they desire to teach

B. Pass an examination of general knowledge, such as Praxis I, or provide an acceptable alternative

C. Pass an examination of content knowledge, such as Praxis II, in the instructional field they desire to teach, if applicable and available

D. Obtain acceptable health and criminal background check clearances

E. Obtain and accept an offer of employment in a position that requires licensure and certification

III. Components of the Alternative Routes Program

A. Summer institute of approximately 120 instructional (clock) hours completed by candidates prior to the beginning of teaching assignments

B. One-year, full-time practicum experience that includes a period of intensive on-the-job mentoring and supervision beginning the first day of classroom teaching and continuing for 30 weeks

C. Seminars on teaching that provide Alternative Routes to Teacher Licensure and Certification teachers with approximately 200 instructional (clock) hours or equivalent professional development during the first year of their teaching assignment and during an intensive seminar the following summer

Standard Certificate

I. Issued to an educator who holds a valid Delaware Initial, Continuing, or Advanced License; or a Limited Standard, Standard, or Professional Status Certificate issued prior to August 31, 2003, who has met the following requirements

II. Preliminary Requirement

A. Certification from the National Board for Professional Teaching Standards in area of certification;
   or

B. Meeting the requirements of the relevant Department or Standards Board regulation for obtaining a Standard Certificate in area of certification;
   or

C. Graduation from a National Council for Accreditation of Teacher Education (NCATE) approved educator preparation program, or from a Delaware-approved educator preparation program using National Association of State Directors of Teacher Education and Certification (NASDTEC) or NCATE standards, with a major or its equivalent in area of certification;
   or

D. Satisfactory completion of the Alternative Routes to Teacher Licensure and Certification Program, the Special Institute for Licensure and Certification, or other approved alternative educator preparation programs;
   or

E. Bachelor's degree from a regionally accredited college or university in any content area including 15 credit hours or their equivalent in professional development related to their area of certification, of which at least 6 credit hours must focus on pedagogy, selected by the applicant with the approval of the employing school district or charter school;

and

III. Additional Requirements

    A. Meet or exceed Praxis II scores in the area of certification, if applicable and available

       or

    B. Hold a valid and current license/certificate in certification area from another state.

Early Childhood Teacher Standard Certificate (Birth–Grade 2)

I. Issued to an applicant who holds a valid Delaware Initial, Continuing, or Advanced License; or a Limited Standard, Standard, or Professional Status Certificate issued prior to August 31, 2003

II. Requirements

    A. See Standard Certificate, I and II, above

    B. If an examination of content knowledge such as Praxis II is not applicable and available in Early Childhood Education, and if the educator is applying for his/her second Standard Certificate, then the applicant must satisfactorily complete 15 credits or its equivalent in professional development related to Early Childhood Education, selected by the applicant with the approval of the employing school district or charter school, which is submitted to the Department of Education.

Elementary Teacher Standard Certificate (Grades K–6)

I. Issued to an educator who holds a valid Delaware Initial, Continuing, or Advanced License; or a Limited Standard, Standard, or Professional Status Certificate issued by the Department prior to August 31, 2003

II. Requirements

    A. See Early Childhood Teacher Standard Certificate, II, A and B, above

Administration

I. School Principal/Assistant Principal

    A. Educational Requirements—satisfy at least 1 of the following:

       1. Master's or doctoral degree in educational leadership, offered by an NCATE specialty organization–recognized educator preparation program or state-approved educator preparation program where the state approval body employed the appropriate NASDTEC or NCATE specialty organization standards, at a regionally accredited college or university

          or

       2. Master's or doctoral degree in any field from regionally accredited college or university and successful completion of one of the following:

          a. School Principal course of study, as defined in 14 DE Admin. Code 1595 Certification Programs for Leaders in Education,

             or

      b.   School Principal certification program pursuant to 14 DE Admin. Code 1595 Certification Programs for Leaders in Education.

  B. Experience Requirement

     1.   Minimum of 5 years of teaching experience at level to be initially assigned, except for middle level, where teaching experience may be at PK–12 level, or as a Principal or Assistant Principal of a school for exceptional students

        a.   Teaching experience means meeting students on a regularly scheduled basis, planning and delivering instruction, developing or preparing instructional materials, and evaluating student performance in any PK–12 setting.

           i.   Experience must be in categories of children served (example: autistic)

          ii.   Principal of Exceptional Children must have teaching experience with exceptional children.

II.   Certified Central Office Personnel

  A. Education Requirements

     Satisfy at least 1 of the following additional education requirements:

     1.   Master's or doctoral degree in educational leadership offered by an NCATE-specialty-organization-recognized educator preparation program or state-approved educator preparation program where the state approval body employed the appropriate NASDTEC or NCATE specialty organization standards, at a regionally accredited college or university,
        or

     2.   Master's degree from a regionally accredited college or university in any field and 1 of the following:

        a.   Successful completion of an approved Program pursuant to 14 DE Admin. Code 1595 Certification Programs for Leaders in Education,
           or

        b.   Hold a Standard Certificate School Principal and successful completion of an additional 9 graduate-level credit hours from a regionally accredited college or university in educational leadership or the equivalent in professional development approved by the Department.

  B. Experience Requirement

     1.   Minimum of 5 years of teaching experience

III. Superintendent or Assistant Superintendent

  A. Satisfy at least 1 of the following additional education requirements:

     1.   Doctoral degree in educational leadership offered by an NCATE-specialty-organization-recognized educator preparation program or state-approved educator preparation program where the state approval body employed the appropriate NASDTEC or NCATE specialty organization standards, at a regionally accredited college or university,
        or

     2.   Master's or doctoral degree from a regionally accredited college or university in any field and 1 of the following:

    a.   Successful completion of an approved Program pursuant to 14 DE Admin. Code 1595 Certification Programs for Leaders in Education,
       or

    b.   Hold a Standard Certificate Certified Central Office Personnel or a Standard Certificate Special Education Director and successful completion of an additional 9 graduate level credit hours from a regionally accredited college or university in educational leadership or the equivalent in professional development approved by the Department.

B. Experience Requirements

    1.   Minimum of 5 years of teaching experience,
       and

    2.   Minimum of 2 years of full-time leadership experience working in any of the following areas:

        a.   A School Principal or an Assistant School Principal,
           or

        b.   A Certified Central Office Personnel Educator,
           or

        c.   A Special Education Director,
           or

        d.   Other leadership position,

IV. Special Education Director

  A. Education requirements

    Satisfy at least 1 of the following additional education requirements:

    1.   Master's or doctoral degree in educational leadership offered by an NCATE specialty organization-recognized educator preparation program or state-approved educator preparation program where the state approval body employed the appropriate NASDTEC or NCATE specialty organization standards, at a regionally accredited college or university,
       and

       Thirty graduate level semester hours from a regionally accredited college or university in Special Education taken either as part of a degree program or in addition to it, or the equivalent in professional development pre-approved by the Department;
       or

    2.   Master's or doctoral degree in special education offered by an NCATE-specialty-organization-recognized educator preparation program or state-approved educator preparation program where the state approval body employed the appropriate NASDTEC or NCATE specialty organization standards, at a regionally accredited college or university,
       and

       Successful completion of any approved Program pursuant to 14 DE Admin. Code 1595 Certification programs for Leaders in Education;
       or

    3.   Master's or doctoral degree from a regionally accredited college or university in any field,

and

Successful completion of an approved Special Education Director Program pursuant to 14 DE Admin. Code 1595 Certification Programs for Leaders in Education.

B. Additional Education Requirements

Satisfy at least 1 of the following:

1. Minimum of 5 years of teaching experience with exceptional children special education students at the PreK to 12 public school level or the equivalent as approved by the Department;
   or
2. Minimum of 5 years professional experience under a Delaware Standard Certificate or other Delaware professional license, including but not limited to school psychologist, speech pathologist, or audiologist, working with exceptional children special education students at the PreK-to-12 level or the equivalent as approved by the Department;
   or
3. Minimum of 5 years administrative experience working with exceptional children special education students at the PreK-to-12 level or the equivalent as approved by the Department;
   or
4. Any combination of the types of experiences prescribed above which totals a minimum of 5 years.

Guidance Counselor

I. Elementary School Counselor
   A. Requirements
      1. Holds a valid Delaware Initial, Continuing, or Advanced License or a Limited Standard, Standard, or Professional Status Certicate issued prior to August 31, 2003; and meets the following requirements:
      2. Graduated from an NCATE-specialty-organization-recognized educator preparation program or from a state-approved educator preparation program offered by a regionally accredited college or university, with a master's degree in Elementary School Counseling,
         or
      3. Holds a master's degree from a regionally accredited college in any field; with a minimum of 27 semester hours of graduate course work in the areas of principles and practices of the counseling program, individual counseling skills, group counseling skills, human development, developmental group guidance, individual and group testing for counselors, supervised practicum in elementary counseling, counseling theory, and consultation;
         and one of the following:
         a. Minimum of 3 years of professional experience in an elementary school setting
            or

   b. Three years of equivalent experience as approved by the Department of Education
    or
   c. Supervised school counseling internship of 1 full year in an elementary school setting as part of a graduate degree program in elementary school counseling or arranged by the Department of Education; may be completed over a 2-year period on a half-time basis.

 II. Secondary School Counselor
  A. Requirements—the same as for Elementary School Counselor, but at the secondary school level

School Psychologist

 I. Licensure Requirements
  A. Bachelor's degree in any content area from a regionally accredited college or university
  B. Graduate-level program of study, approved by the National Association of School Psychologists (NASP) or the American Psychological Association (APA), offered by a regionally accredited college or university titled "School Psychology," consisting of a minimum of 60 graduate-level credit hours, of which at least 54 credits are exclusive of an internship,
   and
   Supervised internship of no less than 1,200 hours, completed at or near the end of the program, and completed either full time or half time over a period of no more than 2 consecutive years, at least 600 hours of which must be in a school setting,
   or
  C. Completion of an organized graduate-level program of study offered by a regionally accredited college or university titled "School Psychology," consisting of a minimum of 60 graduate level credit hours, of which at least 54 credits are exclusive of an internship,
   and
   Evidence of substantial graduate-level preparation.
  D. Valid certificate from the National School Psychology Certification Board,
   or
   Valid certificate in school psychology from another state department of education in the U.S.,
   or
   Valid license as a psychologist issued by the Delaware Board of Examiners of Psychologists.

School Social Worker

 I. Requirements
  A. Standard Certificate as a School Social Worker will be given to an applicant who has the following:

1. Valid Delaware Initial, Continuing, or Advanced License,
   or
   Standard or Professional Status Certificate issued by the Department prior to August 31, 2003;
2. Master of Social Work (MSW) degree from a regionally accredited college or university;
3. Two years of successful full-time work experience as a social worker;
4. One year of supervised experience in a school setting,
   or
   One-year internship of 1,000 hours approved by the Department of Education and supervised by an appropriate school designee.

Library/Media Specialist

I. Licensure Requirements
   A. The Department shall issue a Standard Certificate to an applicant meeting the requirements below who holds
      1. A valid Delaware Initial, Continuing, or Advanced License,
         or
      2. A Standard or Professional Status Certificate issued prior to August 31, 2003.
II. Education Requirements
   A. Bachelor's degree in any content area from a regionally accredited college/ university, with completion of a master's degree from a regionally accredited college/university in an American Library Association (ALA)–approved program in School Library/Media,
      or
   B. Master's degree from a regionally accredited college/university in any other content area, including a general Media Library Specialist (MLS) degree, and completion of a program in School Library/Media approved by the Department pursuant to 14 DE Administrative Code 399 which meets ALA standards

District of Columbia

Teaching Licenses/Credentials

I. Regular I License (valid 2 years; nonrenewable; upgrades to Regular II)
   A. Bachelor's degree;
   B. Verification of current enrollment in state-approved teacher preparation program;
   C. Verification of current employment as the teacher of record in a Washington, D.C. (DC), local education agency (LEA);
   D. Passing scores for the basic skills examination (e.g., Praxis CORE, Praxis I, SAT, ACT, or GRE);
      and
   E. Passing score for Praxis II Content Knowledge exam in content area of teaching assignment; for details, visit the Educator Licensure and Accreditation website at www.osse.dc.gov

II. Regular II License (valid 4 years; renewable)
   A. Bachelor's degree;
   B. Verification of successful completion of state-approved teacher preparation program or completion of all course work and experience requirements found in DC municipal regulations with Praxis testing, including passing scores for all portions of the Praxis I and for all required Praxis II content knowledge and pedagogy exams in the area of licensure;
      or
   C. Obtain licensure via reciprocity. For details about reciprocity eligibility, see www.osse.dc.gov

III. Transitional License (valid 1 year; nonrenewable)
   A. Bachelor's degree;
   B. May only be requested by a DC LEA;
   C. Candidate has never been previously employed as a DC public school teacher;
      and
   D. Candidate has major in content area of teaching assignment (liberal arts for elementary education teaching assignments),
      or
      Candidate has verification of completion of state-approved teacher education program or holds a valid level II license from another state and only needs to complete DC's testing requirements.

IV. Past Licenses: the following changes apply
   A. Three-year Provisional license is now a two-year nonrenewable Regular I license.
   B. Five-year Standard license is now a four-year renewable Regular II license.
   C. Five-year Professional license is now a four-year renewable Regular II license.
   D. Limited Term Substitute licenses are no longer issued or renewed.

      1.   All applicants must hold a bachelor's degree to be eligible for Substitute teacher licensure.

   E.   Licensure changes for current license holders will be effective upon application for licensure renewal or upgrade.

  V.   Adding Additional Teaching Endorsements

   A.   Individuals who currently hold a valid Regular II teaching license may obtain additional teacher certification endorsements by successfully completing required Praxis II Pedagogy exam or by evidence of 3 years of recognized full-time teaching experience at the appropriate grade level(s);
    and

   B.   Successfully completing Praxis II Content Exam,
    or
    Completing content course work required in DC municipal regulations from accredited college/university,
    or
    Completing a degree major or major equivalent (30 semester hours) in the single subject teaching area; visit the Educator Licensure and Accreditation website at www.osse.dc.gov for full details.

 VI.   Service Provider Licenses

   A.   School Psychologist

      1.   Conferred master's degree in school, educational, or clinical psychology from accredited institution, including at least 42 semester hours of graduate-level course work with content in the following:

         a.   Fifteen semester hours to include: introduction to school psychology or seminar in school psychology; child adolescent psychology or developmental psychology; psychology of abnormal behavior/psychopathy of childhood and adolescence (mental hygiene); statistics, tests, and measurements, evaluation, or research methods;

         b.   Six semester hours from among the following: neurology or neuro-psychology and brain behavior; biological basis of behavior; theories of learning; or theories of personality;

         c.   Nine semester hours from the following: history and systems of psychology; psychology of the exceptional child; sociocultural education; survey of problems and issues in special education; or public school law, urban issues, legal and ethical issues;

         d.   Six semester hours to include the following: individual assessment of cognitive abilities; and behavioral assessment (behavioral checklist, classroom observation techniques);
           and

         e.   Six semester hours from the following: evaluation and diagnosis of exceptional children; diagnosis and remedial techniques in arithmetic; the learning disabled child/learning disabilities; or personality assessment;
           and

    2.   At least 500 clock hours of satisfactory field experience in PreK–12 school setting under supervision of certified school psychologist.

B.   School Counselor

    1.   Conferred master's degree in school counseling from accredited institution that includes at least 300 clock hours of graduate-level university-supervised field experience in counseling in PreK–12 grade school setting

        a.   Field experience requirement may be met by completion of degree in school counseling from program approved by Council for Accreditation of Counseling and Related Educational Programs (CACREP) or National Board of Certified Counselors (NBCC) certificate.

            i.   Degree program shall include graduate-level course work with content in the following: philosophy and principles underlying guidance and other pupil personnel services; the theory and practice of counseling, including work with exceptional and culturally diverse students; educational and psychological measurement; career development theory including career planning and decision-making techniques and the use of occupational and educational information; understanding the individual (i.e., the nature and range of human characteristics); group counseling and group guidance processes; research and evaluation; elementary, middle, and secondary school counseling;

C.   School Librarian / Media Specialist

    1.   Conferred master's degree from accredited institution;
        and

    2.   Twenty-one semester hours in library or information science content that includes the following: cataloging and classification; computerized applications of library automation and information access; instructional media design and production; organization of school library media programs and collections; reference sources and services; evaluation, selection and utilization of instructional media for children and young people; and integration of library resources in the curriculum;
        and

    3.   Directed field experience in school library media center with experienced media specialist;
        or
        Two years of successful recognized teaching experience;
        or
        One year of library experience.

D.   The OSSE issues additional service provider licenses; visit the Educator Licensure and Accreditation website at www.osse.dc.gov for full details on the following:

    1.   Attendance Officer

    2.   Pupil Personnel Worker

    3.   School Social Worker

    4.   Audiologist

    5.   Psychometrist

    6.   Speech Pathologist

VII. Teacher and Service Provider Licensure Renewal Requirements
    A. Note for all Standard and Professional license holders regarding renewal:
        1. Standard and professional license holders will receive a 4-year Regular II license upon renewal.
        2. Acceptable renewal credits/hours shall be earned within the previous 4 years from the date the renewal application is being submitted.
    B. To renew a Standard, Professional, or Regular II District of Columbia license, applicants must submit evidence of:
        1. Six semester hours or 90 contact hours (or a combination of the two) of professional development activities completed within the previous 4 years before date of renewal application submission.
            a. Minimum of 3 semester hours/45 clock hours of professional development activities must be directly related to field (subject content) of license being renewed;
            b. Remaining required 3 semester hours/45 clock hours may include any professional development activity relevant to Pre-K–12 education and/or serving Pre-K–12 students.
            c. Examples of acceptable renewal activities include: course work at accredited college or university; workshops, seminars, or conferences sponsored by a local education agency/school district and/or other education/professional organization
            d. For information on translating college/university credit hours, Continuing Education Units (CEUs), and Professional Learning Units (PLUs) into contact hours, visit the Educator Licensure and Accreditation website at www.osse.dc.gov
        2. Individuals with more than 1 license must meet subject matter requirements for each licensure area separately (3 credits or 45 contact hours per license). The same general education credits/hours may be used to renew more than one license.
VIII. School Administrator Licensure
    A. Administrative Services Credential Requirements
        1. Option 1
            a. Bachelor's degree from accredited college or university;
            b. Completion of state-approved program in K–12 School Leadership/Administration;
            c. Successful completion of 2 years of full time PreK–12 school-based teaching or pupil services experience,
              or
              Two years of other full-time PreK–12 school-based instructional leadership work experience;
              and
            d. Official verification of passing score for School Leaders Licensure Assessment (SLLA) as required by DC.
        2. Option 2
            a. Master's degree or higher from accredited college or university;

  b.   Successful completion of 2 years of full-time PreK–12 school-based teaching or pupil services experience,
       or
       Two years of other full-time PreK–12 school-based instructional leadership work experience;
       and
  c.   Official verification of passing score for the SLLA as required by DC.
B. License Types
  1. Regular Administrator (valid 4 years, renewable)
       a.   For applicants who successfully meet all requirements outlined in Option 1 or 2, directly above
  2. Transitional Administrator (valid 1 year; nonrenewable)
       a.   For applicant who holds current out-of-state license that authorizes him/her to operate as full or lead principal in a K–12 grade school but who has not completed the SLLA as required by DC or have not passed a comparable administrator exam in the state where licensed
  3. Please note that DC issues a combined principal/assistant principal license
       a.   License holders from other states who only hold assistant principal's license will not qualify for DC license under the Interstate Licensure Agreement, but may qualify for licensure by meeting requirements as stated directly above in A, 1 and 2.
C. School Administrator License Renewal Requirements
  1. Completion of 200 clock hours of approved professional development activities and services completed within previous 4 years from the date renewal application is filed.
       a.   Professional development hours may be accrued by completion of activities from 1 or more of following options: college credit, professional workshops presented by approved nationally recognized entities, and professional development activities approved by employing local educational agencies.

Florida

The Bureau of Educator Certification at the Florida Department of Education determines individualized testing requirements for certification. After your application for certification is on file, the Bureau will issue you an Official Statement of Status of Eligibility. This statement will indicate your individualized testing requirements; these may include the Florida Teacher Certification Exams (FTCE) or, for candidates seeking certification in educational leadership, the Florida Educational Leadership Exam (FELE). Contact the Bureau (see Appendix 1) for complete information.

Types of Certificates

I. Professional Certificate Eligibility Requirements
    A professional certificate valid for 5 school years, may be issued to an applicant who meets all of the following:
    A. Files a completed application, including official degree transcripts and a complete fingerprint report that has been cleared by the Florida Department of Law Enforcement and the FBI
    B. Holds a bachelor's or higher degree from an acceptable institution of higher learning
    C. Has an acceptable major in a single subject in which Florida offers certification or meets specialization requirements in the subject
    D. Has obtained a 2.5 grade-point average on a 4.0 scale in each subject shown on the certificate
    E. Meets professional preparation requirements (see IV, below)
    F. Has received a passing score on the Florida General Knowledge Test or on the College Level Academic Skills Test (CLAST) earned prior to July 1, 2002.
    G. Has received a passing score on the Professional Education Subtest of the Florida Teacher Certification Examination
    H. Has received a passing score on the Florida state-approved subject area examination for each subject or field shown on the certificate
    I. Successfully demonstrates professional education competencies identified by Florida statutes
II. Temporary Certificate Eligibility Requirements
    A. A nonrenewable, temporary certificate, valid for 3 school years, may be issued to an applicant who satisfies I, A–E, of the above requirements for the professional certificate.
III. Professional Certificate Renewal
    A. Completion of 6 semester hours of appropriate college credit; or 120 approved Florida staff-development points specific to the subject(s) shown on the certificate; or training/course work related to the educational goals and performance standards outlined in Florida statutes during each 5-year validity period

1. Beginning July 1, 2014, credit must include 1 semester hour or 20 approved Florida staff-development points in teaching students with disabilities.

IV. Professional Preparation Requirements for Academic, Administrative, and Speciality Class Coverages (PreK–12)

    A. Completes an undergraduate teacher education program at an institution approved by the Florida State Board of Education or another state

       or

    B. Possesses a valid full-time standard teaching certificate issued by another state or by the National Board for Professional Teaching Standards,

       or

    C. Professional preparation

       1. Completes 15 semester hours in the following professional development areas:

          a. Classroom management, including safe learning environments,

          b. Human development and learning,

          c. Educational assessment, to include the content measured by state achievement tests and the interpretation and utilization of data to improve student achievement,

          d. Effective instructional strategies, including the needs of diverse learners,

          e. For the middle (grades 5–9) and for secondary (grades 6–12) and K–12 level: art, music, dance, computer science, health, foreign languages, humanities, curriculum and special methods of teaching the subject, *and*

          f. For the middle (grades 5–9) and secondary (grades 6–12) level subject coverages, foundations of research-based practices in teaching reading (competency 2 of the State Board–approved reading endorsement competencies).

       2. Practical experience in teaching, satisfied by 1 of the following methods:

          a. One year of full-time teaching experience in an approved elementary or secondary school,

             or

            Six semester hours earned in a college student teaching or supervised internship completed in an elementary or secondary school.

       3. Additional requirements in teaching reading and professional education for grades K–6 and for exceptional education students are included in the separate certification subject specialization State Board Rules.

       4. All the professional education requirements for preschool and prekindergarten–grade 3 subject coverages in lieu of the requirements in C, 1, directly above, are included in the separate certification subject specialization State Board Rules.

       5. The requirements of professional preparation in C, 1, directly above, are not applicable and shall not be required for school social worker or speech-language impaired certification.

    D. Professional preparation for agriculture (grades 6–12)

       1. Complete 15 semester hours with credit in the following professional agricultural education areas:

          a. Curriculum development and educational assessment in agriculture,

        b.   Instructional strategies in teaching agriculture,

        c.   Program planning in agricultural education,

        d.   An agriscience teaching induction course that includes basic principles and philosophy of agricultural education, and strategies for classroom management.

    2. The practical teaching experience requirement may be satisfied as in professional preparation in C, 2 (see above).

 D. For other options, see http://www.fldoe.org/edcert/mast_prof.ASP

Elementary School

I. General Requirements

   A. General and professional preparation. See Professional Certificate Eligibility, above.

II. Specific Requirements

   A. Bachelor's or higher degree with a major in elementary education that includes teaching reading at the elementary or primary level,
or
See www.fldoe.org/edcert/rules/6a-4-0151.asp

Middle Grades (5–9)

I. General Requirements

   A. General and professional preparation. See Professional Certificate Eligibility, above.

II. Specific Requirements

   A. Middle Grades English: a bachelor's or higher degree major in middle grades English or a bachelor's or higher degree in another subject or field and 18 semester hours above the freshman level in English, including specific courses in grammar, composition, and 9 semester hours of literature and speech

   B. Middle Grades Mathematics: a bachelor's or higher degree major in middle grades mathematics or a bachelor's degree in another subject or field and 18 semester hours in mathematics, including specific courses in calculus, geometry, probability, or statistics

   C. Middle Grades General Science: a bachelor's or higher degree major in middle grades general science or a bachelor's or higher degree in another subject or field and 18 semester hours in science, including specific courses in biology, earth-space science, and chemistry or physics

   D. Middle Grades Social Science: a bachelor's or higher degree major in middle grades social science or a bachelor's or higher degree in another subject or field and 18 semester hours in social science, including specific courses in history, economics, United States government, geography, and United States history (6 hours)

Secondary School (6–12)

I. General Requirements

   A. General and professional preparation. See Professional Certificate Eligibility, above.

II. Special requirements for subject fields: agriculture, biology, business education, chemistry, drama, earth-space science, English, family and consumer science, journalism, marketing, mathematics, physics, social science (general), and speech and technology education
   A. Florida offers alternative plans for certification in the subject fields.
      1. For all subject fields, applicants may qualify by having a bachelor's or higher degree with a major or 30 semester hours of specified courses in the field for which certification is being sought.
      2. For English and social science, applicants may also qualify by having a bachelor's or higher degree with at least 30 semester hours in the field or in related fields for which certification is being sought. (Contact Florida's Bureau of Educator Certification—see Appendix 1—for details on specific course distributions.)
      3. For mathematics and the sciences, applicants may also qualify by two additional certification routes. In all cases, the applicant must have a bachelor's or higher degree with at least 30 semester hours of specified courses in the field or related fields for which certification is being sought. (Contact Florida's Bureau of Educator Certification—see Appendix 1—for details on specific course distributions.)

All Grades (K–12)

I. General Requirements
   A. General and professional preparation. See Professional Certificate Eligibility, above.
II. Special requirements for subject fields: art, computer science, dance, English for speakers of other languages, exceptional student education, health, hearing impaired, humanities, music, physical education, reading, speech-language impaired, visually impaired, and world languages
   A. Florida offers alternative plans for certification in the subject fields.
      1. For all subject fields except reading and speech-language impaired, applicants may qualify by having a bachelor's or higher degree with a major of 30 semester hours of specified courses in the field for which certification is being sought.
      2. For world language specializations in Arabic, Chinese, Farsi, French, German, Greek, Haitian Creole, Hebrew, Hindi, Italian, Japanese, Latin, Portuguese, Russian, Spanish, and Turkish, applicants may also qualify by 3 additional certification routes.
      3. For reading, applicants may qualify by having a master's or higher degree with a major or 30 semester hours to include specified course work and a supervised reading practicum. (Contact Florida's Bureau of Educator Certification—see Appendix 1—for details on specific distributions)
      4. For speech-language impaired, applicants may qualify by having a master's or higher degree major or 60 semester hours to include specified course work and a supervised clinical practice. (Contact Florida's Bureau of Educator Certification—see Appendix 1—for details on specific distributions.)

Administration

I. General Requirements
    A. General and professional preparation. See Professional Certificate Eligiblity, above.
II. Educational Leadership, Level One Certificate
    A. Holds a master's or higher degree from an accredited institution
    B. Documentation of successful completion of the Florida Educational Leadership Core Curriculum, through one of the following plans:
        1. Successful completion of a Florida Department of Education–approved preservice program in educational leadership offered by an accredited institution, *or*
        2. A graduate degree major in educational administration, administration and supervision, or educational leadership awarded by a Florida Department of Education–approved institution, *or*
        3. Successful completion of an Educational Leadership training program approved by the Florida Department of Education and offered by a Florida public school district, *or*
        4. A graduate degree with a major in a subject other than educational administration, administration and supervision, or educational leadership, *and* Successful completion of a Department of Education–approved modified Florida program in educational leadership offered by an accredited institution, *or*
        5. A graduate degree with a major in a subject other than educational administration, administration and supervision, or educational leadership awarded by an accredited institution, and 30 semester hours of graduate credit in each of the Florida-specified principal leadership standard areas and an internship or a course with associated field experience in educational leadership.
III. School Principal, Level Two Certificate
    A. Holds a valid professional certificate covering educational leadership, school administration, or school administration/supervision
    B. Documents successful performance of the duties of school principalship
    C. Demonstrates successful performance of the competencies of the school principalship, which shall be documented by the Florida district school superintendent

Educational Media Specialist (PreK–12)

I. General Requirements
    A. General and professional preparation. See Professional Certificate Eligibility, above.
II. Specialization Requirements
    A. Bachelor's or higher degree with a major in educational media or library science, *or*

B. Bachelor's or higher degree with 30 semester hours in educational media or library science, including the following areas:
1. Management of library media programs
2. Collection development
3. Library media resources
4. Reference sources and services
5. Organization of collections
6. Design and production of educational media

Guidance Counselor (Grades PreK–12)

I. General Requirements
    A. General and professional preparation. See Professional Certificate Eligibility, above.
II. Specialization Requirements
    A. Master's or higher degree with a graduate major in guidance and counseling or in counselor education that includes 3 semester hours in a supervised counseling practicum in an elementary or secondary school,
      or
    B. Master's or higher degree with 30 semester hours of graduate credit in guidance and counseling, including (in semester hours)
        1. Principles and administration of guidance.. 3
        2. Student appraisal... 3
        3. Education and career development 3
        4. Learning theory and human development 3
        5. Counseling theories and techniques.. 3
        6. Group counseling... 3
        7. Consultation skills... 3
        8. Legal and ethical issues 3
        9. Counseling techniques for special populations... 3
       10. Supervised practicum in an elementary or secondary school........................ 3

Note: Noncitizens, exchange teachers, and resident aliens and refugees may be issued a certificate on the same basis as citizens of the United States, provided they meet exact and specific qualifications established by the Florida State Board of Education. Proof of eligibility to work in the United States is required for noncitizens.

Georgia

Certification Classification

I. Categories
   A. Renewable (valid 5 years, during which educator must satisfy standard renewal requirements)
      1. Clear Renewable: indicates all professional and Georgia-specific requirements for certification in the field have been met
      2. Performance-Based (PB): issued prior to 1990 under the Teacher Performance Assessment Instrument (TPAI) and remains in effect for certificates originally issued under the system
      3. Performance-Based (P): issued only for Educational Leadership performance-based programs
         a. Individual must be employed in leadership position and have the certificate requested by employing school system.
         b. During validity period of certificate, individual must complete specific requirements of performance-based leadership program.
   B. Non-Renewable (valid from 1 to 3 years, except for Performance-Based Leadership Certificate): issued at request of a Georgia employing school system when 1 or more conditions must be met
      1. Non-Renewable Professional Certificate (valid 3 years, nonrenewable, nonextendable)
         a. Recognizes initial preparation for certification in the field including, but not limited to, former Georgia educators or out-of-state certificate holders who do not meet or exempt Special Georgia Requirements; professional certificate holders assigned to another field who do not meet all certificate requirements for new field; and certificate holders who must obtain higher degree level.
         b. During validity period, individual must complete specific requirements outlined in Georgia Professional Standards Commission (PSC) correspondence that accompanies the certificate.
      2. Non-Renewable Non-Professional Certificate (valid 3 years, nonrenewable, nonextendable)
         a. Issued to applicants who have satisfied minimum content standards but must complete pedagogy and/or Special Georgia Requirements and/or who must obtain a higher degree level.
         b. During validity period, individual must complete specific requirements outlined in PSC correspondence that accompanies the certificate.
      3. Advanced Degree Alternative Certificate (ADAC) (issued in 1-year increments for a total of 3 years; nonextendable)
         a. Issued to individuals accepted into ADAC Program.

      b. During each 1-year validity period, applicant must satisfy specified requirements outlined in the rule and in PSC correspondence that accompanies the certificate.

    4. Core Academic Certificate (valid 3 years; nonrenewable and nonextendable)

      a. Issued to individuals accepted into Core Academic Preparation Program path for middle grades (4–8) or secondary grades (6–12) only

      b. Issued for core academic subjects as defined in section 4.01 of the Georgia Implementation Guidelines for Title II-A which is found on the PSC website at: http://www.gapsc.com/EducatorPreparation/NoChild LeftBehind/Admin/Files/ImpPolicy.pdf

    5. Clinical Practice Certificate (valid 3 years; nonrenewable and nonextendable). Issued to:

      a. Individuals who have held Georgia permit at bachelor's degree or higher level, with exception of JROTC, for a minimum of 3 years,
        or
      Individuals who have completed an education program and are eligible for college or university student teaching but elected to accept a degree without student teaching.

    6. Intern Certificate (valid 3 years; nonrenewable and nonextendable)

      a. Issued to individuals accepted into Teacher Academy for Preparation and Pedagogy (TAPP).

    7. International Exchange Certificate (valid 3 years; nonrenewable and nonextendable)

      a. Issued to educators certified in other nations who wish to teach in Georgia schools

    8. Life Certificate: although discontinued in 1974, valid for current holders

    9. One-Year Supervised Practicum Certificate (valid 3 years; nonrenewable and nonextendable)

      a. Issued to individuals accepted into One-Year Supervised Practicum Program path

II. Certificate Type: consult PSC website at http://www.gapsc.com for specific eligibility requirements

    A. Teaching: issued in fields that prepare individual to teach subject matter offered as part of school curriculum

    B. Service: issued in fields that prepare individual to provide support services to students, school personnel, and school operations

    C. Leadership: issued in fields that prepare individual to administer or supervise a school system, school, or school program

    D. Paraprofessional: issued to eligible individuals hired as paraprofessionals; no assigned level

    E. Noninstructional Aide: issued to eligible individuals hired to perform routine noninstructional tasks; no assigned level

    F. Technical Specialist: issued to eligible individuals in Technology/Career Education areas of Trade & Industry Education and Healthcare Science & Technology Education

1. May be issued to those holding high school diplomas/GED or associate degrees, as well as those with bachelor's degrees or higher
G. Permits: issued at request of employing school system to individuals with specific experience in teaching fields of performing arts (music, dance, drama), foreign language (for native speakers), educational leadership positions of superintendent and JROTC.
H. Support Personnel Licenses: issued at request of employing school system to individuals who serve in position of leadership over support functions in local school system
    1. Such positions include, but are not limited to, finance, transportation, public relations, personnel, staff development, facilities, planning, evaluation, research, assessment, and technology coordination
I. Adjunct Licenses (valid 1 year; renewable): issued at request of employing school system to:

Individuals with specific knowledge, skills, and experience in engineering, medical, dental, pharmaceutical, veterinarian, legal, accounting, or arts profession, or any other professional position approved by PSC,

or

Who have instructional experience in branch of U.S. military (except for JROTC),

or

Who are in a PSC-accepted accredited college or university.

    1. Holders are eligible to provide instruction for one-half day in core academic subjects in grades 6–12 only, as defined in Section 4.01 of Georgia Implementation Guidelines for Title II-A.

III. Certificate Fields
    A. P–5: Pre-Kindergarten through grade 5
    B. 4–8: Middle Grades
    C. 6–12: High School
    D. P–12: special education, art, music, health, physical education, etc.
    E. P–12: service and leadership

IV. Certificate Levels: Determined by highest degree awarded on official transcript from PSC-accepted accredited institution to educator, this single level is assigned to all certificate fields held by that educator.
    A. Level One (Selected Technology/Career Education fields only): completion of high school diploma or GED equivalent
    B. Level Two (Selected Technology/Career Education fields only): completion of associate's degree or 1 of following options:
       1. 54 semester hours of acceptable college credit,
       2. Two-year program consisting of minimum of 2,000 clock hours through regionally accredited postsecondary vocational/technical school in field in which certification is requested,
         or
       3. Minimum of 27 semester hours of acceptable college or university credit and minimum of 1,000 clock hours through accredited vocational/technical school in field in which certification is requested.

C. Level Four: completion of bachelor's degree or PSC's determined degree equivalent

D. Level Five: completion of master's degree or PSC's determined degree equivalent

E. Level Six: completion of education specialist's degree or PSC's determined degree equivalent;

or

Completion of a minimum of 36 semester hours of course work required for level seven doctoral degree, and successful completion of oral and/or written comprehensive examinations or the institution's determined equivalent.

F. Level Seven: completion of Ph.D. or Ed.D. degree or PSC's determined degree equivalent

V. Endorsements

A. Each endorsement requires a prerequisite certificate and may be added by completing course work within an approved college or staff development endorsement program.

1. Most endorsement fields require 10 to 20 quarter hours of credit for completion.

2. Fields carry same expiration date as their prerequisite certificate, and both are renewed at same time.

B. Teaching Endorsements. Contact PSC at http://www.gapsc.com for its official rule for any endorsement or to see a list of Georgia institutions offering preparation in a specific endorsement

1. Birth through five; career exploration (PECE); career technical instruction (CTI); coaching; computer science; coordinated career academic education (CCAE); culinary arts; English to speakers of other languages (ESOL); gifted in-field; intervention specialist; K–5 mathematics: K–5 science; middle grades; online teaching; reading; safety and driver education; special education deaf education; special education physical and health disabilities; special education preschool (ages 3–5); special education transition specialist; special education visual impairment; work-based learning

C. Service Endorsements

1. Teacher support specialist; student support team (SST) coordinator

D. Leadership Endorsements

1. Teacher Leader

VI. Standard Renewal Requirements

A. Clear Renewable and Performance-Based certificates are eligible for renewal. Requirements include:

1. 6 semester hours of college course work; or 10 Professional Learning Units (PLUs); or 10 Continuing Education Units (CEUs), or 10 credits based on U.S. Department of Education Teacher-To-Teacher Workshops; or, completion of 1 full year of acceptable school experience while working in another state on a valid certificate issued by that state;

and

criminal record check by employing school system.

B. Certificate holders employed by Georgia public school must have an individual professional development plan aligned with their system's Comprehensive School

Improvement Plan (CSIP). To be acceptable for certificate renewal, credit must be included in the individual plan and be directly associated with at least 1 of the following:

1. Field(s) of certification held;
2. School/district improvement plan;
3. Annual personnel evaluation;
    or
4. State/federal requirements.

C. Renewal Cycle
    1. Georgia certificates usually have beginning date of July 1 and ending date of June 30.
    2. Valid certificates may be renewed from October 1 in year preceding ending validity date to September 30 of calendar year in which validity date expires.
        a. Grace period between July 1 and September 30 allows completion of acceptable course work during summer period, so validity continues with no break in dates.

Routes to Certification

I. Traditional Routes to Clear, Renewable Certificate
    A. College/university with state-approved educator preparation program
        1. Complete bachelor's or higher degree from institution of higher education along with all program requirements for certificate field
        2. Obtain recommendation from educator preparation program
        3. Complete appropriate content assessment before certification
    B. Holders of bachelor's degree may enroll in state-approved program for certificate only (post-baccalaureate program)
        1. Complete all program requirements
        2. See I, A, 2 and 3, directly above
    C. Interstate Mobility (Reciprocity)
        1. Hold out-of-state professional certificate,
            or
            Have completed and hold recommendation from approved out-of-state educator preparation program.
        2. The PSC will determine specific Georgia requirements to be completed based on individual experience and credentials.
II. Alternative Route Certification
    A. The Georgia Teacher Academy for Preparation and Pedagogy (GaTAPP) oversees multiple program paths to Georgia Clear Renewable Certification. Preliminary requirements include:
        1. Hold a bachelor's degree or higher from an accredited institute
        2. Have not completed teacher education degree programs
    B. All program paths involve:
        1. Structured supervision and coaching by team of qualified mentors and coaches called the Candidate Support Team (CST)

a.   CST is composed of a school-based administrator, a school-based mentor/coach, a program provider supervisor, and a content specialist.

b.   CST assesses the level of knowledge and skills with which a transition teacher enters the program and recommends the appropriate path for the teacher candidate to take in order to meet 24 teaching competencies.

c.   Through continuous monitoring and assessment of the transition teacher's classroom performance, CST provides recommendations for advancement or retention in the program.

d.   Throughout transition, or induction phase, transition teachers provide evidence of the knowledge, skills, and dispositions required in the 24 teaching competencies and for successful completion of the program.

e.   Upon meeting all the required teacher competencies, including the Special Georgia Requirements and a minimum of one year of mentoring/coaching, transition teachers are recommended by the CST for Georgia Clear Renewable Certification.

C.   For full details, consult http://www.gapsc.com/EducatorPreparation/GaTapp/home.asp

Special Georgia Requirements

I.   Content Knowledge

A.   Appropriate content knowledge assessments are required of all persons seeking initial certification, except for those specifically exempted below. Contact the PSC at http:www.gapsc.com for full and current details.

B.   Exemptions from content knowledge assessments

1.   Hold or have held a professional certificate in another state, having passed appropriate statewide or national content knowledge assessment(s) required in that state for that certificate field,

or

Satisfy out-of-state certificate criteria and have 3 full years of acceptable, successful education experience under that certificate in a field comparable to Georgia certificate field within 5 years of application date,

or

Hold valid National Board for Professional Teaching Standards (NBPTS) certification in the specific field, except for the Middle Grades Generalist field,

or

If the PSC has not adopted a content assessment for certificate field being sought.

2.   Graduates of Georgia state-approved programs who have satisfied all program requirements except the content knowledge assessment(s), including a valid recommendation, may be issued a 1-year Waiver certificate at request of employing school system.

3.   See Testing Requirements below for specific details.

II. Standards of Conduct
   A. Applicant must comply with the profession's ethical standards.
   B. FBI background check (fingerprint) required for professional employment in Georgia public schools.
   C. Every 5 years, a Georgia criminal history check required for certificate renewal.
   D. Applicants for certification must also respond to background check questions on application form.

III. Recency of Study
   A. Certification applicants must verify study or experience within 5 years preceding date of application in one of the following ways:
      1. Complete 6 semester hours or 10 PLU credits or 10 CEU credits within 5 years,
         or
      2. Complete 1 year of out-of-state teaching experience on a certificate within 5 years,
         or
      3. Hold either a valid NBPTS certificate or a valid Georgia Master Teacher certificate,
         or
      4. Complete 1 year of full-time college teaching experience within 5 years,
         or
      5. In fields of audiology, school psychology, school social work, and speech and language pathology, provide a valid State of Georgia license issued by the Professional Licensing Boards Division of the Office of the Secretary of State.

IV. Special Education
   A. Any person certified in a teaching field, the leadership field of Educational Leadership, the service fields of Media Specialist and School Counseling, or holders of permits or Technical Specialist certificates shall complete course work approved by the PSC (3 semester hours of college credit or 5 PLUs) in the identification and education of children who have special educational needs,
      or
   B. Hold NBPTS-valid certification in this area.

V. Veteran out-of-state educators moving into Georgia may be eligible to exempt all Special Georgia Requirements except Standards of Conduct. Contact PSC at http:www.gapsc.com for full requirements for exemption.

Testing Requirements

I. Georgia Assessments for the Certification of Educators (GACE) is the educator licensure assessment in Georgia. Full information about the GACE program and certification requirements is available at www.gace.ets.org.
   A. GACE assessments include Program Admission Assessment, Paraprofessional, Professional Pedagogy, and content assessments.
      1. There is no GACE broad field social studies test for high school (6–12); instead separate tests are available for behavioral science, history, economics, geography, and political science that an educator seeking authorization to teach

multiple social science subjects at that level will need to pass. However, GACE includes a middle grades social studies test to support Middle Grades Social Studies (4 – 8) certification.

2. For certification candidates in the field of Speech and Language Pathology, the Praxis II test 0330 will remain the required test.

B. The PSC will not accept Praxis II scores for Educational Leadership assessments that reflect a score report date after March 15, 2008. If a person has a passing score on his/her score report that is dated on or before March 15, 2008, that passing score will be accepted for the appropriate content assessment if that person completed any approved Georgia Educational Leadership program on or before September 30, 2009.

Leadership Certificate Requirements

Requirements for the Performance-Based Leadership Certificate are listed below. For implementation details, including clarification and guidelines for the transition between the previous and current leadership certification systems, consult the PSC at http://www.gapsc.com and reference Rule 505-2-300.

I. Clear Renewable Certificate Requirements

A. Performance-Based Leadership (PL) Certificate (available after September 30, 2009)

1. Complete a PSC-approved Georgia performance-based leadership program at the specialist (level 6) or doctoral (level 7) degree,
   or

2. Hold a level 6 or level 7 degree in another field and complete the performance-based certification requirements
   and
   Be recommended by a PSC-approved program provider.

B. Leadership (L) Certificate

1. Hold a clear-renewable L certificate issued prior to September 30, 2009
   or
   Apply through the out-of-state reciprocity process if never held a Georgia certificate,
   or
   Under specified conditions, convert a permit in leadership to the clear renewable leadership certificate

Hawaii

Since licensure requirements can change as a result of the Hawaii Teacher Standards Board (HTSB) monthly meeting, consult the website at www.htsb.org for updates.

Licenses

I. Provisional 3-Year License (valid 1 year; reapply annually for up to 3 years). For teachers who have completed a teacher preparation program and taken the content test but do not hold a license in any state
    A. Submit the Provisional Hawaii Teaching License Application
        1. If any question in the Professional Fitness Section of the application is answered "yes," applicant will be notified to submit additional documentation.
    B. Submit verification that applicant completed a State-Approved Teacher Education Program (SATEP)
        1. If applicant completed a SATEP in Hawaii prior to 2002 or in another state at any time, submit the Institutional Recommendation;
            or
        2. If applicant completed a SATEP in Hawaii since 2002, applicant's institution will verify applicant's teacher education program completion directly to HTSB, and applicant does not have to submit the Institutional Recommendation;
            or
        3. If applicant completed a non–U.S. SATEP, submit an evaluation of foreign transcript from a transcript evaluation company that is a member of the National Association of Credit Evaluation Services (NACES) and submit this with application. A listing of companies may be found at http://www.naces.org/members.htm
    C. Submit content expertise verification
        1. If applicant passed the Hawaii content licensure test in the field of SATEP, submit official score report. Check the Testing Chart at www.htsb.org for the correct tests.
        2. If applicant completed a SATEP in another state, submit official score report for the licensure content test in that state.
        3. If licensure tests do not exist in applicant's license field, then submit evidence of a major or 30 credit hours in the field of applicant's SATEP. Submit an official transcript or notarized copy with application.
II. Standard 5-Year License (valid 5 years, renewable). For teachers who have completed a teacher preparation program; meet basic skills and content expertise competencies; and meet other requirements below
    A. Applicants who will have completed a SATEP prior to applying for a license but do not yet hold a teaching license in Hawaii or any other state
        1. Submit Hawaii Standard Teaching License application online at www.htsb.org;

or download the paper application (allow additional processing time with paper option).

2. See Licenses I, A and B, directly above.

3. Submit passing scores for Hawaii Praxis basic skills and content knowledge tests. Check the Licensing Chart at www.htsb.org for the correct tests.

B. Applicants who completed a SATEP and hold a teaching license in another state

    1. If licensed for the first time in another state within the past 5 years

        a. Submit Hawaii Standard Teaching License application online at www.htsb .org; or download the paper application (allow additional processing time with paper option). If any question in the Professional Fitness Section of the application is answered "yes," applicant will be notified to submit additional documentation.

        b. Submit a copy of out-of-state teaching license to HTSB;
           or

    2. If applicant was licensed in another state more than 5 years ago

        a. See Licenses, II, B, 1, a and b directly above

        b. Submit documentation of SATEP, licensure testing, and out-of-state license by one of the following methods:

            i. Download HTSB's Confirmation of Licensure and Certification Tests Taken and send it to out-of-state licensing agency. If the agency confirms that applicant completed a SATEP and passed licensure tests in content knowledge, applicant will not have to submit any other documentation;
               or

            ii. Submit HTSB's Institutional Recommendation, a copy of passing scores for out-of-state licensure tests, and a copy of out-of-state license;
               or

            iii. Submit official transcript which shows applicant completed a SATEP; official out-of-state licensure test scores in license field; and a copy of out-of-state teaching license.

C. Applicants who hold a license in another state, but did not complete a SATEP

    1. Submit Hawaii Standard Teaching License application online at www.htsb .org; or download the paper application (allow additional processing time with paper option). If applicant answers "yes" to any question in the Professional Fitness Section of the application, applicant will be notified to submit additional documentation.

    2. Submit a copy of current, valid teaching license from another state with application;

    3. Submit HTSB's Verification of Qualifying Experience Form, showing at least 3 years of full-time, satisfactory teaching experience within the past 7 years. Submit this form to applicant's employer and ask them to send it to HTSB.

    4. Submit passing scores for Hawaii licensure tests in basic skills and content knowledge in the same teaching field on out-of-state license. Check the Licensing Chart at www.htsb.org for the correct tests.

D. Applicants who hold a valid teaching license and a valid National Board for Professional Teaching Standards (NBPTS) Certificate
   1. Submit Hawaii Standard Teaching License application online at www.htsb .org; or download the paper application (allow additional processing time with paper option). If applicant answers "yes" to any question in the Professional Fitness Section of the application, applicant will be notified to submit additional documentation.
   2. Submit a copy of current, valid teaching license from another state with application
   3. Submit a copy of current, valid NBPTS certificate with application. NOTE: NBPTS certified teachers are not required to submit any test scores.

E. Applicants who received the Meritorious New Teacher Candidate (MNTC) Designation on their valid out-of-state teaching license
   1. Submit Hawaii Standard Teaching License application online at www.htsb .org; or download the paper application (allow additional processing time with paper option). If applicant answers "yes" to any question in the Professional Fitness Section of the application, applicant will be notified to submit additional documentation.
   2. Submit a copy of current, valid out-of-state teaching license with the MNTC designation with application. NOTE: MNTC applicants are not required to submit any test scores.

F. Applicants who completed a non–U.S. SATEP
   1. Submit Hawaii Standard Teaching License application online at www.htsb .org; or download the paper application (allow additional processing time with paper option). If applicant answers "yes" to any question in the Professional Fitness Section of the application, applicant will be notified to submit additional documentation.
   2. Submit an evaluation of foreign transcript from a transcript evaluation company that is a member of NACES and submit this with your application. A listing of companies may be found at http://www.naces.org/members.htm. The evaluation must verify that applicant completed a teacher preparation program and list the teaching field(s).
   3. Submit passing scores for Hawaii licensure tests in basic skills and content knowledge in the field of SATEP. Check the Licensing Chart at www.htsb.org for the correct tests.

III. Advanced 10-Year License (valid 10 years). For teachers who have held a Standard License in Hawaii or another state; have at least 5 years of experience within the past 8 years in Hawaii or another state; and meet other requirements below
   1. Submit Hawaii Standard Teaching License application online at www.htsb.org; or download the paper application (allow additional processing time with paper option). If any question in the Professional Fitness Section of the application is answered "yes," applicant will be notified to submit additional documentation.
   2. Submit proof of one of the following with application:
      a. An official transcript verifying a master's, specialist, or doctoral degree from a regionally accredited institution. This degree must be different

from the degree used to obtain a Standard License and must be in an area relevant to the teaching field for which a license is sought or a field that improves the practice of teaching. Examples of a degree that improves the practice of teaching include, but are not limited to: curriculum and instruction; technology; reading; teacher leadership;
or

b. A copy of a current, valid NBPTS certificate and a copy of a current, valid out-of-state teaching license. Hawaii licensed teachers do not need to submit a copy of their Standard License or their NBPTS certificate if earned while they were a Hawaii licensed teacher.

3. Submit the HTSB Verification of Qualifying Experience for Advanced License form to document 5 out of the past 8 years of satisfactory full-time teaching experience in the state which issued the applicant's Standard License.

4. Note that since the Advanced License is valid for a term of 10 years and the fee is $480. Currently, Advanced License applicants using the online system for payment may pay for the first 5 years of the license either in full or at $48 per year. At the 5-year point, the remaining $240 will be due. Advanced License applicants paying directly to the HTSB office must pay the full amount of $480.

Idaho

General Requirements for All Teachers and Administrators

I.   Testing Requirements
   A.   Applicants for certificates/endorsements in Standard Elementary, Standard Secondary, Early Childhood/ Early Childhood Special Education Blended, and/or Standard Exceptional Child must meet or exceed qualifying score(s) for appropriate Praxis II test(s).
      1.   Applicants for certificates in Administration or Pupil Personnel Services are exempted from this requirement.

II. Out-of-State Applications
   A.   Applicants from regionally accredited institutions meeting bachelor's degree–based requirements for certification or equivalent in other states may be certified by the Idaho Department of Education when they substantially meet the requirements for Idaho certification. Contact the Bureau of Certification/Professional Standards (see Appendix 1).

III. Contact the Certification/Professional Standards Commission (see Appendix 1) for full details on State Board of Education–approved alternate routes to Idaho certification that became effective July 1, 2006.
   A.   Alternative Authorization—Teacher to New Certification
   B.   Alternative Authorization—Content Specialist
   C.   American Board for Certification of Teacher Excellence (ABCTE; see abcte.org)

IV. Professional-Technical Education
   A.   Idaho State Division of Professional-Technical Education is authorized to determine whether applicants meet requirements for instructing or administering professional-technical programs at the secondary and postsecondary levels.

V.   Renewal of Certification
   A.   All credentials may be renewed upon completion of at least 6 semester credits of college courses within the 5-year period of validity.

VI. Criminal History and Background Check
   A.   All adults working in Idaho public schools (certificated and noncertificated), or applying for certification, are currently required to have results of a criminal history check on file with the State Department of Education. Proposed temporary rules for these are receiving public comment. Check with the Idaho Certification/Professional Standards Commission (see Appendix 1) for details and current information.

Early Childhood/Early Childhood Special Education (Birth–Grade 3)

I.   Early Childhood/Early Childhood Special Education Blended Certificate (valid 5 years, renewable). Minimum requirements:

    A. Bachelor's degree from accredited college or university
       1. Complete general education requirements
       2. Professional education requirements:
          a. Minimum of 30 semester credit hours, or 45 quarter credit hours, in philosophical, psychological, and methodological foundations; in instructional technology; and in professional subject matter of early childhood and early childhood–special education.
          b. Professional subject matter of early childhood and early childhood–special education shall include course work specific to young child from birth through grade 3 in areas of: child development and learning; curriculum development and implementation; family and community relationships; assessment and evaluation; professionalism; and application of technologies.
          c. Required 30 semester credit hours, or 45 quarter credit hours, shall include not less than 6 semester credit hours, or 9 quarter credit hours, of early childhood student teaching; and 3 semester credit hours, or 4 quarter credit hours, of developmental reading.
       3. Institutional recommendation from accredited college or university, and passage of Idaho Comprehensive Literacy Exam.
       4. Each candidate shall meet or exceed state qualifying score on the following approved early childhood assessments:
          a. Education of Young Children, Praxis II #0021 (qualifying score—169)
          b. Special Education: Pre-School/Early Childhood, Praxis II #0690 (qualifying score—550)

Elementary School (Grades K–8)

I. Standard Elementary Certificate (valid 5 years; renewable)
    A. Bachelor's degree from accredited college or university
    B. Professional requirements to include the following areas, total semester hours 24
       1. Philosophical, psychological, and methodological foundations of education
       2. Elementary student teaching, semester hours 6
          or
          Two years of successful teaching in an elementary school
       3. Developmental reading, semester hours 6
    C. Completion of Idaho Comprehensive Literacy Course or passage of Idaho Comprehensive Literacy Assessment (all applicants)
    D. Completion of Mathematical Thinking for Instruction class
    E. Completion of requirements for a single-subject endorsement

Secondary School (Grades 6–12)

I. Standard Secondary Certificate (valid 5 years; renewable)
    A. Bachelor's degree
    B. Professional requirements, semester hours.. 20

1. Philosophical, psychological, and methodological foundations of education
2. Secondary student teaching, semester hours.. 6
    or
    Two years of successful teaching in a secondary school
3. Reading in the content area, semester hours.. 3

C. Preparation in at least 2 fields of secondary teaching
1. Major subject, semester hours.. 30
    and Minor subject, semester hours 20
    or
2. Preparation in a single area, in lieu of a major and minor, ... 45
    semester hours

The Exceptional Child

I. Standard Exceptional Child Certificate (valid 5 years; renewable)
A. Generalist (Educationally Handicapped) Endorsement
1. Completion of a program in Special Education approved by Idaho State Board of Education, *or* by the state educational agency where the program was completed
2. Special education courses, semester hours 30
    a. To include developmental processes; evaluation; individualization of instruction for exceptional child; instructional experience; individual and group classroom management; knowledge of and coordination with other school personnel; knowledge of state and community ancillary services; work with parents
3. Pass appropriate Praxis II assessments
4. Completion of Idaho Comprehensive Literacy Course or passage of Idaho Comprehensive Literacy Assessment
5. Completion of Mathematical Thinking for Instruction class
B. Specialized Endorsement
1. Hearing and visually impaired
2. Requirements
    a. Bachelor's degree
    b. Completion of approved program in area of endorsement, as recommended by the training institution
3. Pass appropriate Praxis II assessments
C. Consulting Teacher Endorsement (valid 5 years; renewable)
1. Valid Standard Exceptional Child Certificate
2. Valid Standard Elementary or Secondary teaching certificate
3. Completion of fifth-year or master's degree program
4. Three years of teaching experience, with at least 2 years in a special education classroom setting
5. Demonstration of competencies
D. Supervisor/Coordinator Endorsement
1. Master's degree

2. Standard Exceptional Child Certificate, or Pupil Personnel Services Certificate endorsed for School Psychologist, Communication Disorders Specialist, or School Social Worker
3. Three years of experience in special education
4. Demonstration of competencies

Administration

I. Administrative Certificates
   A. School Principal Endorsement (K–12) (valid 5 years; renewable)
      1. Master's degree from an accredited institution
      2. Four years of full-time experience (under certification) working with K–12 students while under contract in a school setting
      3. Completion of an administrative internship or 1 year of experience as an administrator
      4. Completion of a state-approved program of at least 30 semester hours of graduate study in school administration for the preparation of school principals at an accredited institution
         a. To include competencies in supervision of instruction; curriculum development; school finance; administration; school law; student behavior management; and education of special populations
      5. Institutional recommendation
      6. Completion of Mathematical Thinking for Instruction class
   B. Superintendent Endorsement (valid 5 years; renewable)
      1. Educational specialist or doctorate degree or a comparable post-master's sixth-year program at an accredited institution
      2. See School Principal Endorsement I, A, 2 and 3, directly above.
      3. Completion of a state-approved program of at least 30 semester hours of post-master's graduate study in school administration for the preparation of school superintendents at an accredited institution
         a. In addition to the competencies required for the principal (see I, A, 4, a, above), this program will include competencies in advanced money management, budget, and accounting principles; district-wide support services; employment practices and negotiations; school board and community relations; and special services and federal programs.
      4. Institutional recommendation
      5. Completion of Mathematical Thinking for Instruction class
   C. Director of Special Education Endorsement (K–12)
      1. See School Principal Endorsement I, A, 1 and 2, above.
      2. Institutional verification of competencies in organization and administration of special services; school finance and school law as related to special education; supervision of instruction; practicum experience in special education administration; counseling parents of exceptional children; foundations of special education; curriculum and methods in special education; and diagnosis and remediation in special education

3. Competency checklist forms from the applicant's institution may be requested by the Certification Division.
4. Completion of Mathematical Thinking for Instruction class

Pupil Personnel Services

I. Standard Counselor Endorsement (K–12) (valid 5 years; renewable)
   A. Requirements
      1. Master's degree plus verification of completion of approved program of graduate study in school guidance and counseling from an institution approved by the Idaho State Board of Education or the state educational agency of the state in which the program was completed
         a. The program must include successful completion of 700 hours of supervised field experience, 75 percent of which must be in a K–12 school setting to include substantial amounts of experience in elementary, middle/ junior high, and high school
      2. Institutional recommendation
II. School Psychologist Endorsement (valid 5 years; renewable)
   A. Requirements
      1. Graduate semester hours 60
         a. Master's degree program of 30 semester hours in education or psychology, plus 30 hour School Psychology Specialist degree program,
            or
         b. Sixty semester hours in master's degree program in School Psychology,
            or
         c. Sixty semester hours in School Psychology Specialist program that does not require a master's degree; laboratory experience; and a minimum 1200 clock-hour internship.
      2. Institutional recommendation
III. Speech-Language Pathologist Endorsement (valid 5 years; renewable)
   A. Requirements
      1. Completion of state-approved program in speech-language pathology
      2. Master's degree in speech-language pathology
      3. Institutional recommendation
IV. Audiology Endorsement (valid 5 years; renewable)
   A. Same as for Speech-Language Pathologist Endorsement, but substitute "audiology" for "speech-language pathology."
V. School Social Worker Endorsement (valid 5 years; renewable)
   A. Requirements
      1. Master's degree in social work from an approved program,
         or
      2. Master's degree in guidance and counseling, sociology, or psychology, plus graduate work in social work education, semester hours 30
      3. Valid social work license issued by the Idaho Bureau of Occupational Licenses
      4. Institutional recommendation

VI. School Nurse Endorsement (valid 5 years; renewable)
    A. Requirements
        1. Valid registered nursing license issued by the Idaho State Board of Nursing
        2. Bachelor's degree in nursing, education, or a health-related field.
           or
           Nine semester credits in at least 3 of the following areas: health program management; child and adolescent health issues; counseling/psychology/social work; and methods of education instruction.

Illinois

On July 1, 2013, Illinois implemented a new system of educator licensure that replaced the previous system of educator certification. All Illinois teaching, administrative, and school service personnel certificates have been converted to a corresponding license.

Requirements for Illinois Licenses and Endorsements

I. Professional Educator License (PEL) (valid for 5 fiscal years; renewable upon completion of professional development requirements)
   A. Requirements for a Professional Educator License:
      1. Proof of completion of a comparable state-approved program;
      2. Appropriate degree from a regionally accredited institution;
      3. One course in cross-categorical special education methods;
      4. Six semester hours of course work in methods of reading and reading in the content area;
      5. One course in English as a Second Language/bilingual methods;
      6. A passing score on Illinois's test of basic skills—the Test of Academic Proficiency (TAP 400)—or, in lieu of the TAP, proof of an ACT Plus Writing composite score of at least 22 or an SAT (critical reading and mathematics) composite score of 1030;
         a. The test score report may be no more than 10 years old at the time form ISBE 73–60 is submitted.
         b. Those who seek to add a subsequent endorsement and have already passed the TAP (or achieved the required composite score on the ACT Plus Writing or SAT) are not required to pass the test again.
      7. A passing score on the applicable content-area-test(s); full details available at http://www.il.nesinc.com/IL17_testselection.asp;
      8. A passing score on the Assessment of Professional Teaching (APT) test if applying for a teaching endorsement;
      and
      9. Satisfactory completion of student teaching or an equivalent experience.
   B. The following endorsements can be added to a professional educator license; all require completion of a state-approved educator preparation program
      1. Early Childhood Education (birth–grade 3); Elementary Education (K–9); Secondary Education (6–12); Special (K–12, endorsed in one content area); Special Education (PK–age 21); School Counselor (PK–age 21); School Social Worker (PK–age 21); School Psychologist (PK–age 21); School Nurse (PK–age 21); Speech Language Pathologist (non-teaching) (PK–age 21); General Administrative (K–12); Principal (PK–2); Chief School

Business Official (PK–age 21); Director of Special Education (PK–age 21); Superintendent (PK–age 21)

2. See III, Content Area Endorsement Structure, below for full area and grade range list

C. Requirements for Professional Educator License endorsements for those trained out-of-state or out-of country

1. For specific details on PEL teaching endorsements for those trained out-of-state or out-of country, consult www.isbe.net/licensure/requirements/oos-pel-end.pdf

2. For specific details on administrative endorsements for those trained out-of-state or out-of country, consult www.isbe.net/licensure/requirements/oos-pel-admin-end.pdf

3. For specific details on school support personnel endorsements for those trained out-of-state or out-of country, consult www.isbe.net/licensure/requirements/oos-pel-school-support-end-1113.pdf

II. Educator License with Stipulations (ELS) Endorsed as a Provisional Educator for Out-of-State or Out-of-Country Applicants (valid until June 30 immediately following 2 years of the license being issued; nonrenewable)

A. Requirements for an Educator License with Stipulations:

1. Valid, comparable out-of-state license;

2. Transcript from a regionally accredited institution of higher education demonstrating a bachelor's degree (unless a master's degree is required), with a minimum of 15 semester hours in content course work;

3. See I, A, 6, a and b), directly above;
   and

4. See I, A, 7, directly above.

5. For specific details on Educator License with Stipulations Endorsement Requirements, consult www.isbe.net/licensure/requirements/ed-lic-w-stip.pdf

   a. No provisional endorsements on an educator license with stipulations shall be issued for principal.

B. The following endorsements—all requiring completion of a state-approved educator preparation program—can be added to an ELS:

1. Early Childhood Education (birth–grade 3); Elementary Education (K–9); Secondary Education (6–12); Special (K–12, endorsed in one content area); Special Education (PK–age 21); School Counselor (PK–age 21); School Social Worker (PK–age 21); School Psychologist (PK–age 21); School Nurse (PK–age 21); Speech Language Pathologist (non-teaching) (PK–age 21); General Administrative (K–12); Principal (PK–12); Chief School Business Official (PK–age 21); Director of Special Education (PK–age 21); Superintendent (PK–age 21)

C. The following endorsements, which do not require completion of a state-approved educator preparation program—can be added to an Educator License with Stipulations:

1. Career and Technical Educator (9–12); Provisional Career and Technical Educator (9–12); Part-time Provisional Career and Technical Educator (9–12); Transitional Bilingual Educator (PK–12); Visiting International Teacher (grade range varies); Paraprofessional Educator (all grades)

      D.   See III, Content Area Endorsement Structure, below for full area and grade range list

III.   Content-Area Endorsement Structure

      A.   Primary Endorsements

          1.   To add a primary content endorsement, you must already hold one of the following endorsements on your license:

              a.   Early childhood education (Birth–Grade 3)

              b.   Elementary education (K–9)

              c.   Special (K–12 or PK–age 21)

          2.   To add such a grade-range endorsement, applicant must complete a state-approved educator preparation program.

          3.   Endorsements available include: Bilingual Education (language required); English as a Second Language; Foreign Language (language required); Library Information Specialist; Reading Teacher; and Technology Specialist

          4.   Specific requirements for each endorsement are listed at http://www.isbe.net/licensure/requirements/endsmt_struct.pdf

      B.   Middle School Endorsements

          1.   To add a middle school content endorsement, you must already hold one of the following endorsements on your license:

              a.   Elementary education (K–9)

              b.   Secondary education (9–12)

              c.   Special (K–12 or PK–age 21)

          2.   To add such a grade-range endorsement, applicant must complete a state-approved educator preparation program.

          3.   Endorsements available include: Agricultural Education; Art; Bilingual Education (language required); Biological Science; Business/Marketing/Management; Computer Applications; Computer Science; Dance; English as a Second Language; Family & Consumer Science; Foreign Language (language required);General Science; General Geography; Health Education; Industrial Technology Education; Language Arts; Library Information Specialist; Mathematics; Music; Physical Education; Physical Science; Reading Teacher; Social Science; Speech; Speech/Theatre; Technology Specialist (Computer Related); Theatre/Drama

          4.   Specific requirements for a middle school endorsement is listed at http://www.isbe.net/licensure/middle_grade/msinfo.htm

      C.   Senior High School Endorsements

          1.   To add a senior high school content endorsement, you must already hold one of the following endorsements on your license:

              a.   Elementary education (K–9)

                 i.   If you hold only an elementary education (K–9) endorsement, the senior high content endorsement will be valid for 9th grade only.

              b.   Secondary education (9–12)

              c.   Special (K–12 or PK–age 21)

          2.   To add such a grade-range endorsement, applicant must complete a state-approved educator preparation program.

3. Endorsements available include: Agricultural Education; Bilingual Education (language required); Business, Marketing, and Computer Education; Business, Marketing, and Computer Education-Business Computer Programming; Computer Applications; Computer Science; Dance; Drama/Theatre Arts; English/Language Arts; English as a New Language; English as a New Language-Bilingual Education (language listed); English as a Second Language; Family & Consumer Science-Apparel and Textiles; Family & Consumer Science-Living Environments; Family & Consumer Science-Nutrition, Wellness, and Hospitality; Foreign Language (language required); Health Education; Library Information Specialist; Mathematics; Music; Physical Education; Reading Teacher; Safety and Driver's Education; Science-Biology; Science-Chemistry; Science-Earth & Space Science; Science-Environmental Science; Science-Physics; Social Science-Economics; Social Science-Geography; Social Science-History; Social Science-Political Science; Social Science-Psychology; Social Science-Sociology and Anthropology; Technology Education (Industrial Arts); Technology Specialist (Computer Related); Visual Arts

4. Applicants receiving a second designation in the senior high school sciences or social sciences must either complete 12 semester hours of course work in the designation and pass the test required for the designation

   or

   Complete a major in the content area of the designation; no upper division course-work is required.

D. Learning Behavior Specialist I (LBS I) Endorsement (valid for 3 calendar years)

   1. Issued to educators who have completed all necessary course work for the endorsement but have not yet passed the LBS I (155) test.
   2. LBS I approvals will not be issued on or after September 1, 2015.
   3. The endorsement is available for the following grade levels:
      a. Grade K–3—for educators who already hold an early childhood education endorsement
      b. Grade K–9—for educators who already hold an elementary education endorsement
      c. Grade 6–12—for educators who already hold a secondary education endorsement
      d. Grade K–12—for educators who already hold a special teaching (K–12) or special education (PK–age 21) endorsement
   4. The LBS I endorsement requires a passing score on the LBS I (155) test and completion of course work addressing the following topics:
      a. Survey of the exceptional child
      b. General characteristics of children with disabilities within the LBS I scope
      c. General methods for teaching children with disabilities within the LBS I scope
      d. Psychological assessment of children with disabilities within the LBS I scope

5. Some Illinois colleges/universities only require one course for each of the above areas, while others require the completion of multiple courses for each area; so be sure to check with the institution to fully understand and comply with requirements for the endorsement.

E. Exceptions to the Endorsement Structure
    1. Specific exceptions exist for the following endorsements: Bilingual; English as a Second Language; Family and Consumer Science; Middle School Mathematics; Middle School Reading Teacher; Middle School Safety and Driver Education; Science; Social Science
    2. Specifics for the above are available at: http://www.isbe.net/licensure/ requirements/exc_endsmt_struct_feb12-rev0114.pdf

Indiana

Stages and Titles of Teaching Certificates

I. Reciprocal Permit
   A. Issued on the basis of:
      1. Completion of an out-of-state teacher preparation program,
      2. Valid (unexpired) out-of-state license comparable to either the Indiana Initial Practitioner or Proficient Practitioner license when there are licensing deficiencies such as the appropriate Praxis II exam(s),
      3. CPR/AED Certification—http://www.doe.in.gov/licensing/cpr-heimlich-maneuver-aed-certification
         and
      4. Suicide Prevention Training—http://www.doe.in.gov/licensing/suicide-prevention-training

II. Initial Practitioner (valid 2 years)
   A. Issued on the basis of:
      1. Completion of bachelor's or higher degree,
      2. Teacher preparation program,
      3. Institution of higher education (IHE) recommendation,
      4. Passing scores on the appropriate Praxis II exam(s) or Indiana Core Assessment after February 10, 2013,
      5. CPR/AED Certification—http://www.doe.in.gov/licensing/cpr-heimlich-maneuver-aed-certification
         and
      6. Suicide Prevention Training—http://www.doe.in.gov/licensing/suicide-prevention-training

III. Proficient Practitioner (valid 5 years; renewable)
   A. Issued on the basis of:
      1. Successful completion of Indiana Mentoring and Assessment Program (IMAP) or 2 years of full-time, out-of-state, creditable teaching experience under a valid out-of-state license,
      2. Passing scores on the appropriate Praxis II exam(s) or Indiana Core Assessment after February 10, 2013,
      3. CPR/AED Certification—http://www.doe.in.gov/licensing/cpr-heimlich-maneuver-aed-certification,
         and
      4. Suicide Prevention Training—http://www.doe.in.gov/licensing/suicide-prevention-training
   B. Renewable every 5 years with completion of:
      1. 90 Professional Growth Plan (PGP) points
         or

Six semester hours of course work from an accredited higher education institution,
and

2. CPR/AED Certification—http://www.doe.in.gov/licensing/cpr-heimlich -maneuver-aed-certification

IV. Accomplished Practitioner (valid 10 years initially; renewable)
  A. Issued on the basis of:
    1. The appropriate graduate degree,
    2. Appropriate years of full-time, creditable teaching experience at an accredited school,
    3. Passing scores on the appropriate Praxis II exam(s) or Indiana Core Assessment after February 10, 2013,
    4. CPR/AED Certification—http://www.doe.in.gov/licensing/cpr-heimlich -maneuver-aed-certification
    and
    5. Suicide Prevention Training—http://www.doe.in.gov/licensing/suicide -prevention-training
  B. Renewable every 10 years with completion of:
    1. 90 PGP points
    or
    Six semester hours of course work from an accredited higher education institution,
    and
    2. CPR/AED Certification—http://www.doe.in.gov/licensing/cpr-heimlich -maneuver-aed-certification

Requirements for Teaching Certificates

Consult http://www.doe.in.gov/licensing/educator-preparation for a complete listing of the content/developmental areas available for teaching.

I. Reciprocal Permit (valid 1 year)
  A. Available only to candidates who have completed an out-of-state education program at a 4-year, regionally accredited IHE
  B. Requirements include:
    1. Bachelor's or higher degree,
    2. Teacher preparation program,
    3. Valid (unexpired) out-of-state license equivalent to the Indiana Initial or Proficient Practitioner license with an equivalent content (subject area) and school setting (grade level),
    4. Field experience, practicum, and/or student teaching,
    5. Passing scores on the appropriate Praxis II exam(s) or Indiana Core Assessment after February 10, 2013,
    6. CPR/AED Certification—http://www.doe.in.gov/licensing/cpr-heimlich -maneuver-aed-certification

> *and*
>
> 7. Suicide Prevention Training—http://www.doe.in.gov/licensing/suicide
>   -prevention-training

II. Initial Practitioners License (valid 2 years)
  A. Requirements include:
    1. Recommendation of the Indiana IHE approved to offer the program,
    2. Out-of-state graduates may be eligible if all Indiana licensure requirements are met and the applicant has less than 2 years of full-time, creditable teaching experience at an accredited school,
    3. Passing scores on the appropriate Praxis II exam(s) or Indiana Core Assessment after February 10, 2013,
    4. CPR/AED Certification—http://www.doe.in.gov/licensing/cpr-heimlich -maneuver-aed-certification
       and
    5. Suicide Prevention Training—http://www.doe.in.gov/licensing/suicide -prevention-training

III. Proficient Practitioner License (valid 5 years)
  A. Requirements include:
    1. Successful completion of IMAP or recommendation of the Indiana IHE approved to offer the program,
       a. Conditional upon applicant completing a beginning teacher internship under a valid Indiana license issued under a prior bulletin or rules; or upon applicant having 2 years of full-time, creditable teaching experience under a valid Indiana license issued under a prior bulletin or rules
    2. Out-of-state graduates may be eligible if all Indiana licensure requirements are met and the applicant has at least 2 years of full-time, creditable out-of-state teaching experience under a valid out-of-state license from an accredited school.
    3. Passing scores on the appropriate Praxis II exam(s) or Indiana Core Assessment after February 10, 2013,
    4. CPR/AED Certification—http://www.doe.in.gov/licensing/cpr-heimlich -maneuver-aed-certification
       and
    5. Suicide Prevention Training—http://www.doe.in.gov/licensing/suicide -prevention-training

IV. Accomplished Practitioner License (valid 10 years; renewable)
  A. Requirements include:
    1. Recommendation of the Indiana IHE approved to offer the appropriate graduate degree and verification of 2 years of full-time, creditable teaching experience under a valid license,
    2. Out-of-state graduates may be eligible if all Indiana licensure requirements are met and the applicant holds the appropriate graduate degree and has 2 years of full-time, creditable teaching experience under a valid out-of-state license,
    3. An individual who obtains national board certification (NBCT) is immediately eligible for the accomplished practitioner license,

4. Passing scores on the appropriate Praxis II exam(s) or Indiana Core Assessment after February 10, 2013,
5. CPR/AED Certification—http://www.doe.in.gov/licensing/cpr-heimlich-maneuver-aed-certification
   and
6. Suicide Prevention Training—http://www.doe.in.gov/licensing/suicide-prevention-training

V. Renewal Requirements
   A. Six semester hours of course work;
   or
   Ninety PGP points;
   or
   National Board of Professional Teaching Standards Certification;
   and
   B. CPR/AED Certification—http://www.doe.in.gov/licensing/cpr-heimlich-maneuver-aed-certification

Requirements for Administrative/Supervisory Certificates

I. The following areas are available for administration and supervision licensure:
   A. Building Level Administrator (Principal)
   B. Superintendent
   C. Director of Exceptional Needs
   D. Director of Curriculum and Instruction
   E. Director of Career and Technical Education
II. All administrative licenses are P–12.
III. Types of Certificates
   A. Reciprocal Permit (valid 1 year)
     1. Available only to candidates who have completed an approved out-of-state program at an institution of higher education (IHE) regionally accredited to offer the appropriate graduate degree.
     2. Requirements include:
       a. Master's or higher degree,
       b. Education leadership program,
       c. Two years of full-time, creditable teaching experience,
       d. Valid (unexpired) out-of-state license equivalent to the Indiana Initial or Proficient Practitioner license,
       e. CPR/AED Certification—http://www.doe.in.gov/licensing/cpr-heimlich-maneuver-aed-certification
         and
       f. Suicide Prevention Training—http://www.doe.in.gov/licensing/suicide-prevention-training
   B. Initial Practitioner License (valid 2 years)
     1. Requirements include:
       a. Recommendation of the Indiana IHE approved to offer the program

      b.   Out-of-state graduates may be eligible if all Indiana licensure requirements are met, including passing score on Praxis School Leaders Licensure Assessment (SLLA) exam, and the applicant has less than 2 years of full-time, creditable administration and supervision experience,

      c.   Passing scores on the appropriate Praxis II exam(s) or Indiana Core Assessment after February 10, 2013,

      d.   CPR/AED Certification—http://www.doe.in.gov/licensing/cpr-heimlich -maneuver-aed-certification
           and

      e.   Suicide Prevention Training—http://www.doe.in.gov/licensing/suicide -prevention-training

C.   Proficient Practitioner License (valid 5 years)

   1.   Requirements include:

      a.   Successful completion of IMAP or recommendation of the Indiana IHE approved to offer the program if the candidate holds another Indiana administrative license issued under a prior bulletin or rules,

      b.   Out-of-state graduates may be eligible if all Indiana licensure requirements are met (including passing score on Praxis SLLA exam) and the applicant has at least 2 years of full-time, creditable out-of-state administration and supervision experience under a valid out-of-state license,

      c.   Passing scores on the appropriate Praxis II exam(s) or Indiana Core Assessment after February 10, 2013,

      d.   CPR/AED Certification—http://www.doe.in.gov/licensing/cpr-heimlich -maneuver-aed-certification
           and

      e.   Suicide Prevention Training—http://www.doe.in.gov/licensing/suicide -prevention-training

D.   Accomplished Practitioner License (valid 10 years; renewable)

   1.   Requirements include:

      a.   For Building Level Administrator: 5 years of full-time, creditable administration and supervision experience under the appropriate license;

      b.   For District Level Administrator: 5 years of full-time, creditable administration and supervision experience under the appropriate license;
           and

      c.   60 credit hours of graduate course work

E.   Renewal Requirements

   1.   Six semester hours of course work;
       or
       90 PGP points;
       or
       National Board of Professional Teaching Standards Certification;
       and

   2.   CPR/AED Certification—http://www.doe.in.gov/licensing/cpr-heimlich -maneuver-aed-certification

Requirements for School Services Certificates

I. The following content/developmental areas are available for school services:
    A. School Counselor
    B. School Nurse
    C. School Social Worker
    D. School Psychologist

II. Types of Certificates
    A. Reciprocal Permit (valid 1 year)
        1. Available only to candidates who have completed an out-of-state education program at a four year, regionally accredited IHE.
        2. Requirements include:
            a. Bachelor's or higher degree for school nurse and appropriate license from the Indiana Professional Licensing Agency (see IPLA at www.pla.in.gov);
            b. Master's or higher degree for school social work and accompanying license from the Indiana Professional Licensing Agency (see IPLA at www.pla.in.gov);
            c. Master's or higher degree for school counseling and school psychology and equivalent out-of-state license;
            d. CPR/AED Certification—http://www.doe.in.gov/licensing/cpr-heimlich-maneuver-aed-certification
                and
            e. Suicide Prevention Training—http://www.doe.in.gov/licensing/suicide-prevention-training
    B. Initial Practitioner License (valid 2 years)
        1. Requirements include:
            a. Recommendation of the Indiana IHE approved to offer the program,
            b. Out-of-state graduates may be eligible if all Indiana licensure requirements are met and the applicant has less than 2 years full-time, creditable experience in the school services area,
            c. CPR/AED Certification—http://www.doe.in.gov/licensing/cpr-heimlich-maneuver-aed-certification
                and
            d. Suicide Prevention Training—http://www.doe.in.gov/licensing/suicide-prevention-training
    C. Proficient Practitioner License (valid 5 years)
        1. Requirements include:
            a. Successful completion of IMAP,
            b. Out-of-state graduates may be eligible if all Indiana licensure requirements are met and the applicant has at least 2 years of full-time, creditable out-of-state school services experience under a valid out-of-state license,
            c. CPR/AED Certification—http://www.doe.in.gov/licensing/cpr-heimlich-maneuver-aed-certification

and
  d. Suicide Prevention Training—http://www.doe.in.gov/licensing/suicide
      -prevention-training
D. Accomplished Practitioner License (valid 10 years; renewable)
    1. Requirements include:
        a. Recommendation of the Indiana IHE approved to offer the appropriate
            graduate degree and verification of creditable experience under a valid
            license,
        b. Out-of-state graduates may be eligible if all Indiana licensure requirements
            are met and the applicant holds the appropriate graduate degree and
            appropriate number of years of creditable experience in the school services
            area under a valid out-of-state license,
        c. CPR/AED Certification—htttp://www.doe.in.gov/licensing/cpr-heimlich
            -maneuver-aed-certification
            and
        d. Suicide Prevention Training—http://www.doe.in.gov/licensing/suicide
            -prevention-training
E. Renewal Requirements:
    1. Six semester hours of course work;
        or
        90 PGP points;
        or
        Indiana Professional Licensing Agency License (IPLA);
        or
        National Board of Professional Teaching Standards Certification;
        and
    2. CPR/AED Certification—http://www.doe.in.gov/licensing/cpr-heimlich
        -maneuver-aed-certification
F. License Renewal Requirements:
    1. For information regarding the renewal of licenses, go to http://www.doe.in.gov/
        licensing/renewing-indiana-educator-license

Iowa

Types of Licenses

I. Initial License (valid 2 years: renewable under prescribed conditions)
   A. Baccalaureate degree from a regionally accredited institution;
   B. Completion of an approved teacher preparation program;
   C. Completion of an approved human relations component;
   D. Completion of requirements for a teaching endorsement;
   E. Completion of the Iowa mandated tests (for applicants who graduated after January 1, 2013)
      or
      Completion of the mandated tests in the state in which the applicant is currently licensed (for applicants who graduated before January 1, 2013); and
   F. Meets the recency requirement of either 6 college credits or teaching experience within the last 5 years.
II. Standard License (valid 5 years; renewable under prescribed conditions)
   A. Completion of requirements for the initial license—see I, A–F, directly above; *and*
   B. Evidence of 2 years of successful teaching experience in a public school in Iowa, or of 3 years in any combination of public, private, or out-of-state schools.
III. Master Educator License (valid 5 years; renewable under prescribed conditions)
   A. Completion of requirements for the initial license—see I, A–F, directly above;
   B. Five years of teaching experience; *and*
   C. Master's degree in a recognized endorsement area or in curriculum, effective teaching, or a similar degree program which has a focus on school curriculum or instruction.
IV. Initial Administrator License (valid 1 year; renewable under prescribed conditions)
   A. Hold or be eligible for a standard license—see II, A and B, directly above;
   B. Three years of teaching experience;
   C. Does not have administrative experience;
   D. Completion of the requirements for an administrative endorsement; and
   E. Completion of a master's degree.
V. Professional Administrator License (valid 5 years; renewable under prescribed conditions)
   A. Hold or be eligible for a standard license; — see II, A and B, directly above;
   B. Three years of teaching experience;
   C. Completion of the requirements for an administrative endorsement; *and*
   D. Meets the recency requirement listed under the one-year conditional license.

VI.   Exchange License (valid 1 year; nonrenewable)
 A. Must complete a teacher preparation program from a state approved and regionally accredited institution, then submit transcripts to verify;
 B. Baccalaureate degree from a regionally accredited institution;
 C. Hold a valid teaching license in the state in which the teacher preparation program was completed;
 D. No disciplinary action pending;
 E. Completion of the mandated tests in the state in which the applicant is currently licensed (for applicants who graduated before January 1, 2013)
  or
  Completion of the Iowa mandated tests (for applicants who graduated after January 1, 2013);
  and
 F. Has not completed all Iowa requirements for a teaching endorsement.

VII. Initial Professional Service License (valid 2 years; renewable under prescribed conditions)
May be issued to an applicant for licensure to serve as a school audiologist, school psychologist, school social worker, speech-language pathologist, supervisor of special education (support), director of special education of an area education agency, or school counselor who:
 A. Has a master's degree in a recognized professional educational service area from a regionally accredited institution;
 B. Has completed a state-approved program which meets the requirements for an endorsement in a professional educational service area;
 C. Has completed the requirements for one of the professional educational service area endorsements;
  and
 D. Meets the recency requirement
  1. For details, see 282—subrule 13.10(3) at http://www.boee.iowa.gov/agency_282.pdf

VIII. Standard Professional Service License (valid 5 years; renewable under prescribed conditions)
 A. Completes requirements listed for the initial professional service license; see VII, A–D directly above;
  and
 B. Shows evidence of successful completion of a state-approved mentoring and induction program by
  1. Meeting the Iowa standards as determined by a comprehensive evaluation;
   and
  2. Two years of successful service experience in an Iowa public school.
  3. In lieu of completion of an Iowa state-approved mentoring and induction program, the applicant must provide evidence of 3 years of successful service area experience in an Iowa nonpublic school or 3 years of successful service area experience in an out-of-state K–12 educational setting.

Teaching Endorsements

I. General requirements for the issuance of a license with an endorsement
    A. Baccalaureate degree from a regionally accredited institution;
    B. Completion of an approved human relations component;
    C. Completion of the exceptional learner program, which must include preparation that contributes to the education of individuals with disabilities and the gifted and talented;
    D. Professional education core, with completed course work or evidence of competency in:
        1. Student learning: the practitioner understands how students learn and develop, and provides learning opportunities that support intellectual, career, social, and personal development;
        2. Diverse learners: the practitioner understands how students differ in their approaches to learning and creates instructional opportunities that are equitable and are adaptable to diverse learners;
        3. Instructional planning: the practitioner plans instruction based upon knowledge of subject matter, students, the community, curriculum goals, and state curriculum models;
        4. Instructional strategies: the practitioner understands and uses a variety of instructional strategies to encourage students' development of critical thinking, problem solving, and performance skills;
        5. Learning environment/classroom management: the practitioner uses an understanding of individual and group motivation and behavior to create a learning environment that encourages positive social interaction, active engagement in learning, and self-motivation;
        6. Communication: the practitioner uses knowledge of effective verbal, nonverbal, and media communication techniques, and other forms of symbolic representation, to foster active inquiry, collaboration, and support interaction in the classroom;
        7. Assessment: the practitioner understands and uses formal and informal assessment strategies to evaluate the continuous intellectual, social, and physical development of the learner;
        8. Foundations, reflection and professional development: the practitioner continually evaluates the effects of the practitioner's choices and actions on students, parents, and other professionals in the learning community, and actively seeks out opportunities to grow professionally;
        9. Collaboration, ethics and relationships: the practitioner fosters relationships with parents, school colleagues, and organizations in the larger community to support students' learning and development;
        10. Computer technology related to instruction;
        11. Completion of pre–student teaching field-based experiences;
        12. Methods of teaching, with an emphasis on the subject and grade level endorsement desired;

13. Student teaching in the subject area and grade level endorsement desired;
14. Preparation in reading programs, including reading recovery, and integration of reading strategies into content area methods course work; and

E. Content/subject matter specialization: the practitioner understands the central concepts, tools of inquiry, and structure of the discipline(s) the practitioner teaches and creates learning experiences that make these aspects of subject matter meaningful for students.

1. This is evidenced by completion of a 30-semester-hour teaching major that must minimally include the requirements for at least 1 of the basic endorsement areas, special education teaching endorsements, or secondary level occupational endorsements.
2. For specific endorsement requirements, consult www.boee.iowa.gov – endorsements

Administrator Licenses

Note: Applicants for the administrator license must first comply with the requirements for all Iowa practitioners set out in 282—Chapter 13 (for details, consult http//www.boee.iowa.gov/agency_282.pdf) Additionally, the requirements of rules 282—13.2(272) and 282—13.3(272) and the license-specific requirements set forth under each license must be met before an applicant is eligible for an administrator license.

I. Initial Administrator License (valid 1 year) may be issued to an applicant who:
  A. Is the holder of or is eligible for a standard license;
  B. Has 3 years of teaching experience;
  C. Has completed a state-approved PK–12 principal and PK–12 supervisor of special education program;
    1. For details, see subrule 18.9(1)) at http://www.boee.iowa.gov/agency_282.pdf
  D. Is assuming a position as a PK–12 principal and PK–12 supervisor of special education for the first time or has 1 year of out-of-state or nonpublic administrative experience;
    1. For details, see subrule 18.9(1)) at http://www.boee.iowa.gov/agency_282.pdf
  E. Has completed an approved human relations component;
  F. Has completed an exceptional learner component;
    and
  G. Has completed an evaluator approval program.
II. Superintendent / AEA Administrator
  The holder of this endorsement is authorized to serve as a superintendent for PreK–12 or as an Area Education Agency (AEA) administrator.
  A. Program requirements
    1. Specialist degree (or its equivalent: a master's degree plus at least 30 semester hours of planned graduate study in administration beyond the master's degree);
    2. Content: through completion of a sequence of courses and experiences which may have been part of, or in addition to, the degree requirements, the administrator has knowledge and understanding of:

    a. Models, theories, and practices that provide the basis for leading educational systems toward improving student performance;

    b. Federal, state and local fiscal policies related to education;

    c. Human resources management, including recruitment, personnel assistance and development, evaluation and negotiations;

    d. Current legal issues in general and special education;

    e. Non-instructional support services management including but not limited to transportation, nutrition and facilities; *and*

    f. Practicum in PreK–12 school administration in which, or in related course work, the administrator facilitates processes and engages in activities for:

        i. Developing a shared vision of learning through articulation, implementation, and stewardship;

        ii. Advocating, nurturing, and sustaining a school culture and instructional program conducive to student learning and staff professional growth;

        iii. Ensuring management of the organization, operations, and resources for a safe, efficient, and effective learning environment;

        iv. Collaborating with school staff, families, community members and boards of directors; responding to diverse community interests and needs; and mobilizing community resources;

        v. Acting with integrity, fairness, and in an ethical manner; *and*

        vi. Understanding, responding to, and influencing the larger political, social, economic, legal, and cultural context.

B. Administrative experience

    1. The applicant must have had 3 years of experience as a building principal.

        a. PreK–12 or area education agency administrative experience is acceptable if the applicant acquires the 3 years of experience while holding a valid administrator license.

Kansas

License Types and Requirements

I. Initial Teaching License (valid 2 years; renewable)
   A. In-state applicants
      1. Bachelor's degree from a regionally accredited college or university
      2. Completion of a state-approved teacher preparation program
      3. Recency: have at least 8 credit hours or 1 year of accredited teaching experience completed within the last 6 years
      4. Passing scores on the content assessment in each of the endorsement areas on license
      5. Passing scores on the pedagogy assessment: Principles of Learning and Teaching (PLT)
   B. Out-of-state applicants
      1. See I, A, 1–3, directly above;
         and
      2. Passing scores on content and pedagogy tests: tests completed to achieve the out-of-state license may be acceptable;
         or
      3. May be issued a 2-year exchange license, if applicable;
         or
      4. May be issued a 1-year nonrenewable license;
         or
      5. May be issued a substitute license;
         or
      6. Meet experience requirements to come in at the professional license level.
II. Professional Teaching License (valid 5 years; renewable)
   A. In-state applicants
      1. Hold a currently valid Initial teaching license
      2. During its validity period, successfully complete the prescribed performance assessment
   B. Out-of-state applicants
      1. Bachelor's degree
      2. Completion of a state-approved preparation program in subject or field in which licensure is sought
      3. Recency: at least 1 year of accredited teaching experience or 8 semester hours of college credit within the 6 year period immediately prior to application
      4. Out-of-state professional license,
         and
      5. Three years of recent accredited experience under a standard teaching license
         or

Meet recency and verify at least 5 years of accredited experience under an intial or professional license

or

Passing scores on assessments in content and pedagogy, with an already completed performance assessment.

III. Accomplished Teaching License (valid 10 years; renewable)
  A. Available only to teachers who have achieved National Board certification from the National Board for Professional Teaching Standards (NBPTS) through completion of their advanced-level performance assessment process.
     1. Kansas licensed teachers must also hold a currently valid Kansas professional level teaching license as well as achieving National Board certification.
     2. National Board–certified teachers coming from out-of-state may apply for this license as their initial Kansas license, as long as they also hold a currently valid professional-level teaching license in another state.
        a. Accomplished license will be valid for the validity length of National Board certification.

IV. One-Year Nonrenewable Teaching License (valid only for current school year)
  A. Meet all requirements for an Initial license (see I, A, 1–5, directly above) except for all or part of the prelicensure tests
  B. Tests in which individual is deficient must be completed during the school year in order to upgrade to the Initial license.

V. Two-Year Exchange (Teaching or School Specialist) License (valid 2 years)
  A. Exchange Teaching
     1. Complete a state-approved teacher education program through college in home state
     2. Hold a standard valid license in that state
     3. Rectify all deficiencies in initial Kansas requirements during 2-year period
  B. Exchange School Specialist (school counselor, library media, reading specialist)
     1. Complete a state-approved school specialist program in home state
     2. Hold a standard valid school specialist license in that state
     3. Rectify all deficiencies in initial Kansas requirements during 2-year period
        a. Deficiencies may include completion of the content licensure examination; a 3.25 cumulative GPA in graduate course work; and/or recency credit.
     4. Hold a Kansas professional-level teaching license
     5. Neither leadership licenses nor alternative routes to licensure are eligible for exchange licensure.

VI. Substitute Licenses
  A. Standard Substitute License (valid 5 years; renewable)
     1. Hold a bachelor's degree
     2. Complete a teacher preparation program
     3. Submit 1 fingerprint card for an FBI and Kansas Bureau of Investigation (KBI) background clearance report
  B. Emergency Substitute License (valid for current school year)
     1. Complete a minimum of 60 semester credit hours from regionally accredited college or university

2.   Submit 1 fingerprint card for an FBI and KBI background clearance report

VII.   Provisional License (valid 2 years; renewable)

A.   Provisional Teaching Endorsement License

1.   Hold a valid Kansas license and have a plan of study for completing an approved program for a new teaching subject

2.   Fifty percent of the program for the new teaching area is complete

3.   A Kansas district must verify assignment of teacher in the provisional subject area at the appropriate level.

4.   To qualify for a second provisional, complete half the remaining course work deficiencies (have 75 percent of approved program completed).

5.   For Provisional Teaching Endorsement License in Special Education, see VII, A, 2, directly above.

a.   A valid license for general education is required.

b.   Course work in areas of methodology, characteristics, and a practicum is already completed.

c.   Kansas district must verify assignment of teacher in provisional special education area at the appropriate level.

B.   Provisional School Specialist License for school counselor, library media, or reading specialist

1.   Hold a valid 5-year professional teaching license

2.   Fifty percent of the school specialist program is completed

3.   Kansas district must verify assignment of applicant as a school specialist.

C.   Provisional license is not available for school leadership licenses.

VIII.   Restricted Teaching License Alternative Pathway (valid 3 years while employed in school system)

A.   Meet all eligibility requirements:

1.   Hold a bachelor's degree or higher from a regionally accredited university

2.   Degree must be in a regular education content area in which applicant desires to teach or equivalent content course work must be completed.

3.   Most recent 60 semester credits of college course work show a cumulative GPA of 2.75

4.   Passing score on the appropriate content assessment

B.   Request that the university hosting the alternative route program evaluate transcript to ensure that content requirements for subject matter teaching area are adequate

1.   Develop a plan of study with the alternative certification program staff; program length may vary depending on situation.

C.   Locate and apply for a teaching position, verifying that a restricted license is appropriate for it

D.   Apply for restricted license, coordinating application among individual, employing school district, and higher education institution providing the course work.

E.   Once license is issued, applicant will teach full time while completing required professional education course work towards full licensure.

F.   Submit a progress report every year verifying appropriate progress towards a full license; otherwise, restricted license will be cancelled

G.   Apply for a full Kansas license with institutional recommendation once applicant successfully completes all course work and testing requirements on plan of study

    H.   Complete the PLT assessment

IX.   School Specialist License

    A.   Initial School Specialist License

        1.   Graduate degree from a regionally accredited college

        2.   Complete graduate-level state-approved program

        3.   3.25 cumulative GPA in graduate course work

        4.   Recency: have at least 8 credit hours or 1 year of accredited experience completed within the last 6 years

        5.   Currently valid Kansas professional teaching license (if applying for library media, reading specialist)

        6.   Successfully complete a school specialist content assessment

            a.   School counselor content test: complete Praxis II test number 0420—School Guidance and Counseling—with score of 600 or above

            b.   Library media specialist content test: complete Praxis II test number 0311—Library Media Specialist—with score of 630 or above

            c.   Reading specialist content test: complete Praxis II test number 0300—Reading Specialist—with score of 560 or above

    B.   Professional School Specialist License

        1.   In-state applicants

            a.   Hold a currently valid Initial School Specialist License; see IX, A, 1–6, directly above

            b.   Complete the performance assessment while employed as a school specialist

        2.   Out-of-state applicants

            a.   See IX, A, 1–5, directly above,
and

            b.   Successfully complete a school specialist content and performance assessment,
or
Three years of recent accredited experience in a school specialist position with a valid professional level license.

X.   School Leadership Licenses: includes Program Leadership (supervisor/coordinator); Building Leadership (principal); District Leadership (superintendent)

    A.   Initial School Leadership License (valid 2 years)

        1.   Graduate degree from a regionally accredited college

        2.   Complete graduate-level state-approved program in school leadership

        3.   3.25 cumulative GPA in graduate course work

        4.   Recency: at least 8 credit hours or 1 year of accredited experience completed within the last 6 years

        5.   Minimum of 3 years of accredited experience under a valid professional license/certificate

        6.   School leadership licensure assessment

B. Professional School Leadership license (valid 5 years)
   1. Hold a currently valid Initial School Leadership License
   2. Complete performance assessment while employed as an administrator
C. Out-of-state applicants
   1. See X, A, 1–6, directly above
      and
   2. Successfully complete a school leadership content and performance assessment
      or
      Three years of recent accredited experience in a school leadership position with a valid professional school leadership license

XI. New Licenses: Contact the Kansas State Department of Education (see Appendix 1) for full details
A. Transitional License (valid 1 year)
   1. Provides immediate access to practice for:
      a. Out-of-state applicant without recent credit or experience
      b. Kansas educator with expired full license who is retired or out of practice
B. Interim Alternative License (valid 1 year; renewable for another year)
   1. Guarantees license for immediate access to practice to out-of-state applicant whose preparation was through an alternative pathway
C. Restricted School Specialist License (for school counselor or library media)
   1. Requires graduate degree and 3 years of professional experience in the counseling or library field
   2. Must complete professional education during 3-year restricted license period while employed in school system

Endorsements by Levels

I. Early Childhood: Birth–Grade 3 or Birth–K
A. Requires combined general education and special education curriculum: Early Childhood Unified
B. Must be done with a general education license: Deaf or Hard-of-Hearing; Visually Impaired; School Psychologist
II. Early Childhood–Late Childhood: K–6
A. Elementary
B. Provisional is available for: Adaptive; Functional; Gifted; English for Speakers of Other Languages (ESOL)
III. Late Childhood–Early Adolescence: Grades 5–8
A. Provisional is available for: History Comprehensive; Science; English Language Arts; Mathematics
IV. Early Adolescence–Late Adolescence/Adulthood: Grades 6–12
A. Provisional is available for: English Language Arts; Mathematics; Agriculture; Biology; Business; Chemistry; Earth and Space Science; Family & Consumer

Science; History and Government; Journalism; Physics; Psychology; Speech/Theatre; Technology Education; Communication Technology; Power, Energy, Transportation Technology; Production Technology; Adaptive; ESOL; Functional; Gifted

V.   Early Childhood–Late Adolescence/Adulthood: PreK–12

    A.   School Psychologist; Building Leadership; District Leadership; Program Leadership

    B.   Provisional is available for: Deaf or Hard-of-Hearing; Visually Impaired; Adaptive, Functional; Gifted; ESOL; Library Media Specialist; Music; Instrumental Music; Vocal Music; Physical Education; Reading Specialist; School Counselor

Kentucky

General Requirements

I. Recency of preparation
   A. Completed program of preparation within 5 years preceding date of receipt of certification application form,
   or
   Completed 6 semester hours of additional graduate credit within preceding 5 years.
   1. Applicants who have completed a 5th-year program and have 2 years of successful teaching experience within the last 10 years are exempt from the 6-hour requirement.
   B. Initial 1-year certification for special circumstances
   1. Those not meeting recency requirements in I, A, directly above, who have not previously held a regular Kentucky teaching certificate, but who otherwise qualify for certification shall be issued a 1-year initial certificate that
      a. Ends June 30 of next calendar year
      b. Is conditional on 6 semester hours of graduate credit applicable toward the usual renewal requirements being completed by September 1 of year of expiration

II. Duration of teaching certificates
   A. Issued for 5 years, with provisions for subsequent 5-year renewals, provided that by September 1 of the year of expiration, the applicant has completed
   1. Three years of successful teaching experience,
      or
   At least 6 semester hours of graduate credit or the equivalent.
   B. One-year certificates shall be issued for
   1. Beginning teacher internship
      a. Upon successful completion of such internship as judged by majority vote of beginning teacher committee, 1-year certificate will be extended for remainder of the 5-year period.
   2. Initial certification for applicants not meeting recency requirements in I, A, directly above.

III. Renewal of teaching certificates
   A. Requirements for subsequent 5-year renewals
   1. Completion by September 1 of the year of expiration of
      a. Three years of successful teaching experience,
         or
      Six semester hours of graduate credit or the equivalent.
   2. Those who have not yet completed the planned 5th-year program shall
      a. Complete at least 15 semester hours of graduate credit applicable to the program for the first renewal,

and

      b.   Complete the remainder of the program for the second renewal.

    3.   Credits for certificate renewal shall be earned after the issuance of the certificate.

      a.   Any credits earned in excess of minimum requirements shall accumulate and apply toward subsequent renewals.

    4.   Applicants holding a lapsed regular Kentucky teaching certificate shall not be required to take the written tests or to participate in the beginning teacher internship program.

IV.   Out-of-State Applicants

    A.   Those who have completed 2 or more years of acceptable teaching experience outside of the Commonwealth of Kentucky and who otherwise qualify for certification shall not be required to take the written tests or to participate in the beginning teacher internship program.

V.   Requirements for 1-year certificate for beginning teacher internship

    A.   Completion of an approved program of preparation that corresponds to the certificate desired

    B.   Passing scores on the Praxis II Subject Assessment appropriate for each content area in which certification is requested, in addition to the appropriate Principles of Learning and Teaching (PLT) test

      1.   All new teachers are required to take the PLT test in addition to the specialty(ies) test appropriate for the certification they are seeking. Contact the Education Professional Standards Board (see Appendix 1) for detailed information.

    C.   Evidence of full-time employment in a Kentucky school as attested by the prospective employer

VI.   Upon successful completion of the approved program of preparation and upon completion of the designated tests with acceptable scores, the Education Professional Standards Board shall issue a statement of eligibility for employment that shall serve as evidence of eligibility for the 1-year certificate once a teaching position is secured. The statement of eligibility shall be valid for a 5-year period.

Approved Programs

The Commonwealth of Kentucky follows the "approved program" approach to certification. An individual should follow the program in effect at the college or university with the guidance of the college advisor and meet the General Requirements (see above). Applicants interested in certification should contact the Division of Certification (see Appendix 1) for the latest information.

    I.   Interdisciplinary Early Childhood Education (Birth to Primary)

    II.   Elementary School (Primary through Grade 5)

    III.   Middle School (Grades 5 through 9)

      A.   Preparation in one major or equivalent,
        or

      B.   Preparation in two teaching fields selected from the following: English and communications, mathematics, science, and social studies

      1.   Candidates who choose to prepare simultaneously for teaching in the middle school and for teaching exceptional children are required to complete only one middle school teaching field.

IV.   Secondary School (Grades 8 through 12)

    A.   Preparation includes one or more of the following specializations: English, mathematics, social studies, biological science, physics, chemistry, or earth science.

V.   Middle/Secondary School (Grades 5 through 12)

    A.   Preparation includes one or more of the following specializations: agriculture, business and marketing, family and consumer science, industrial education, technology education.

VI.   Elementary/Middle/Secondary School (Primary through Grade 12)

    A.   Preparation includes one or more of the following specializations: art, foreign language (Arabic, Chinese, French, German, Japanese, Latin, Russian, or Spanish), health, physical education, integrated music, vocal music, instrumental music, school media librarian.

VII.   Exceptional Children (Primary through Grade 12, and for collaborating with teachers to design and deliver programs for pre-primary children)

    A.   Preparation includes one or more of the following specializations: learning and behavior disorders; moderate and severe disabilities; hearing impaired or hearing impaired/sign proficiency; visually impaired; communication disorders (master's level); speech language pathology assistant (bachelor's level).

VIII.   Endorsements to Certificates (Primary through Grade 12)

    A.   Computer science (8–12), English as a second language (P–12), gifted education (P–12), driver education (8–12), reading and writing (P–12), instructional computer technology (P–12), learning and behavior disorders (8–12), school nutrition (P–12), and school safety (P–12)

    B.   Restricted Base Certificates: psychology (8–12), sociology (8–12), journalism (8–12), speech/media communications (8–12), theater (P–12), dance (P–12), computer information systems (P–12), English as a second language (P–12), school nurse (P–12), school social worker (P–12), junior reserve officer training corps (8–12)

IX.   Professional Certificate for Instructional Leadership

    A.   Certification is offered for the following positions: Supervisor of Instruction, Level 1; Supervisor of Instruction, Level 2; Principal, All Grades, Level 1; Principal, All Grades, Level 2; Director of Special Education; Director of Pupil Personnel; School Psychologist; Guidance Counselor; and School Superintendent.

Principal, All Grades

I.   Requirements for Principal, All Grades, Level 1

    A.   As prerequisites for the Level 1 program of preparation for the initial Professional Certificate for Instructional Leadership, the candidate shall

        1.   Have been admitted to the preparation program on the basis of criteria, developed by the teacher-education institution,

        2.   Have completed 3 years of full-time teaching experience,

3. Have completed a 30-hour post-master's degree program in school administration,
4. Qualify for a Kentucky teaching certificate.
5. Successfully complete the School Leaders Licensure Assessment (SLLA) and the Kentucky specialty test of instructional and administrative practices.
   a. Applicants with out-of-state principal certification and 2 years of verified full-time principal experience are exempt from the SLLA.
6. All applicants without 2 years of verified full-time principal experience must successfully complete a 1-year Kentucky principal internship program.

B. The initial Professional Certificate for Instructional Leadership shall be issued for a period of 1 year upon successful completion of Level 1 preparation and the tests prescribed and upon obtaining employment for an internship position as principal or assistant principal. Upon proof of employment as a principal /assistant principal, the certificate shall be extended for 4 years.

C. The certificate shall be renewed subsequently for 5-year periods. The first renewal shall require the completion of the curriculum identified as the Level 2 program in the curriculum standards. Each 5-year renewal thereafter shall require the completion of 2 years of experience as a principal, or 3 semester hours of additional graduate credit related to the position of school principal, or 42 hours of approved training selected from programs approved for the Kentucky Effective Leadership Training Program.

D. If a lapse in certification occurs because of lack of completion of the Level 2 preparation, the certificate may be reissued for a 5-year period upon successful completion of the Level 2 preparation. If a certificate lapses with Level 2 preparation, but because of lack of the renewal requirements, the certificate may be reissued after the completion of an additional 6 semester hours of graduate study appropriate to the program.

E. Persons applying for the Professional Certificate for Instructional Leadership who satisfy the curriculum requirements and all other prerequisites and who have completed at least 2 years of successful full-time experience, including at least 140 days per year, as a school principal, within a 10-year period prior to making application will be exempt from the internship requirements for school principals but shall be required to pass the written examinations.

II. Standards for School Principal
   A. Individuals must meet the standards for principals taken from the Standards for School Leaders developed by the Interstate School Leaders Licensure Consortium (ISLLC). Please contact the Kentucky Division of Certification (see Appendix 1) for additional information.

Guidance Counselor

I. Provisional Certificate Requirements, Primary–Grade 12 (valid 5 years)
   A. Complete an approved master's level program in guidance counseling
   B. Renewable with proof of completion of at least 9 semester hours of graduate credit in areas of counseling or guidance counseling

II.   Standard Certificate Requirements, Primary–Grade 12 (valid 5 years)

   A. Option 1

      1. Successfully complete an approved master's level program in guidance counseling

      2. Successfully complete additional 3–6 credit hours from an approved graduate-level counseling or guidance counseling program

      3. One year of full-time employment as a provisionally certified guidance counselor in an accredited public or private school

      4. Hold a valid Kentucky Professional teaching certificate, *and*

      5. Complete at least 1 year of full-time classroom teaching experience

   B. Option 2

      1. See II, A, 1 and 2, directly above

      2. Complete at least 2 years of successful employment as a provisional full-time certified guidance counselor

   C. Renewable upon completion of Effective Instructional Leadership Act (EILA) hours as specified by the Kentucky Department of Education by September 1 of the year of expiration

Library Media Specialist

I.   This standards- and performance-based credential is awarded for work with all grade levels after the following requirements have been met:

   A. Transcript reflecting appropriate grades and courses,

   B. Recommendation of the college or university,

   C. Praxis II: Library Media Specialist test with satisfactory score, *and*

   D. Internship.

II.   For applicants with 2 years of experience as a Library Media Specialist, C and D, directly above, may be waived. Contact the Education Professional Standards Board (see Appendix 1) for more detailed information.

School Psychologist

I.   Provisional Certificate for School Psychologist

   A. Requirements

      1. Recommendation of the applicant's preparing institution

      2. Successful completion of the institution's approved program of preparation

      3. Passing score on the required assessment

   B. Issued for a duration period of 1 year; may be renewed for an additional year if the individual is serving in the position of the school psychologist on at least a half-time basis.

   C. Individual serves under the supervision of the preparing institution. During this first year of service, the employer of the Provisional Certificate shall permit the individual to engage in the preparing institution's internship component.

D. Internship may be served full-time during 1 school year or half-time during 2 consecutive years.

II. Standard Certificate for School Psychologist
   A. Option 1
       1. Completion of an approved program of preparation that corresponds to the certificate at a teacher-education institution that adheres to the National Association of School Psychologists Standards for Training Programs
       2. Completion of the appropriate assessment and a passing score as established in state regulations
   B. Option 2
       1. Possession of a valid certificate as a nationally certified school psychologist issued by the National School Psychology Certification System
   C. The Standard Certificate for School Psychologist shall be issued for a period of 5 years and may be renewed for subsequent 5-year periods with completion of one of the following:
       1. At least 3 years of experience as a school psychologist within each certification period and 72 hours of continuing professional development activities, *or*
       2. Six semester hours of graduate training related to school psychology.

Teacher for Gifted Education

I. Standards for Certificate Endorsement
   A. Classroom teaching certificate
   B. One year of teaching experience
   C. The completion of an approved graduate-level curriculum
       1. At least 9 semester hours of credit giving emphasis to the following content:
           a. Nature and needs of gifted education
           b. Assessment and/or counseling of the gifted
           c. Curriculum development for the gifted
           d. Strategies and materials for teaching the gifted
           e. Creative studies
       2. At least 3 semester hours of credit in a supervised practicum for gifted education; however, with 2 years of experience as a teacher for gifted, the practicum requirement may be waived.

Louisiana

Standard Certificates

I. Type C/Level 1 (valid for 3 years)
   A. Baccalaureate degree, including an approved teacher-education program, student teaching, and 1-year internship,
   or
   3 years of teaching experience in the program area
   B. Credits distributed among general education, content focus area, knowledge of the learner, and methodology in teaching
   C. Appropriate NTE /Praxis scores for initial certification
II. Type B (valid for life for continuous service)/Level 2 (valid for 5 years)
   A. Baccalaureate or higher degree, including completion of an approved teacher-education program
   B. See I, B, directly above
   C. Three years of successful teaching experience in certified field
   D. Successful completion of the State Evaluation Program
III. Type A (valid for life for continuous service)/Level 3 (valid for 5 years)
   A. Baccalaureate degree, including completion of an approved teacher-education program
   B. See I, B, directly above
   C. Master's or higher degree from an approved institution
   D. Five years of successful teaching experience in certified field
   E. Successful completion of the State Evaluation Program

Basic Certification

I. Grades PK–3
   A. General education course work hours: English (12), mathematics (9), sciences (9), social studies (6), and arts (3)
   B. Focus areas course work hours: nursery school and kindergarten (12); reading/language arts (12); and mathematics (9)
II. Grades 1–5
   A. General education course work hours: English (12), mathematics (12), sciences (15), social studies (12), and arts (3)
   B. Focus areas course work hours: reading/language arts (12); and mathematics (9)
III. Grades 4–8
   A. Focus on greater depth in content in generic or 2 in-depth teaching areas
   B. General education course work hours: English (12), mathematics (12), sciences (15), social studies (12), and arts (3)

   C. Focus areas course work hours
      1. In-depth teaching areas #1 and #2 each require:
         a. Seven or more hours in English/social studies/mathematics *or* science, *and*
         b. Nineteen total hours in general education and focus area courses.

IV. Grades 6–12
   A. Focus on greater depth in content in primary and secondary teaching area
   B. General education course work hours: English (6), mathematics (6), sciences (9), social studies (6), and arts (3)
   C. Primary teaching area requires 22 or more hours if in science,
      or
      Twenty-five or more hours if in English, social studies, or mathematics,
      or
      Thirty-one or more hours if in other areas.
      1. General education (if applicable) and focus area hours should equal 31 total hours.
   D. Secondary teaching area requires 13 or more hours if in English, social studies, or mathematics,
      or
      Ten or more hours if in science,
      or
      Nineteen or more hours if in other areas.
      1. General education (if applicable) and focus area hours should equal 19 total hours.

New Certification Areas and Courses

I. Common Elements of Basic Certification for All Grade Levels
   A. General education course work
      1. Same general course work areas and hours (e.g., 54 hours) for grades 1–5 and 4–8
   B. Knowledge of the learner and learning environment: 15 hours
      1. Same general course work areas and hours (e.g., 15 hours) for all PK–12 teachers
   C. Teaching Methodology
   D. Student Teaching
      1. Same requirements and hours (e.g., 9 hours) for all PK–12 teachers
   E. Total hours: 124
II. Grades PK–3
   A. Methodology and Teaching
      1. Teaching Methodology: 6 hours
      2. Student Teaching: same requirements and hours (e.g., 9 hours) for all PK–12 teachers
         a. Students must spend a minimum of 270 clock hours in student teaching with at least 180 of such hours spent in actual teaching, a substantial portion of which shall be on an all-day basis.

B. See I, B, 1, directly above
C. Flexible hours for the university's use: 22 hours
   1. It is recommended that preservice teachers be provided a minimum of 180 hours of direct teaching experience in field-based settings prior to student teaching.
D. See I, E, directly above

III. Grades 1–5
   A. See II, A–D, directly above, except that flexible hours for university's use are 19

IV. Grades 4–8
   A. Methodology and Teaching
      1. Teaching Methodology: 9 hours
      2. Student Teaching: See II, A, 2, a, directly above
      3. Reading: 6 hours
   B. See I, B, 1, directly above
   C. Flexible hours for the university's use
      1. Two in-depth teaching areas: 17–20 hours
   D. See I, E, directly above

V. Grades 6–12
   A. Methodology and Teaching
      1. Teaching Methodology: 6 hours
      2. Student Teaching: See II, A, 2, a, directly above
      3. Reading: 3 hours
   B. See I, B, 1, directly above
   C. Flexible hours for the university's use: 17–26
   D. See I, E, directly above

General/Special Education, Mild-Moderate Certification

I. Elementary Grades 1–5
   A. Complete approved blended general/special education mild-moderate program for elementary grade levels 1–5, with program focus on areas of reading/language arts and mathematics. Total required semester hours in program 126
      1. General education, semester hours 54
         To include English (12), mathematics (12), sciences (15), social studies (12), and arts (3)
      2. Focus area, special education semester hours 21
         Must meet Council for Exceptional Children (CEC) performance-based standards for accreditation and licensure
      3. Knowledge of the learner and learning environment, with emphasis on the elementary school student, semester hours 15
         Course work to address needs of regular and exceptional child, including child/adolescent development or psychology, educational psychology, the learner with special needs, classroom organization and management, and multicultural education

4. Methodology and teaching, semester hours.................................... 33
   Teaching methodology and strategies, including science and social science (6), math content/methodology (6), student teaching, 50% of which must include working with and actual teaching of students with disabilities (9)
5. Flexible hours for university's use, semester hours 3
6. In addition to the student teaching experience, actual teaching experiences (in addition to observations) in classroom settings during sophomore, junior, and senior years within schools with varied socioeconomic and cultural characteristics are required.
   a. A minimum of 180 hours of direct teaching experience in field-based settings prior to student teaching is required.

II. Middle Grades 4–8
   A. Complete approved blended general/special education mild-moderate program for middle grades 4–8, with program focus on special education and one middle school content area. Total required semester hours in program.............. 123
      1. See I, A, 1, directly above
      2. Focus area, special education and 1 middle school content area, semester hours.. 42
         Combined general education and focus area (19); middle school content area—English, mathematics, science, or social studies (21); special education content, which must meet CEC performance-based standards for accreditation and licensure (21).
      3. See I, A, 3, directly above, except with emphasis on the middle school student
      4. Methodology and teaching, semester hours.................................... 21
         Reading and literacy content/methodology (6), teaching methodology and strategies (6), student teaching, 50% of which must include working with and actual teaching of students with disabilities (9)
      5. Flexible hours for university's use, semester hours 3–16
      6. In addition to the student teaching experience, actual teaching experiences (in addition to observations) in classroom settings during sophomore, junior, and senior years within schools with varied socioeconomic and cultural characteristics are required.
         a. A minimum of 180 hours of direct teaching experience in field-based settings prior to student teaching is required.

III. Secondary Grades 6–12
   A. Complete approved blended general/special education mild-moderate program for secondary grade levels 6–12, with program focus on special education and one high school content area. Total required semester hours in program 123
      1. General education, semester hours 30
         To include English (6), mathematics (6), sciences (9), social studies (6), and arts (3)
      2. Focus area, special education and 1 high school content focus area, semester hours.. 51

Combined general education and focus area (31); secondary school content area (30); special education content, which must meet CEC performance-based standards for accreditation and licensure (21).

3. See I, A, 3, directly above, except with emphasis on the secondary school student
4. Methodology and teaching, semester hours... 21
    Reading and literacy content/methodology (6), teaching methodology and strategies (6), student teaching, 50% of which must include working with and actual teaching of students with disabilities (9)
5. Flexible hours for university's use, semester hours 16–29
6. In addition to the student teaching experience, actual teaching experiences (in addition to observations) in classroom settings during sophomore, junior, and senior years within schools with varied socioeconomic and cultural characteristics are required.
    a. A minimum of 180 hours of direct teaching experience in field-based settings prior to student teaching is required.

Administrators, Supervisors, and Special Service Personnel

I. Educational Leadership Certificate—Level 1. For school and district leadership positions such as principal, assistant principal, parish or city supervisor of instruction, supervisor of child welfare and attendance, or comparable positions
    A. Eligibility Requirements
        1. Hold or be eligible to hold valid Louisiana Type B or Level 2 teaching certificate; see Standard Certificates, III, A–E, above
        2. Have completed competency-based graduate degree preparation program in area of educational leadership from regionally accredited institution of higher education
        3. Earn passing score on School Leaders Licensure Assessment (SLLA), in accordance with state requirements
        4. Those meeting requirements in I, A, 1 and 2, directly above, are eligible for a Level 1 Educational Leader Certificate and must meet the standards of effectiveness as an educational leader for 3 years pursuant to Bulletin 130 and R.S.17:3902.
II. Educational Leadership Certificate—Level 1 (Alternate Path). For same positions as in I, directly above.
    A. Eligibility Requirements
        1. See I, A, 1, directly above
        2. Have completed a graduate degree program from a regionally accredited institution of higher education
        3. Have met competency-based requirements by completing individualized program of educational leadership—based on screening of each candidate's competencies when entering program—from a regionally accredited institution of higher education
        4. Earn passing score on SLLA in accordance with state requirements

    5. See I, A, 4, directly above, except candidates must meet requirements listed in II, A, 1–4, directly above

III. Educational Leadership Certificate—Level 2: Professional (valid for 5 years; renewable)
  A. Eligibility Requirements for Initial Certification
    1. Hold a valid Level 1 Educational Leader Certificate
  B. Renewal Requirements
    1. Meet the standards of effectiveness as an educational leader for 3 years pursuant to Bulletin 130 and R.S.17:3902.

IV. Education Leader Certificate—Level 3: Superintendent (valid 5 years; certification period activated with candidate's first full-time appointment as Superintendent)
  A. Eligibility Requirements
    1. Hold valid Louisiana Level 2 Educational Leader Certificate
    2. Have completed 5 years of successful administrative or management experience in education at level of principal or above
    3. Earn passing score on the School Superintendent Assessment (SSA), in keeping with state requirements
  B. Renewal Requirements
    1. See III, B, 1, directly above

V. Teacher Leader Endorsement (Optional). Teachers who hold valid Type B or Level 2 or higher Louisiana teaching certificate may add this endorsement to their certificate. Contact Louisiana Department of Education (see Appendix 1) for eligibility requirements and renewal guidelines.

Counselor K–12

I. Counselor in a School Setting (valid for 5 years; renewable)
  A. Complete a standards-based master's degree program in school counseling from a regionally accredited college or university approved by the Council for Accreditation of Counseling and Related Educational Program (CACREP)
  B. Complete a practicum/internship:
    1. Practicum in school counseling to include 100 contacts hours in a school setting; *or*
    2. Internship in school counseling to include 600 contact hours in a school setting;
  C. Complete the PRAXIS examination in school guidance and counseling (0420).

II. Renewal Requirements
  A. Meet the standards of effectiveness as an educational leader for 3 years pursuant to Bulletin 130 and R.S.17:3902.

School Librarian

I. Requirements
  A. Elementary or secondary school teaching certificate
  B. Library science courses, semester hours 18
    To include elementary and/or secondary school library materials (9); organization,

administration, and interpretation of elementary and/or secondary school library services (6); and elementary and/or secondary school library practice (3)

Regulations for Out-of-State Application for Classroom Teacher

I. Requirements for Level 1 Certificate
    A. Bachelor's degree from a regionally accredited institution, completion of an approved teacher-education program, including student teaching, and a regular certificate from the state where the applicant completed the program,
        or
        Bachelor's degree from a regionally accredited institution, a regular certificate from another state, and student teaching or 3 years of teaching in certified field
    B. If applicant has not taught within 5 years immediately preceding date of application or if this will be a first employment in Louisiana, he or she must complete 6 hours of resident credit, or extension credit, in areas relative to his or her field.
    C. Appropriate NTE/Praxis scores
    D. These certificates are governed by laws and regulations applying to certification in Louisiana.
    E. An applicant who lacks the appropriate NTE/Praxis scores but meets all other requirements may be issued a 3-year nonrenewable certificate.

Maine

Fingerprinting through a Maine-approved site/process is required prior to issuing any certificate, whether new or renewing, regardless of whether the applicant is employed. The same process is required for all contracted personnel, such as speech clinicians, psychologists, and occupational therapists, as well as substitute teachers and all support staff.

Teacher and Educational Specialist Certificates

I. Targeted Need Certificate (valid 1 year; renewable twice)
   A. Bachelor's degree from accredited college
   B. Teaching in a subject area designated as a shortage area
   C. Six semester hours in the content area
   D. Affidavit of employment from local school district
II. Conditional Certificate (valid 1 year; renewable twice)
   A. Bachelor's degree from a regionally accredited college
   B. Completion of all content area (24 semester hours) course requirements
   C. Affidavit of employment from local school district
III. Provisional Certificate (valid 2 years; renewable in special circumstances)
   A. Bachelor's degree from regionally accredited institution with a 2-year concentration in liberal arts
   B. Completion of an approved teacher-education program (professional and subject matter), including student teaching
   C. Qualifying scores on the Praxis I
   D. Qualifying scores on Praxis II
IV. Professional Certificate (valid for 5 years; renewable)
   A. Meet requirements of a provisional certificate
   B. Two years of teaching experience
   C. Recommendation for professional certificate from support system following successful completion of a Teacher Action Plan, including 6 classroom observations
V. Master Certificate (valid for 5 years; optional; renewable)
   A. Recommendation for a master certificate from the support system following completion of a Teacher or Educational Specialist Action Plan based on the standards for National Board certification as developed by the National Board of Professional Teaching Standards

Endorsements

I. Elementary Teacher (K–8)
   A. Bachelor's degree from an accredited institution in an approved program for the education of elementary teachers which includes at least 6 semester hours in each

of the 4 liberal arts areas (math, English, science, social sciences), together with the formal recommendation of the preparing institution, Praxis I and Praxis II,
or
Bachelor's degree from an accredited institution with at least 6 semester hours in each of the 4 areas noted above, professional course work, student teaching, Praxis I, Praxis II, and PLT (Principles of Learning and Teaching);
and
Affidavit of employment from local school district.

    B.   Professional education courses, to include:
        1.   Teaching exceptional children in the regular classroom
        2.   Effective instruction through content area methods
            a.   At least 12 semester hours to include all of the following: mathematics, reading, science, and social studies
            b.   At least 3 semester hours from one of the following: language arts, process writing, children's literature, and whole language
        3.   One academic semester or 15 weeks of full-time student teaching experience or a combination of part-time and full-time student teaching equivalent to 15 weeks
    C.   Renewal for a professional certificate
        1.   Completion of 6 hours of approved study, preferably academic study in the endorsement area
        2.   Recommendation of the support system

  II. Middle Level (5–8): endorsements for English/language arts, mathematics, science, social studies, or a world language
    A.   Possession of a valid provisional or professional Maine teaching certificate (K–8, K–3, 7–12, or K–12),
    B.   7–12 endorsement area of authorization, semester hours 24
        1.   Science endorsement must include at least 9 semester hours each in life science and physical science
    C.   Other K–12 or foreign-language endorsement areas, semester hours 24
    D.   Praxis II middle level content exam

 III. Secondary Level (7–12): endorsements for English/language arts, mathematics, life science, physical science, and social studies
    A.   Bachelor's degree from an accredited institution in an approved program for teachers in the relevant subject area that includes a major in that subject area, together with the formal recommendation of the preparing institution,
        or
        Bachelor's degree from an accredited institution with a concentration in the liberal arts, plus
        1.   At least 24 semester hours of credit in the relevant subject area for English/language arts, mathematics, social studies, and life science or physical science
    B.   Professional education courses
        1.   Teaching exceptional children in the regular classroom
        2.   Content area methods
        3.   One academic semester or 15 weeks of full-time student teaching experience

C. Praxis I, Praxis II, and PLT
D. Renewal for a professional certificate
  1. See Endorsements, I, C, 1.

Administration Certificates

I. Superintendent Certificate (valid for 5 years; renewable with specific requirements)
   A. Bachelor's degree and master's degree (at a minimum) from an accredited institution. It is recommended, but not required, that the master's degree be in educational administration.
   B. Evidence of 3 years of satisfactory teaching experience or 3 years of equivalent teaching experience in an instructional setting
   C. Evidence of 3 years of previous administrative experience in schools or equivalent experience as an administrator in an institutional setting
      D. Evidence of a basic level of knowledge appropriate to the certificate demonstrated by course work in 13 specified categories
      1. Past experience—such as performance upon examinations or completion of specialized programs approved for this purpose—may be accepted, upon documentation, in lieu of one or more of these course requirements.
   E. A candidate may demonstrate a basic knowledge of I, D, directly above, through course work, equivalent training experiences, or by meeting a minimum score of 165 on the School Superintendent Assessment. For details, contact the Maine Department of Education (see Appendix 1).
   F. Knowledge of Maine education laws
   G. Completion of an approved internship or practicum in a school setting
      1. Graduate-level, state-approved administrator internship or practicum program of at least 15 weeks,
         or
         One full year of employment as an assistant supervisor or a superintendent,
         or
         Mentorship program lasting 1 academic year in which the mentor is a school superintendent
II. Assistant Superintendent Certificate (valid for 5 years)
   A. See Administration Certificates, I, A–F, directly above, except that only 1 year of previous administrative experience (or an approved 1-year administrative internship) is required.
III. Principal Certificate (valid for 5 years)
   A. See Administration Certificates, I, A, B, and D, directly above
IV. Assistant Principal Certificate (valid for 5 years)
   A. Bachelor's degree from an accredited institution
   B. Evidence of 3 years of satisfactory public school teaching experience or 3 years of equivalent teaching experience
   C. Evidence of a basic level of knowledge appropriate to the certificate demonstrated by course work in 3 specified areas

V.   Other Administrative Certificates (valid for 5 years) Teaching principal, curriculum coordinator/instructional supervisor, director of special education, director of secondary vocational education, assistant director of secondary vocational education, adult and community education director, and assistant adult and community education director. For details, contact the Maine Department of Education (see Appendix 1).

School Guidance Counselor (K–12)

I.   Requirements
   A.   Master's or doctorate degree from an accredited institution and an approved program to prepare school guidance counselors, together with the formal recommendation of the preparing institution
   B.   Minimum of 33 semester units in specified areas
   C.   Completion of an approved graduate-level, K–12 internship of 1 academic year that relates to the duties of a school guidance counselor in a school setting
   D.   Praxis II
   E.   Renewal
       1.   Completion of 6 hours of approved study, preferably academic study in the certificate area, and recommendation by local support system

Library-Media Specialist (K–12)

I.   Academic Requirements
   A.   Holder of a Maine provisional or professional-level certificate with a subject area endorsement
   B.   Completion of an approved graduate program for the preparation of school library-media specialists,
       and
       Specified area courses in library science, semester hours 24
   C.   Praxis II
II.   Valid 2 years
III.   Renewal
   A.   See School Guidance Counselor, I, F, 1, above.

Maryland

Certificates are issued with either a January or July date. Maryland does not issue a permanent certificate. Full regulations and application instructions are accessible at www.medcert.org

Types of Certificates

I. Professional Eligibility Certificate (PEC). Valid for 5 years
    A. Issued to an applicant who meets all certification requirements and is not currently employed in a Maryland local school system.
II. Standard Professional Certificate I (SPC I). Valid for 5 years
    A. Issued to an applicant who meets all certification requirements and is employed by a Maryland local school system or an accredited nonpublic school.
III. Standard Professional Certificate II (SPC II). Valid for 5 years
    A. Issued to an applicant who completes the SPC I, is employed by a Maryland local school system or an accredited nonpublic school, and submits the following:
        1. Verification of 3 years of satisfactory professional experience;
        2. Six semester hours of acceptable credit;
            and
        3. A professional development plan for the Advanced Professional Certificate (APC).
IV. Advanced Professional Certificate (APC). Valid for 5 years
    A. Issued to an applicant who submits the following:
        1. Verification of 3 years of full-time professional school-related experience;
        2. Six semester hours of acceptable credit;
            and
        3. A master's degree, or a minimum of 36 semester hours of post-baccalaureate course work, which must include at least 21 semester hours of graduate credit.
            a. The remaining 15 semester hours may include graduate or undergraduate course work and/or Maryland State Department of Education Continuing Professional Development (CPD) credits.
                or
            b. Obtains National Board Certification and earns a minimum of 12 semester hours of approved graduate course work after the conferral of the bachelor's or higher degree.
V. Resident Teacher Certificate (RTC). Valid for 2 years
    A. Issued to an applicant who has been selected by a local school system to participate in an alternative teacher preparation program.
VI. Conditional Certificate (COND). Valid for 2 years
    A. Issued only at the request of a local school system superintendent to an applicant employed in a local school system who does not meet all certification requirements.

Teacher Areas Overview

I. Maryland issues certificates in the following teaching areas:
    A. Early Childhood Education (PreK–3)
    B. Elementary Education, grades 1–6
    C. Mathematics Instructional Leader, PreK–6 (endorsement only)
    D. Middle School Areas: (4–9)
        1. English Language Arts; Mathematics; Science; Social Studies; Mathematics Instructional Leader (endorsement only)
    E. Secondary Academic Areas: (7–12)
        1. Agriculture/Agribusiness and Renewable Natural Resources; Biology; Business Education; Chemistry; Computer Science; Earth/Space Science; English; Environmental Science; Family and Consumer Sciences; Geography; History; Marketing; Mathematics; Physical Science; Physics; Professional and Technical Education; Social Studies; Specialized Professional Areas; Speech Communication; Theater; Work-Based Learning Coordinator (endorsement only)
    F. Special Education
        1. Infant/primary (birth–grade 3); Elementary/middle (grades 1–8); Secondary/adult (grades 6–12); Hearing Impaired; Severely and Profoundly Disabled; Visually Impaired
    G. Specialty Areas (PreK–12)
        1. American Sign Language; Art; Dance; English for Speakers of Other Languages; Environmental Education; Health; Music; Physical Education; World Languages

Paths to Certification

I. One of the following:
    A. Complete a college or university state-approved educator preparation program;
    B. Hold a valid, out-of-state professional certificate and submit verification of 3 years of full-time satisfactory professional experience;
    C. Meet transcript analysis requirements;
        or
    D. Complete a Resident Teacher Certificate program.
II. Special Maryland requirements
    A. Individuals applying for a Maryland certificate are required to complete additional reading course work.
        1. Early childhood, elementary education, and special education at those levels are required to complete 12 semester hours.
        2. Secondary education, PreK–12, and secondary special education teachers are required to complete 6 semester hours.
III. Adding another certification area to certificate
    A. Complete either course work requirements (30 credits depending upon the area)
        or

B. Submit a qualifying score on the appropriate content assessment. No pedagogy assessment is required to add an endorsement to a professional Maryland teacher's certificate.

Testing

I. All candidates applying for an initial teacher certificate are required to present qualifying scores on the Praxis I Academic Skills Assessments, ACT, SAT, or GRE and the appropriate content and pedagogy assessments where required (Praxis II or ACTFL). The tests may be taken at any valid test site in the nation.

II. Out-of-state candidates who do not hold a professional certificate from their respective state must meet Maryland's qualifying scores. Some out-of-state candidates may be eligible for a test exemption.

III. Applicants who have taken the teacher certification tests must submit their scores when applying for a Maryland certificate. Test scores must be sent to the Maryland State Department of Education in one of the following ways:
A. Notation on an official college transcript;
B. Photocopy of examinee's score report;
or
C. Verification from a state department of education.

Administrative or Supervisory Areas

Consult http://www.marylandpublicschools.org/MSDE/divisions/certification/certification_branch/certification_inf/areas/administrative_supervisory_areas for full regulations and for references to regulations, chapter, COMAR, and §B below.

I. Superintendent. For certification as a superintendent, deputy superintendent, associate superintendent, assistant superintendent or equivalent position, candidates should
A. Meet the requirements for certification in early childhood education, elementary education, or a secondary education area;
B. Have a master's degree from an IHE;
C. Have 3 years of successful teaching experience and 2 years of administrative or supervisory experience;
and
D. Have successfully completed a 2-year program with graduate courses in administration and supervision in institution(s) approved by an accrediting agency recognized by the State Superintendent of Schools.
1. Graduate work under §B may be applied toward these requirements, provided that a minimum of 60 semester hours of graduate work is presented.

II. Supervisors of Instruction, Assistant Principals, and Principals. For certification as an Administrator I or Administrator II
A. Administrator I. To be assigned as a supervisor of instruction or assistant principal, candidates should
1. Have a master's degree from an IHE;

2. Have 27 months of satisfactory teaching performance or satisfactory performance on a professional certificate or satisfactory performance as a certified specialist
and

3. Complete 1 of the following:
   a. Department-approved program which leads to certification as a supervisor of instruction, assistant principal, or principal that includes the outcomes in the Maryland instructional leadership framework;
   or
   b. Approved program that leads to certification as a supervisor of instruction, assistant principal, or principal in accordance with the interstate agreement;
   or
   c. 18 semester hours of graduate course work taken at an IHE at the post-baccalaureate level to include a balance of content in the following categories: curriculum, instruction, and assessment; development, observation, and evaluation of staff; legal issues and ethical decision-making; school leadership, management and administration; and practicum, internship, or a collaboratively designed and supervised experience by the local school system and IHE to include department-approved instructional leadership outcomes with verification of this experience submitted by the applicant.

B. Administrator II. For an individual to be assigned as a school principal
   1. The applicant, before initial appointment as principal, shall:
      a. Complete the requirements for Administrator I;
      and
      b. Present evidence of a qualifying score as established by the state board on a department-approved principal certification assessment.
   2. A principal who enters Maryland from another state may obtain an Administrator II certificate if that principal held a valid professional state certificate and verifies at least 27 months of satisfactory performance as a principal during the past 7 years on the basis of which application is being made for a like or comparable Maryland certificate.

C. If a principal in a regular school transfers to become a principal in a special education school, the principal shall have special education certification; however, if a principal in a special education school transfers to become a principal in a regular school, no additional certification requirements are applicable.

D. Special Provisions
   1. An applicant who successfully completes the requirements under Regulation .05D of the chapter cited in link above for the resident principal certificate may obtain an Administrator II certificate; consult link above for full details.
   2. A Standard Professional certificate or Advanced Professional certificate shall be considered valid for service as principal of an elementary school of not more than 6 teachers if the principal teaches at least 50 percent of the school day.
   3. A person who holds the position of assistant principal on the date this regulation becomes effective shall meet the requirements of §B of the regulation cited in

link above not later than the end of the first full validity period after the renewal of the currently held certificate.

III.   Library Media Administrator. To be certified, the applicant shall:

A.   Meet the requirements for certification as a library media specialist;

1.   Have a master's degree from an IHE;

2.   Have 3 years of satisfactory library media program experience; however, at the recommendation of the local school superintendent, 2 years of related satisfactory experience may be substituted for 2 years of library media program experience;
and

3.   Complete one of the options listed under Regulation .04B(3) of the chapter cited in link above that would lead to certification as Administrator I.

B.   Certificate Renewal. In addition to meeting the requirements of COMAR 13A.12.01.11B (see link above), a library media administrator or a holder of a valid certificate for an education media administrator (Level III) shall satisfy the required reading course work contained in COMAR 13A.12.01.11A(5)(c) to renew the certificate.

IV.   Supervisor of Guidance. For certification, the applicant shall:

A.   Meet the requirements for certification as a guidance counselor;

B.   Have 3 years of satisfactory performance as a guidance counselor;
and

C.   Have 12 semester hours of graduate credit from an IHE in any of the following areas, with at least 6 of those semester hours in school supervision or school administration: management; school supervision; school administration; program development; and program evaluation

V.   Supervisor of School Psychological Services. For certification, the applicant shall:

A.   Meet the requirements for certification as a school psychologist under COMAR 13A.12.03.07 (see link above);

B.   Have a doctoral degree:

1.   From a state or regionally credited school psychology program or National Association of School Psychologists (NCATE), or American Psychological Association–accredited school psychology program,
or

2.   In psychology or education or human development;

C.   As part of or in addition to §B of the regulation cited in link above, have 9 semester hours of graduate credits, including 3 semester hours in school law and 6 semester hours in supervision, management, or administration of schools;
and

D.   Have 3 years of experience as a school psychologist under COMAR 13A.12.03.07 (see link above).

VI.   Supervisor of Pupil Personnel. For certification, the applicant shall:

A.   Meet the requirements for certification as a pupil personnel worker;

B.   Have a master's degree from an IHE;

C.   As part of or in addition to §B of the regulation cited in link above, have a graduate course in the area of administration and supervision;

and

D. Have 3 years of successful teaching experience. At the recommendation of the local superintendent of schools, 2 years of related experience may be counted for 2 years of teaching experience.

VII. Supervisor of Special Education

A. Principal (Handicapped Facility). For certification, the applicant shall:
1. Meet the requirements for certification in special education;
and
2. Meet the requirements for certification as an Administrator II.

B. Supervisor of Special Education (Sole Assignment). For certification, the applicant shall:
1. Meet the requirements for certification in special education;
and
2. Meet the requirements for certification as an Administrator I.

C. Special Provision. Supervisors with multiple area assignments shall meet the requirements set forth in Regulation .04 of the chapter cited in link above.

VIII. Supervisor of Teachers of Hearing Impaired. The applicant shall:

A. Meet the requirements for certification as a teacher of the hearing impaired;

B. Have a master's degree from an IHE with at least 1 course in administrative and supervisory techniques and 1 course in curriculum development;
and

C. Have experience which includes:
1. Three years of successful teaching experience with the hearing impaired,
or
2. Four years of paid experience or its equivalent in a school setting, with 2 years of successful teaching experience with the hearing impaired.

Specialist Areas

For full requirements, consult link above.

I. Gifted & Talented Specialist
II. Guidance Counselor
IIII. Library Media Specialist
IV. Pupil Personnel Worker
V. Reading Specialist
VI. Reading Teacher
VII. Psychometrist
VIII. School Psychologist
IX. School Social Worker

Massachusetts

Academic (PreK–12) Licenses

I. Preliminary License (valid for 5 years of employment; nonrenewable). For applicant who has not completed Approved Educator Preparation Program
   A. Hold a bachelor's degree
   B. Pass the Massachusetts Tests for Educator Licensure (MTEL)
   C. Meet other eligibility requirements as required
      1. To access a list of all academic educator licenses and determine the requirements for a particular license, consult http://www.doe.mass.edu/licensurehelp/. Once you select the field, level, and type of license, Licensure Help will display all possible requirement paths available, listing the specific requirements to satisfy each path.
         a. Paths available to a specific applicant will vary depending upon licenses held.
   D. Elementary and Early Childhood
      1. In addition to other requirements, applicant must verify
         a. Seminars or courses that address the teaching of reading, English language arts, and mathematics
         b. Seminars or courses on ways to prepare and maintain students with disabilities for general classrooms
   E. Special Education
      1. Typically, a Competency Review is required for applicants seeking a Preliminary or additional Initial or Professional license in special education. Find out more about this process for determining whether the subject matter knowledge requirements for a license have been met in a field for which there is no subject matter knowledge test, and elsewhere as required within licensure regulations at http://www.doe.mass.edu/educators/sped_review.pdf
II. Temporary License (valid for 1 calendar year from date of issue). For experienced educators from another state or District of Columbia
   A. Three years of teaching under valid out-of-state license
   B. Possession of a valid educator license/certificate from another state/jurisdiction that is comparable to at least an Initial license in Massachusetts
   C. Meet the terms of the National Association of State Directors of Teacher Education and Certification (NASDTEC) Interstate Contract; for full details, consult http://www.doe.mass.edu/edprep/nasdtec.html
III. Initial License (valid for 5 years of employment; renewable one time for additional 5 years of employment).
   A. Hold a bachelor's degree

      B.   Secure passing score(s) on the MTEL
          1.   Consult http://www.doe.mass.edu/mtel/
      C.   Complete an Educator Preparation Program approved by the commissioner
          1.   For teacher induction programs, consult http://www.doe.mass.edu/educators/ mentor/teachers.html
          2.   For administrator inductions programs, consult http://www.doe.mass.edu/ educators/mentor/admins.html
      D.   Meet other eligibility requirements as required
          1.   See I, C, 1, directly above
          2.   Typically, applicants who hold a Preliminary license and are advancing to their first academic Initial teacher license are required to complete an approved educator preparation program. To search a directory and learn more about these programs offered through Massachusetts colleges and universities as well as approved alternative educator preparation programs, consult http://www.doe.mass.edu/educators/directory.html
          3.   Educator candidates who complete an approved educator preparation program outside of Massachusetts will meet the Initial License requirement by completing one of the following:
               a.   A state-approved educator preparation program in a state with which Massachusetts has signed the National Association of State Directors of Teacher Education and Certification (NASDTEC) Interstate Contract
                  or
               b.   An educator preparation program sponsored by a college or university outside Massachusetts that has been accredited by the National Council for Accreditation of Teacher Education (NCATE)
                  or
               c.   Possession of the equivalent of at least an Initial license/certificate issued by a state with which Massachusetts has signed the NASDTEC Interstate Contract and 3 years of employment under such license/certificate during the previous 7 years.
  IV. Professional License (valid for 5 calendar years; renewable for 5-year terms based on professional development)
      A.   Three years of employment under an Initial license
      B.   Complete a Teacher Induction Program in first year of employment
          1.   Consult http://www.doe.mass.edu/educators/mentor/teachers.html
              and
      C.   One of the following:
          1.   Approved district program of at least 50 contact hours of content-based seminars;
              or
          2.   Approved program for the Professional License;
               a.   Usually but not necessarily a master's degree in education, with half the credits in arts/sciences or professional schools other than education that are appropriate to the field of the license; *or*

       b.   Master's degree in discipline or other advanced graduate program, except education, from an accredited college or university
         or

  3.   For those who already hold at least a master's degree in any field
       a.   Approved 12-credit Program for the Professional License, with at least 9 credits in the academic discipline appropriate to instructional field of the license; *or*
       b.   Twelve graduate level credits in the academic discipline; these may include credits earned prior to application for the license;
         or

  4.   Master teacher status, as verified by the National Board for Professional Teaching Standards (NBPTS) and others accepted by the Commissioner;
     or

  5.   State performance assessment program; when available.

V.   Other Licenses
  A.   For information on licenses in vocational technical education or adult basic education, consult http://www.doe.mass.edu/educators/e_license.html

VI. Relicensure
  A.   Primary License: 150 Professional Development Points (PDPs)
  B.   For each additional license: 30 PDPs
    1.   An invalid status requires 150 PDPs
  C.   Continuing professional development is required to renew Professional licenses every 5 calendar years.
  D.   For complete information on recertification, consult http://www.doe.mass.edu/recert/2000guidelines/guidelines.pdf and http://www.doe.mass.edu/recert/qa.html

License Fields

Note: Each license is valid for employment at a particular grade level or several grade levels; and there are several grade level combinations including (but not limited to) "All," "PreK–8," and "8–12." For full details, consult https://gateway.edu.state.ma.us/elar/licensurehelp/License RequirementsCriteriaPageControl.ser

I.   Fields for Academic Teacher Licenses
  A.   Biology, Business, Chemistry, Dance, Deaf and Hard-of-Hearing—[ASL/TC], Deaf and Hard-of-Hearing—[Oral/Aural], Early Childhood: Students with and without Disabilities, Earth Science, Elementary, English as a Second Language, English, Foreign Language [American Sign Language; Arabic; Armenian; Cambodian; Cape Verdean; Chinese; Creole Haitian; French; German; Greek; Hebrew; Hmong; Hungarian; Italian; Japanese; Khmer; Korean; Polish; Portuguese; Russian; Spanish; Ukrainian; Vietnamese], General Science, Health/Family and Consumer Sciences, History, Instructional Technology, Latin and Classical Humanities, Library, Mathematics, Middle School Humanities, Middle School Mathematics/Science, Moderate Disabilities, Music: Vocal/Instrumental/General, Physical Education,

Physics, Political Science/Political Philosophy, Severe Disabilities, Speech, Technology/Engineering, Theater, Visual Art, Visually Impaired

II. Fields for Academic Specialist Teacher Licenses
   A. Academically Advanced, Reading, Speech Language and Hearing Disorders

III. Fields for Academic Administrator Licenses
   A. Principal/Assistant Principal, School Business Administrator, Special Education Administrator, Superintendent/Assistant Superintendent, Supervisor/Director—Core [Arts; Civics and Government/Economics/Geography; English; Foreign Languages; History; Mathematics; Reading/Language Arts; Science], Supervisor/Director—Non-Core, Supervisor/Director—[Guidance Director], Supervisor/Director—[Pupil Personnel Service]

IV. Fields for Academic Professional Support Personnel
   A. School Guidance Counselor, School Nurse, School Psychologist, School Social Worker/School Adjustment Counselor

Michigan

Teaching Certificate Validity Levels

I. Elementary: An elementary certificate issued after September 1, 1988, is valid for teaching all subjects grades K–5, all subjects grades K–8 in a self-contained classroom, and subject area endorsements, as listed on the certificate, in grades 6–8.

II. Secondary: A secondary certificate issued after September 1, 1988, is valid for teaching subject area endorsements, as listed on the certificate, in grades 6–12.

Types of Certificates

I. Provisional Certificate (Initial teaching license/credential; valid for 6 years)
    A. Issued upon successful completion of a state-approved teacher preparation program and a passing score on the appropriate Michigan Test for Teacher Certification (MTTC) exams, including the Basic Skills Test (BST).
        1. Note: After January 1, 2013, the BST will become known as the Professional Readiness Examination (PRE), and this terminology will be phased in within the year.
        2. For information on Michigan-approved Educator Preparation Institutions (EPI) and programs, consult https://mdoe.state.mi.us/proprep/
    B. Programs completed through colleges/universities outside of Michigan must be approved for the certification of teachers by another state; contact that state's education department for information. Upon completion of the out-of-state program, candidates must apply for a Michigan teacher certification, and their credentials must be evaluated by the Office of Professional Preparation Services (OPPS).
    C. Alternate routes to certification completed in another state may require the completion of 3 years of teaching experience within the validity of the out-of-state regular standard teaching certificate.

II. Provisional Temporary Teacher Employment Authorization [T2EA]; (valid for 1 year; nonrenewable)
    A. The Provisional T2EA allows out-of-state candidates 1 year to meet Michigan testing requirements, for which the MTTC is the only acceptable examination. Issued to candidates after they have been evaluated by the Michigan Office of Professional Preparation Services to determine if they meet the following criteria:
        1. Hold a valid, acceptable teaching certificate from another state;
        2. Have never held a Michigan teaching certificate;
        3. Have applied for initial provisional certification;
            and
        4. Meet all the requirements for the Provisional Certificate, except for passing the MTTC.

B. Candidates do not apply for the T2EA; it is issued upon evaluation for initial certification.
   1. Note: Once a T2EA has been issued, the candidate must complete testing requirements in order to be issued any Michigan teaching certificate.

III. Professional Education Certificate (Initial advanced teaching license/credential; valid for 5 years)
Requirements after September 1, 2013:
A. Three years of successful teaching experience since the issue date and within the validity and grade level of the Provisional Certificate;
B. The appropriate reading credit(s):
   1. In-state applicants who have completed a Methods program through a Michigan University must meet the basic reading requirements (6 semester hours of teaching of reading or of reading methods for elementary; or 3 semester hours for secondary);
   2. Out-of-state applicants applying for initial Michigan Certification with a program completed through a state other than Michigan must also meet the basic reading requirements (6 semester hours of teaching of reading or of reading methods for elementary; and 3 semester hours for secondary);
      a. Candidates from other states who hold a regular, valid teaching certificate from another state and meet all of the requirements for the Professional Education Certificate at the time of application are not required to take the Michigan Test for Teacher Certification (MTTC) for initial Michigan certification.
         and
   3. All teachers progressing to the Professional Education Certificate must complete 3 semester credits of reading diagnostics and remediation, which includes a field experience, in accordance with Michigan Revised School Code MCL 380.1531(4). For approved Michigan courses that meet this requirement, consult http://www.michigan.gov/teachercert
C. In addition, 1 or a combination of the following are required within the 5-year period preceding the date of application and since the issue date of the Provisional Certificate or Provisional Renewal:
   1. Six semester hours in a planned program at an approved EPI; or 6 semester credit hours of academic credit appropriate to the grade level and content endorsement(s) of the certificate at any approved college or university;
      and/or
   2. 180 State Continuing Education Clock Hours (SCECHs) appropriate to the grade level and content endorsement(s) of the certificate held;
      and/or
   3. 150 annual District Provided Professional Development (DPPD) hours, in accordance with Michigan School Code Sections 380.1527, completed through professional development programs that are appropriate to the grade level and content endorsement (s) of the certificate.
      a. Note: SCECHs (30 SCECHs equate to 1 semester credit hour) and/or DPPD hours (30 clock hours of DPPD equates to 1 semester credit hour

or 30 SCECHs) must be earned since the issue date of the Provisional Certificate.

IV. Temporary Teacher Employment Authorization [T2EA] (valid for 1 year; nonrenewable)

   A. The Professional T2EA allows out-of-state candidates 1 year to meet Michigan's basic reading requirements. Issued to out-of-state candidates who hold a valid, acceptable certificate from another state who:

   1. Have never held a Michigan teaching certificate;
      and

   2. Meet all the requirements for the Michigan Professional Education Certificate, except for the reading methods course work.

   B. Candidates do not apply for this authorization; it is issued upon evaluation for initial certification.

   1. Once the T2EA has been issued the candidate must complete the reading requirements within the year in order to be issued a Michigan Professional Education Certificate.

   2. If the reading Methods requirement is not met within the year, the candidate must be evaluated for the Provisional Certificate and pass the appropriate MTTC exams.

V. Interim Occupational Certificate (Initial license; valid for 6 years) (Formerly Temporary Vocational Authorization)

   A. An applicant may be recommended by the occupational EPI if he/she has met the following requirements:

   1. Has a bachelor's degree;

   2. Has a major or minor in the field of specialization in which occupational certification is being requested;

   3. Has a minimum of 2 years (4,000 hours) of experience in the occupational area concerned or has completed a planned program of directed, supervised, relevant, and recent occupational experience approved by the superintendent of public instruction;

   4. Has passed both the MTTC Professional Readiness Examination (formerly known as the Basic Skills Test) and appropriate subject area exam(s) available at the time of application;
      and

   5. Has successfully completed a minimum of 6 semester credit hours of professional or occupational education credit.

   6. The Interim Occupational Certificate is valid for teaching in those courses in which instruction is limited to the occupation specified on the certificate in approved occupational programs.

VI. Occupational Education Certificate (Advanced license; valid for 5 years)

   A. Three years of successful teaching experience within the validity of the Interim Occupational Certificate (formerly Temporary Vocational Authorization);

   B. Completion of 9 additional semester hours of professional occupational education credit since the issue date of the Interim Occupational Certificate at an approved occupational institution, or an approved master's or higher degree earned at any time.

   C. The Occupational Education Certificate has the same validity and renewal conditions as the Professional Education Certificate.

VII. Preliminary School Psychologist Certificate (Initial certificate; valid 3 years; renewable once upon completion of 6 additional semester credit hours)
 A. Complete a minimum of 45 graduate semester hours in an approved school psychologist program;
  and
 B. Complete a supervised internship of not less than 600 hours under the supervision of a certified school psychologist.
 C. In order to advance to the School Psychologist certificate, the candidate must complete at least an additional 15 semester credits in an approved program.

VIII. School Psychologist Certificate (Advanced; valid for 5 years)
 A. Complete at least 15 additional semester credit hours in an approved school psychology program since Preliminary School Psychologist certificate was issued,
  or
  Have a specialist's or equivalent degree in school psychology earned at any time from an approved institution.
 B. Complete 1 year of satisfactory work experience as a school psychologist under the supervision of a fully certified school psychologist since Preliminary School Psychologist certificate was issued.
 C. An additional 600-hour internship to meet the total 1,200-hour requirement for a certificate.
 D. School Psychologist Certificate (Renewal valid for 5 years)
  1. Requires 1 or a combination of the following:
   a. Complete 6 semester hours at any 4-year or community college listed in the Directory of Michigan Institutions of Higher Education. Credits completed at approved out-of-state 4-year EPI are also acceptable.
   b. 180 State Continuing Education Clock Hours (SCECHs). Note: Semester credits or SCECHs (formerly SB-CEUs) must have been completed within the 5-year period preceding the date of application and after the issue date of the previous certificate.

IX. Interim Teaching Certificate (valid for 5 years; nonrenewable)
 An individual may qualify for this certificate under the following conditions:
 A. Participate in a state-approved alternate route teaching program;
 B. Hold a bachelor's, master's, doctorate, or professional degree from a regionally accredited college or university, with a grade-point average of at least 3.0 on a 4.0 scale (or equivalent);
 C. Pass the MTTC Professional Readiness Examination (Basic Skills Test) and appropriate subject area exam(s) prior to acceptance or admission to an alternate route program;
  and
 D. While working under the Interim Certificate, the individual must:
  1. Submit to and pass a criminal history check, including Federal Bureau of Investigation fingerprinting in accordance with Michigan School Safety law, prior to employment by a local district or school;
  2. Receive intensive observation and coaching;
  3. Complete 3 years of satisfactory teaching experience under the Interim

Certificate in order to be recommended for a Michigan Provisional Certificate or Professional Education Certificate (which requires completion of 3 semester credit hours of diagnostic reading and 18 semester credit hours in a planned or a master's degree program);
and

4. Individuals must be recommended by the approved alternate route provider.

5. Additional endorsements shall not be added to an Interim Teaching Certificate.

X. School Guidance Counselor License (valid for 5 years)

    A. Requirements for in-state applicant, who completed a program through a Michigan university:

        1. Complete a minimum of 30 graduate level semester hours in an approved school counseling program, including an internship;

        2. Complete a 600 clock hour internship, based on an approved school counselor program with school-aged pupils, under the supervision of a credentialed school counselor or a school counselor educator;

            a. At least 300 of the 600 clock hours shall be in a school setting;
            and

        3. Pass the MTTC (School Counselor exam).

    B. Requirements for out-of-state applicant, who completed a program through a state other than Michigan:

        1. At least 5 years of successful experience serving in the role of a school counselor in another state within the immediate preceding 7 years;

        2. Hold a bachelor's degree;

        3. Pass the MTTC;
        and

        4. Provide documentation from another state as to authorization to work as a school counselor;
        or

        Complete all requirements of an approved school counselor education program from an out-of state institution and earn an advanced degree in guidance counseling or its equivalency; and pass the MTTC.

    C. School Guidance Counselor License Renewal (valid for 5 years)

        1. Requires one or a combination of the following:

            a. Complete 6 semester hours at any 4-year or community college listed in the Directory of Michigan Institutions of Higher Education;
            and/or

            b. 180 State Continuing Education Clock Hours (SCECHs). Note: Semester credits or SCECHs (formerly SB-CEUs) must have been completed within the 5-year period preceding the date of application and after the issue date of the previous certificate.

            c. Credits completed at approved out-of-state 4-year EPI are also acceptable.

XI. Temporary School Counselor Authorization (Valid for 1 year; nonrenewable)

    A. Allows out-of-state candidates 1 year to meet Michigan testing requirements; issued to out-of-state candidates who meet either the educational and/or experience requirement but have yet to take and pass the required examination.

    B. Candidate does not apply for this authorization; it is issued upon evaluation for initial license as a school counselor.

XII. Preliminary Authorization to Work as a School Counselor (valid for 3 years; nonrenewable)

    A. Available to a candidate of a Michigan EPI who has completed 30 semester hours of course work in an approved school guidance counseling program and has passed the guidance counselor subject area exam on the MTTC.

    B. During the 3-year validity period, a person is expected to complete the remainder of any outstanding courses/practicum in order to be recommended for the school counselor endorsement or School Guidance Counselor License.

XIII. Administrator Certificate (Initial license; valid for 5 years)

    A. Two basic endorsements available: Elementary/Secondary Administrator K–12 (Building) or Central Office (District)

    B. Certification requires completion of master's or higher degree from an approved program in educational leadership or administration offered by an IHE.

    C. A superintendent, principal, assistant principal, or other person whose primary responsibility is administering instructional programs:

        1. If employed as a school administrator after January 4, 2010, must hold a valid Administrator Certificate in accordance with SB 981.

        2. If employed as a school administrator on or before January 4, 2010, does not need to hold the Administrator Certificate for their current position, but must meet the professional development requirements as described in the Administrative Certificate renewal requirements directly below.

        3. A noncertified school administrator may be employed by a school district if enrolled in a program leading to certification as a school administrator not later than 6 months after date of employment.

           a. The school administrator has 3 years to meet the certification requirements.

    D. Administrator Certificate Renewal (valid for 5 years)

        1. Requires one or a combination of the following:

           a. Complete 6 semester hours at any 4-year or community college listed in the Directory of Michigan Institutions of Higher Education;
and/or

           b. 180 State Continuing Education Clock Hours (SCECHs). Note: Semester credits or SCECHs (formerly SB-CEUs) must have been completed within the 5-year period preceding the date of application and after the issue date of the previous certificate
or
Holders of a Professional Educators Teaching Certificate may use that certificate to renew their Administrator certificate.

XIV. Previously Issued Certificates

    A. Michigan no longer issues the following certificates; however, they are still valid for those who hold them:

        1. 18-Hour and 30-Hour Continuing Certificate

        2. Permanent Certificate

        3. Full Vocational Authorization

Certificate Renewal Requirements after September 1, 2013

I. Provisional Certificate Renewal (each renewal is valid for 3 years)
   A. First renewal requires completion of 1 of the following within the 3 years preceding application:
      1. 6 semester hours in a planned course of study at a state-approved EPI or 6 semester credit hours of academic credit appropriate to the grade level and content endorsement(s) of the certificate at any regionally accredited college or university since the issue date of the first Provisional Certificate renewal;
         a. Credit completed outside the state of Michigan must be in an approved master's degree program or in an endorsement program (requiring a minimum of 20 semester credit hours to obtain endorsement) at a state-approved EPI.
         or
      2. 180 State Continuing Education Clock Hours (SCECHs) appropriate to the grade level and content endorsement(s) of the certificate held since the issue date of the initial Provisional Certificate;
         or
      3. Combination of semester credit hours and SCECHs (30 SCECHs equate to 1 semester credit hour) since the issue date of the initial Provisional Certificate.
   B. Second renewal requires completion of 1 of the following within the 3 years preceding application:
      1. 6 semester hours in a planned course of study at an approved EPI or 6 semester credit hours of academic credit appropriate to the grade level and content endorsement(s) of the certificate at any regionally accredited college or university since the issue date of the first Provisional Certificate renewal;
         a. See I, A, 1, a, directly above
         or
      2. 180 State Continuing Education Clock Hours (SCECHs) appropriate to the grade level and content endorsement(s) of the certificate held since the issue date of the first Provisional Certificate renewal;
         or
         Combination of semester credit hours and SCECHs (30 SCECHs equate to 1 semester credit hour) since the issue date of the first Provisional Certificate renewal;
   C. Third renewal requires sponsorship by the local school district or private school, completion of all academic requirements for the Professional Education Certificate, and approval of the Michigan Department of Education.
      1. This renewal will not be issued to individuals who meet all the requirements for the Professional Education Certificate.
   D. An individual who holds an expired Provisional, Temporary Vocational Authorization, or Interim Occupational Certificate, and who has not met the credit requirements for a first or second renewal may qualify for a 3-year renewal of the certificate if he/she:

1. Holds an acceptable valid teaching certificate from another state; *and*
2. Has taught in that state within the grade level and subject area endorsement or endorsements to the validity of the certificate for at least 1 year in the preceding 5-year period.

II. Two-Year Extended Provisional Certificate (valid for 2 calendar years; nonrenewable) Individuals with expired Provisional Certificates who do not meet the requirements for a provisional renewal may be eligible for a Two-Year Extended Provisional Certificate if the following conditions are met:

A. Initial Provisional Certificate expired less than 10 years ago;
B. At least 1 year of satisfactory teaching experience within the validity of his/her teaching certificate;
C. The individual is currently enrolled in a planned program at an approved college/university;
   1. Enrollment must be verified by the approved EPI. To be enrolled, the individual must be registered for at least 1 class during the current semester/trimester or the upcoming semester/trimester and have paid enrollment fees.
D. A Michigan public or private school is employing and sponsoring the individual for the Two-Year Extended Provisional Certificate; *and*
E. The sponsoring school agrees to monitor the teacher's progress towards the completion of the Professional Education Certificate requirements.
F. Individuals who fail to complete all requirements for the professional education certificate during the 2-year validity period of the Two-Year Extended Provisional Certificate will not be granted additional renewals or extensions of their Provisional Certificates.

Minnesota

First-Time Licensure Requirements

I. Teachers and School Administrators
    A. Completion of a state-approved teacher education and/or administrative preparation program through a regionally accredited institution
        1. Certifying officer of the college/university through which the state-approved program was completed must recommend the applicant for Minnesota licensure.
    B. Testing Requirements
        1. The Minnesota Teacher Licensure Examinations (MTLE) are the sole means of assessing the basic skills, pedagogical, and content-area knowledge of candidates for Minnesota licensure.
        2. All candidates for an initial license will be required to pass the MTLE basic skills tests as well as pedagogy and content area tests; for full details, including information about registration and exceptions, consult http://education.state.mn.us/mde/Teacher_Support/Educator_Licensing/index.html, in the document titled "Teacher Testing Requirements and Testing Chart"
    C. Minnesota Human Relations Program
        1. Human Relations Requirement is a state mandate directing licensure applicants to show evidence of the following:
            a. Understanding the contributions and lifestyles of the various racial, cultural, and economic groups in our society
            b. Recognizing and dealing with dehumanizing biases, discrimination, and prejudices
            c. Creating learning environments that contribute to the self-esteem of all persons and to positive interpersonal relations
            d. Respecting human diversity and personal rights
            e. The study of American Indian language, history, government, and culture
        2. Applicants may fulfill this requirement through one of the following options:
            a. Graduate from a Minnesota teacher preparation program—verified by licensure recommendation;
            b. Graduate from a teacher preparation program in states with which Minnesota has reciprocity of Human Relations, including Iowa, Ohio, Nebraska, South Dakota, or Wisconsin—verified by licensure recommendation;
            c. Evidence of program completion through Peace Corps, AmeriCorps, Vista, or Teacher Corps;
              or
            d. Certifying officer for out-of-state programs verifies human relations requirement has been met using checkbox on application form.

3. Applicants prepared outside of Minnesota may be granted a 1-year temporary license to teach while completing a human relations program.

4. Applicants who have not completed one of the options above but believe that they can demonstrate meeting all 5 Human Relations components/objectives may submit evidence by completing the Human Relations Verification Chart and attaching verifying documents.

5. For detailed information and list of approved Human Relations courses offered in Minnesota, consult http://education.state.mn.us/mde/Teacher_Support/ Educator_Licensing/index.html

D. Fingerprinting Requirements

1. All applicants for an initial educator license in Minnesota are required by state law to obtain a criminal background check including a fingerprint check. Contact the Educator Licensing office (651/582-8691 or via e-mail at mde .educator-licensing@state.min.us) with your name and mailing address to request a fingerprint card, a list of local agencies providing these services and their fees, and detailed instructions on how to complete the card.

II. Teachers and School Administrators (outside Minnesota)

A. Minnesota does not have licensure reciprocity with any other state.

B. Applicants prepared out of state may be granted a Minnesota professional license when the following criteria are met:

1. The teacher preparation institution is accredited by the regional association for the accreditation of colleges and secondary schools;

2. The program leading to licensure, including alternative programs, has been recognized by the other state as qualifying the applicant completing the program for current licensure within that state;

3. The program leading to licensure completed by the applicant is essentially equivalent in content to approved Minnesota programs and the grade-level range of preparation is the same as, greater than, or not more than 1 year less than the grade-level range of the Minnesota licensure field for which application is made;

4. The preparing institution verifies applicant completion of the approved licensure program and recommends the applicant for a license in the licensure field and at the licensure level;

5. Program completion is verified by an official transcript or equivalent issued by the recommending institution or program;

6. The applicant has completed instruction in methods of teaching in the licensure field and at the licensure level of the program;
and

7. The applicant has completed student teaching or essentially equivalent experience.

C. Applicants who complete online preparation programs meeting these 7 criteria may be eligible to apply for a limited teaching license which provides time for the applicant to complete Minnesota-specific licensure requirements in II, D and E, directly below. Such online programs must be:

1. Regionally accredited (see http://www.ncahighlerlearningcommission.org/) and approved by the state in which the program is offered;

2. In a licensure field for which Minnesota has licenses and rules;
3. Essentially equivalent in content and scope to approved programs offered by Minnesota institutions;
4. Able to qualify the graduate for full licensure in the state in which the program was offered;
5. Providing supervised clinical experiences, including 10 weeks of full-time student teaching in the subject and grade level of licensure requested;
6. Including instruction in methods of teaching in the licensure field and at the licensure level;
   and
7. Providing evidence that the applicant has a bachelor's degree with a major, or the equivalent, in the field of intended licensure.

D. In addition to the above stipulations, applicants for teacher and administrative licenses must satisfy Minnesota requirements for:
1. MTLE testing; see I, B, directly above;
2. Minnesota Human Relations Program; see I, C, directly above;
   and
3. Fingerprinting requirements; see I, D, directly above

E. For teachers educated out of state or online whose initial Minnesota teaching license has a renewal condition requiring completion of one or more reading courses, consult http://www.education.state.mn.us/MDE/Teacher_Support/Educator_ Licensing/Licensing_Info/License_Renew/index.html for a current list of reading programs which will meet the specific requirement for licensure.

III. Related Services Personnel
A. Includes School Counselors, School Nurses, School Psychologists, School Social Workers, and Speech/Language Pathologists
B. Licensure in these fields does not require compliance with the Minnesota Human Relations or MTLE testing requirements.
C. In addition, applications for School Counselor (if the program completed is accredited by the Council for the Accreditation of Counseling and Related Educational Programs [CACREP]), School Nurse, School Psychologist, School Social Worker, and Speech/ Language Pathologists do not require a recommending signature.
D. An applicant seeking School Counselor licensure through a non–CACREP accredited program must be recommended for licensure by the certifying officer of the college/ university through which the program was completed. For full details, contact Educator Licensing at the Minnesota Department of Education (see Appendix 1). Consult http:// education.state.mn.us/mde/Teacher_Support/Educator_Licensing/index.html
E. See Fingerprinting Requirements, I, D, 1, directly above.

Licensure Requirements and Levels

I. For the most accurate information on the approximately 32 programs approved for licensing in Minnesota, view the Teacher Preparation Institutions with contact information document at http://education.state.mn.us>Educator Licensing>First-Time Licensure.

II. For a detailed listing of the 77 teacher licensure fields, 4 administrative licenses, and

5 related licenses, contact Educator Licensing at http://education.state.mn.us/mde/
Teacher_Support/Educator_Licensing/index.html

Administration

I. Licensure for superintendent, principal, or special education director. Requirements for all three positions include:
- A. Three years of successful classroom teaching experience while holding a classroom teaching license valid for the position or positions in which the experience was gained;
  and
- B. Completion of a specialist or doctoral program, or a program consisting of 60 semester credits beyond the bachelor's degree that includes a terminating graduate degree and topics preparatory for educational administration and specified Minnesota competencies.
  1. Each program must be approved by the Board of School Administrators and be offered at a regionally accredited Minnesota graduate school.
- C. Additional position-specific requirements include:
  1. An applicant for licensure as a superintendent or principal must have field experience of at least 320 hours or 40 eight-hour days to be completed within 12 continuous months in elementary, middle or junior high, and high schools as an administrative aide to a licensed and practicing school principal or superintendent, depending on the licensure sought.
     a. The field experience must include at least 40 hours or one week at each level not represented by the applicant's primary teaching experience.
        i. A person licensed as an elementary school principal must complete a field experience of at least 200 hours in secondary administration to qualify for licensure as a K–12 principal.
        ii. A person licensed as a secondary school principal must complete a field experience of at least 200 hours in elementary administration to qualify for licensure as a K–12 principal.
  2. An applicant for licensure as a director of special education must have a practicum or field experience that includes a minimum of 320 hours in an administrative position under the immediate supervision of a licensed and practicing director of special education.
     a. The field experience will include at least 40 hours or one week at a special education administrative unit other than the primary experience of the applicant.
II. Provisional license (valid 2 years, nonrenewable)
- A. Currently licensed elementary and secondary school principals seeking entry into a position as a K–12 principal may apply for a provisional license.
  1. Applicant must provide evidence of enrollment in an approved administrative licensure program for licensure as a K–12 principal.
III. Administrative Licensure Without Teaching Experience for Superintendents, Principals, and Directors of Special Education. Requirements include:

A. Meet the degree requirement specified in I, B, directly above;

B. Satisfactorily complete a field experience in school administration as an intern in the license area sought:

   1. In a school district setting appropriate for the license sought,

   2. Under the supervision of educators from an approved college or university school administration program and a licensed practicing school administrator working in the area of the intern's field experience,
       and

   3. The field experience must consist of at least 320 hours, of which at least 40 must be in each school level: elementary, middle grades, and high school, and is in addition to the teaching internship requirement below;

C. Demonstrate required basic teaching knowledge and skills by:

   1. Presenting a portfolio or other appropriate presentation as determined by the approved school administration program demonstrating appropriate teaching knowledge and skills;
       or

   2. Meet the examination requirement of part 8710.0510, subpart 1, items A and B, and subpart 3, items A and B;
       and

D. Fulfill teaching internship requirement insuring that applicant shall have experience and knowledge in curriculum, school organization, philosophy of education, early childhood, elementary, junior high, middle school, and senior high schools through an internship that:

   1. Includes 1 school year with a minimum hour equivalency of 1,050 hours of classroom experiences, including 8 weeks of supervised teaching;

   2. Is under the supervision of a licensed practicing school administrator;

   3. Includes supervision provided by educators from an approved school administration program;
       and

   4. Is based on a written agreement between the intern, the approved school administration preparation institution, and the school district in which the internship is completed.

IV. Licensure for Directors of Community Education For specific requirements, consult http://educaton.state.mn.us/mde/Teacher_Support/Educator_Licensing/index.html

School Counselor (K–12)

I. Requirements for Entrance License

A. Hold a master's degree from a college or university that is regionally accredited by the association for the accreditation of colleges and secondary schools.

B. Complete an approved teaching preparation program leading to the licensure of school counselors or provide evidence of having completed a preparation program in school counseling accredited by the Council for the Accreditation of Counseling and Related Educational Programs.

C. Complete a preparation program that must demonstrate specific knowledge and skills. For details, contact the Minnesota State Department of Education (see Appendix 1).

II.   Renewal of Continuing License

A.   See detailed rules governing continuing licensure at http://education.state.mn.us/mde/Teacher_Support/Educator_Licensing/index.html

Mississippi

Standard Educator Licenses

I. Five-year Educator License, Traditional Teacher Education Route
   A. Class A Five-Year Educator License (valid for 5 years; renewable)
      1. Bachelor's degree in teacher education from a state-approved or a National Council for Accreditation of Teacher Education (NCATE)–approved program from a regionally/nationally accredited institution of higher learning
      2. Passing scores on Praxis II (Principles of Learning and Teaching Test)
      3. Passing scores on Praxis II (Specialty Area Test) in degree program
   B. Class AA Five-Year Educator License (valid for 5 years; renewable)
      1. See I, A, 1–3, directly above
      2. Master's degree in the endorsement area in which license is requested *or* Master of Education degree
   C. Class AAA Five-Year Educator License (valid for 5 years; renewable)
      1. See I, A, 1–3, directly above
      2. Specialist degree in the endorsement area in which license is requested
         or
         Specialist of Education degree
   D. Class AAAA Five-Year Educator License (valid for 5 years; renewable)
      1. See I, A, 1–3, directly above
      2. Doctoral degree in the endorsement area in which license is requested
         or
         Doctor of Education degree
II. Five-Year Educator License, Alternate Route
   A. Class A Five-Year Educator License
      1. Route One
         a. Bachelor's degree (noneducation) from a regionally/nationally accredited institution of higher learning
         b. Passing scores on Core Academic Skills for Educators Test (CASE)
         c. Passing scores on Praxis II Specialty Area Test
         d. Successful completion of a 1- or 3-year state-approved alternate route program; for details, consult www.mde.kl2.ms.us/ed_licensure/alternate _path.html
         e. Application for a 5-year educator license,
            or
      2. Route Two
         a. Hold a bachelor's degree with a minor or concentration in secondary education (7–12)
         b. Passing scores on CASE

    c. Passing scores on Praxis II Specialty Area Test

    d. Documentation of completion of student teaching from a state- or NCATE-approved program.

  B. Class AA, Class AAA, and/or Class AAAA Five-Year Educator License

   1. Meet the requirements for a Class A license

   2. Master's, specialist, or doctoral degree in the endorsement area in which license is requested,

    or

    Master's of Education degree or Specialist of Education degree,

    or

    Doctor of Education degree.

III. Reciprocity

  A. Class A Five-Year Educator Reciprocity License (valid 5 years; renewable)

   1. Granted to applicants who hold a valid standard out-of-state license (K–12) in an area in which Mississippi issues an endorsement if it meets minimum Mississippi license requirements or equivalent requirements

   2. Applicants must submit to the Office of Educator Licensure:

    a. Original valid out-of-state license;

    b. Sealed copy of all college transcripts;

     and

    c. Documentation showing a passing score on a core subject test required for certification by issuing state, or documentation that verifies the out-of-state license was obtained in a manner equivalent with current Mississippi license guidelines for that license.

  B. Class AA, AAA, or AAAA Five-Year Educator Reciprocity License

   1. Meet requirements for Class A Five-Year Educator Reciprocity License; see III, A, 1 and 2, directly above

   2. Original valid out-of-state Standard Class AA (master's degree); Class AAA (specialist degree); or Class AAAA (doctoral degree) License in a Mississippi endorsement area

  C. Two-Year Reciprocity License (valid current teaching year plus 1 additional school year, to expire June 30; nonrenewable)

   1. For applicant with a valid credential less than a standard license or certificate from another state. Applicant must submit to the Office of Educator Licensure:

    a. See III, A, 2, a and b, directly above

   2. To convert this provisional license to a five-year renewable license, the applicant must meet all requirements for a five-year license in Mississippi.

IV. Five-Year Educator License—Guidance and Counseling

  A. Class AA Option One (valid 5 years; renewable)

   1. Hold a Five-Year educator license

   2. Complete a master's degree program in guidance and counseling

   3. Passing score on Praxis II (Specialty Area for Guidance Counselor)

  B. Class AA Option Two (valid 5 years; renewable)

        1. Complete an approved master's degree program for guidance and counseling that includes a full year internship

        2. Passing score on CASE

        3. Passing score on Praxis II (Specialty Area Test for Guidance Counseling)

  C. Class AA Option Three (valid 5 years, renewable)

        1. Hold National Certified School Counselor (NCSC) credential issued by National Board of Certified Counselors (NBCC)

  D. Class AAA (valid 5 years; renewable)

        1. Meet requirements for Class AA License (see IV, A–C, directly above)

        2. Specialist degree in guidance and counseling

  E. Class AAAA (valid 5 years; renewable)

        1. Meet requirements for Class AA License (see IV, A–C, directly above)

        2. Doctoral degree in guidance and counseling

V. Five-Year Library/Media License (valid 5 years; renewable)

  A. Class A Requirements: *Either*

        1. Complete bachelor's degree program or higher in Library/Media; and attain passing scores on CORE (Core Academic Skills for Educators), Praxis II (Principles of Learning and Teaching), and Praxis II (Specialty Area for Library/Media);
or

        2. Hold a Five-Year Educator license and complete an approved Library/Media program;
or

        3. Hold a Five-Year-Educator license and attain passing score on Praxis II (Specialty Area for Library/Media);

  B. Class AA, AAA, or AAAA Requirements

        1. Meet requirements for Class A license (see V, A, 1–3, directly above) and complete an approved master's (Class AA), specialist (Class AAA), or doctorate (Class AAAA) in library/media from a state-approved or regionally/nationally accredited institution of higher learning

VI. Licenses Available

  I. Mississippi Educator Teacher Education Route License

    A. Five-Year Educator License

 II. Alternate Route Licenses

    A. MS Alternate Path to Quality Educators/One-Year Alternate Route License

    B. Teach MS Institute/One-Year License

    C. Master of Arts in Teaching/Three-Year License

    D. American Board Certification

    E. Five-Year Alternate Route License

III. Special Subject Five-Year Educator Licenses

    A. Audiologist, Child Development, Dyslexia Therapy, Early Oral Intervention Hearing Impaired B-K, Emotional Disability, Guidance and Counseling, Library Media, Performing Arts, Psychometrist, School Psychologist, Speech/Language Clinician, Speech/Language Therapist, Special Education Birth-Kindergarten, Special Education Mild/Moderate Disability K–12

IV. Career Technical Educator Licenses
   A. Career Technical Non–Education Degree (Associate's Degree)/Three-Year License
   B. Career Technical Non–Education Degree (Bachelor's Degree)/Three-Year License
   C. Career Technical Educator License Non-Degree or Non–Education Degree/Five-Year License
IV. Licenses by District Request Only
   A. JROTC Non-practicing
   B. One-Year License for Veteran Teachers Entry Level
   C. Expert Citizen Career Level

Administrator Licenses

I. Nonpracticing Administrator License (Class AA, AAA, or AAAA; 5 years renewable): issued to an educator not currently employed in an administrative position
   A. Hold 5-year standard educator license
   B. Verfication of 3 years of education experience
   C. Completion of an approved master's, specialist, or doctoral degree in educational administration/leadership from a state-approved or regionally/nationally accredited institution of higher learning
   D. Successful completion of School Leaders Licensure Assessment (SLLA), Educational Testing Service
   E. Institutional recommendation documenting completion of an approved planned program in educational leadership/supervision through a state-approved or regionally/nationally accredited institution of higher learning
   F. Validity is based upon validity of period of standard license currently held.
II. Entry Level Administrator License (Class AA, AAA, or AAAA; valid 5 years; nonrenewable): issued to an educator employed as a beginning administrator
   A. See I, A–E, directly above.
   B. Application for Entry Level license upon obtaining first job as administrator (Orientation to School Leadership—OSL)
   C. Letter from District stating the administrative position and date of administrative employment
III. Standard Career Level Administrator License (Class AA, AAA, or AAAA; 5 years renewable)
   A. Complete School Executive Management Institute (SEMI) entry-level requirements (Orientation to School Leadership—OSL)
IV. Alternate Route Administrator License (Class AA, AAA, or AAAA)
   A. One-year Alternate Route Administrator License (Class AA; valid 1 year; convertible to IV, B, directly below)
      1. Requirements
         a. Completion of master's of education (MED) or higher education degree
         b. Passing score on Core Academic Skills for Educators Test (CASE) and Praxis II (Principles of Learning and Teaching Test)
         c. Three years teaching experience for MED

         d.   Successful completion of alternate route training

         e.   Priority will be given to Superintendent/Board recommendation for admittance into an alternate route program.

    2.   Conversion to Five-Year Entry Level Alternate Route Administrator License

         a.   Complete Alternate Route program

         b.   See I, D , directly above.

B. Five-Year Entry Level Alternate Route Administrator License (Class AA; valid 5 years; nonrenewable)

    1.   Requirements

         a.   See IV, A, 1, a–e, directly above.

         b.   See I, D, directly above.

    2.   Conversion to Standard Career Level Alternate Route Administrator License within 5 years—see III, A, directly above.

         a.   Completion of SEMI entry-level OSL requirements

         b.   Completion of 6 hours of educational leadership course work from an approved educational leadership administrator program; courses must be in school law, school finance, instructional improvement or leadership, curriculum and instruction

C. Standard Career-Level Alternate Route Administrator License (Class AA, AAA, AAAA)

    1.   Requirements

         a.   See IV, A, 1, a–c, directly above

         b.   Completion of School Executive Management Institute (SEMI) entry-level requirements

D. Five-Year Alternate Route Administrator License, Business Track (Class AA valid 5 years; nonrenewable)

    1.   Requirements:

         a.   Complete one of the following: Master of Business Administration (MBA); or Master of Public Administration (MPA); or Master of Public Planning and Policy (MPP);
and

         b.   CORE (Core Academic Skills for Educators) and Praxis II (Principles of Learning and Teaching) Tests;
and

         c.   Five years of administrative/supervisory experience, meaning direct supervision of individuals and/or programs within a business, industry, and/or organization;
and

         d.   Successful completion of School Leaders Licensure Assessment (SLLA)-Educational Testing Service;
and

         e.   Successful completion of Alternate Route training.

         f.   Priority will be given to Superintendent/Board recommendation for admittance into an Alternate Route program.

     2.   Conversion to Career Level Standard License within 5 years—see IV, B, 2, directly above.

E.   Other Administrative Licenses; for further information, consult http://www.mde.kl2 .ms.us/docs/educator-licensure/licensure-guidelines.pdf?sfvrsn=0

     1.   Athletic Administrator

     2.   School District Business Administrator

Missouri

Educator Certification, Classification, and Renewals

I. General Qualifications for Certification
Identical for all teaching certificates, except for some areas of Vocational Education
   A. Baccalaureate degree from college/university with teacher education program approved by Missouri Department of Elementary and Secondary Education (DESE) or with teacher education program approved by state education agency in states other than Missouri
      1. No formal reciprocity for certification with other states; however, graduates from approved teacher-education programs within other states may obtain Missouri certificate based on meeting certain requirements.
   B. Recommendation for certification from designated official for teacher education in college/university where program was completed; not required with possession of a valid out-of-state certificate
   C. Grade-point average of 2.5 on a 4.0 scale, both overall and in content area.
   D. Successful completion of required Praxis test(s)
      1. Consult DESE website (see Appendix 1) for list of the Missouri Specialty Area Tests and qualifying scores
   E. Meet educational, professional, and subject area requirements as specified
   F. Applicants are required to complete a Missouri background check, including fingerprinting; for details, consult http://dese.mo.gov/eq/cert/index.html

II. Classifications
   A. Initial Professional Certificate (valid 4 years)
      1. Assigned to new graduates of teacher-education programs and to individuals with less than 4 years of DESE-approved teaching experience who meet the minimum requirements and qualifications
      2. See I, A–E, directly above.
      3. To advance to next level, during valid dates of classification, the teacher must meet all of following requirements:
         a. Participate in district-provided and -approved mentoring program for 2 years
         b. Successfully complete 30 contact hours of professional development that may include college credits
         c. Participate in Beginning Teacher Assistance Program
         d. Successfully participate in a yearly performance-based teacher evaluation
         e. Complete 4 years of approved teaching experience
   B. Career Continuous Professional Certificate, or CCPC
   C. Administrative Classification
      1. Elementary Principal and Secondary Principal

    a.   Initial Administrator Certificate (valid for 4 years)

        i.   Permanent or professional Missouri teaching certificate
or
Baccalaureate degree and recommendation from state-approved teacher-preparation program; and qualifying score on designated assessment for initial certification

        ii.   Minimum of 2 years of approved teaching experience

        iii.   Complete designated building-level administrator's assessment

        iv.   Course in psychology and education of the exceptional child

        v.   Master's degree in educational leadership from approved college/university

        vi.   Recommendation for certification from approved college/university program

    b.   Transition Administrator Certificate—Principal (valid for 6 years)

        i.   4 years of state-approved administrator experience

        ii.   2 years of designated district-provided mentoring.

        iii.   Development, implementation, and completion of approved professional development plan

        iv.   Annual performance-based evaluation that meets or exceeds Missouri Performance Based Principal's Evaluation

        v.   Completion of 8 semester hours towards advanced degree in educational leadership or 120 contact hours in professional development activities

    c.   Career Continuous Administrator Certificate—Principal

        i.   Educational specialist degree or higher in educational leadership, reading/literacy or curriculum/instruction.

        ii.   Performance-based principal evaluation

        iii.   30 contact hours of professional development annually

2.   Superintendent

    a.   Initial Administrator certificate (valid for 4 years)

        i.   Must complete Ed.S. or Ed.D. in educational administration and be recommended by the degree-granting University; must complete designated district level administrator's assessment.

        ii.   Minimum of 1 year of experience as a building- or district-level administrator at public or accredited nonpublic school

        iii.   See II, C, 1, a, i–vi, directly above

    b.   Career Certificate Administrator

        i.   See II, C, 1, c, i–iii, directly above

4.   Special Education Administrator K–12

    a.   Initial Administrator Certificate—Special Education Director (valid for 4 years)

        i.   Professional teaching certificate for an area of special education or student services
or
Baccalaureate degree and recommendation from state-approved

teacher-preparation program in an area of special education; and qualifying score on designated assessment

    ii.   Minimum of 2 years of approved special education or student services teaching experience

    iii.   See II, C, 1, a, i–vi, directly above

  b. Transition Administrator Certificate—Special Education Director (valid for 6 years)

    i.   See II, C, 1, b, i–v, directly above

  c. Career Administrator Certificate—Special Education Director

    i.   See II, C, 1, c, i–iii, directly above

  5. Career Education Director

    a. Initial Administrator Certificate—Career Education Director (valid for 4 years)

      i.   Permanent or professional or career education Missouri teaching certificate

      or

      Baccalaureate degree and recommendation from state-approved teacher-preparation program; and qualifying score on designated assessment

      ii.   See II, C, 1, a, ii–vi, directly above

    b. Transition Administrator Certificate—Career Education Director (valid for 6 years)

      i.   See II, C, 1, b, i–v, directly above

    c. Career Administrator Certificate—Career Education Director

      i.   See II, C, 1, c, i–iii, directly above

D. Student Services Classification

  1. Counselor K–8 (valid for 4 years)

    a. Recommendation for certification from approved college/university with a school counseling program

    b. Master's degree with major emphasis in school guidance and counseling from approved college/university based upon completion of approved program of at least 24 semester hours of approved graduate courses in guidance and counseling, with at least 12 semester hours focused upon guidance in elementary schools

    c. Qualifying score on designated assessment

  2. Counselor 7–12 (valid for 4 years)

    a. See II, D, 1, a–c, directly above

  3. Career Student Services (valid for 99 years)

    a. Four years of state-approved school counseling experience

    b. Participation in 2 years district-provided mentoring during the first 2 years of student services experience

    c. Development, implementation, and completion of a professional development plan of at least 40 contact hours of professional development or 3 semester hours of graduate credit towards an advanced degree

    d. Successful participation in an annual performance-based evaluation

4. For related certificates listed here, contact Educator Certification at Missouri's Department of Elementary and Secondary Education (http://dese.mo.gov/eq/cert/index.html)
   a. Psychological Examiner K–12
   b. School Psychologist K–12
   c. Speech-Language Pathologist
E. Classifications involving district application. For detailed information on these, contact Missouri Department of Elementary and Secondary Education (http://dese.mo.gov/divteachqual/teachcert/)
   1. Provisional (valid 2 years)
   2. Temporary Authorization Classification (valid 1 year)
F. Career (Vocational) Classification Applicants may seek certificates below; for full details, contact Missouri Department of Elementary and Secondary Education (http://dese.mo.gov/eq/cert/index.html)
   1. Secondary Career Education Certificate
   2. Postsecondary/Adult Career Education Certificate
   3. Career Continuous Career Education (CCCE) Certificate

Areas and Types of Certification

I. Certification Levels
   A. Early Childhood (Birth–Grade 3)
   B. Elementary Education (1–6)
   C. Middle School (5–9)
      1. Language Arts
      2. Mathematics
      3. Science
      4. Social Studies
      5. Other Middle School Endorsements
   D. Secondary Education (9–12) (except as noted)
   E. Special Education (K–12)
   F. Student Services
   G. Administration
   H. Career Education (vocational)
   I. Other
II. Subject Areas
   Agriculture; Art (K–12, 9–12); Blind & Partially Sighted (B–12); Building-Level Administrator; Business Education; Deaf and Hearing Impaired (B–12); District-Level Administrator (Superintendent, K–12); Early Childhood Education (B–Grade 3); Early Childhood Special Education (B–Grade 3); English; English for Speakers of Other Languages (ESOL) (K–12); Family and Consumer Science (B–12); Foreign Languages [French (K–12); German (K–12); Spanish (K–12)]; Gifted Education (K–12); Health (K–12, K–9, 9–12); Library Media Specialist (K–12); Marketing Education; Mathematics; Music (Instrumental, Vocal) (K–12); Physical Education (K–9, K–12, 9–12); Principal (K–8, 5–9, 7–12); School Counselor (K–8, 7–12); School

Psychologist K–12; Science (Biology; Chemistry; Earth Science; General Science; Physics); Severely Developmentally Disabled (B–12); Social Science; Special Education Administrator; Mild/Moderate Cross-Categorical K–12; Special Reading (Remedial) (K–12); Speech and Language Pathologist (B–12); Speech/Theater; Unified Science (Biology; Chemistry; Earth Science; Physics); Technology and Engineering; Vocational School Director

Montana

Educator Licensure

I. Minimal educator licensure requirements
    A. Bachelor's degree from regionally accredited college or university,
    B. Six semester credits in department of education course work from accredited education preparation program either in Montana or elsewhere,
        and
    C. Verification of student teaching or 1 year of teaching experience in elementary and/or secondary school or school district either in Montana or elsewhere,
        or
        Eligibility for a Class 5 alternative license to complete this requirement.

Teacher Licenses

I. Class 2 Standard Teacher's License (valid 5 years)
    A. Applicant must submit verification of all of the following:
        1. Meeting or exceeding minimal educator licensure requirements; see Educator Licensure, I, A–C, above,
        2. Completion of accredited professional educator preparation program,
            and
        3. Qualification for 1 or more endorsements as outlined in Class 1 and 2 Endorsements; see III, directly below.
    B. Class 2 standard teacher's license shall be renewable with 1 of the following combinations of college credit and renewal units:
        1. Three semester credits and 15 renewal units,
        2. Four semester credits,
        3. Four quarter credits and 20 renewal units,
        4. Five quarter credits and 10 renewal units,
            or
        5. Six quarter credits.
    C. A lapsed Class 2 standard teacher's license may be reinstated by showing verification of 60 renewal units, 40 of which must be earned by college credit during the 5-year period preceding the validation date of the new license.
II. Class I Professional Teacher's License (valid 5 years)
    A. Applicant must submit verification of all of the following:
        1. Eligibility for the Class 2 standard teacher's license; see I, A, 1–3, directly above,
        2. Master's degree in professional education or endorsable teaching area(s) from accredited college or university,
            and
        3. Three years of successful teaching experience employed in accredited school

organization consistent with Montana's K–12 pattern during school fiscal year as licensed member of instructional staff.

    a. Experience gained prior to basic eligibility for initial licensure is not considered.

B. Class 1 standard teacher's license shall be renewable with 60 renewal units.

C. A lapsed Class 1 professional teacher's license may be reinstated by showing verification of 60 renewal units earned during 5-year period preceding validation date of new license.

III. Class 1 and 2 Endorsements

A. Areas approved for endorsement on Class 1 and 2 licenses include the following: agriculture, art K–12, biology, business education, chemistry, computer science K–12, drama, earth science, economics, elementary education, English, English as a second language K–12, family and consumer sciences, geography, health, history, history–political science, industrial arts, journalism, library K–12, marketing, mathematics, music K–12, physical education K–12, school counseling K–12, science (broadfield), social studies (broadfield), sociology, special education P–12, speech-communication, speech-drama, technology education, trade and industry, traffic education K–12, and world languages

B. License holder may qualify for a statement of specialized competency by completing at least 20 semester college credit hours or equivalency in approved areas of permissive specialized competency, including: early childhood education, gifted and talented education, and technology in education.

C. To obtain elementary endorsement, applicant must provide verification of completion of accredited elementary teacher education program, including student teaching, or university-supervised teaching experience.

D. To obtain secondary endorsement, applicant must provide verification of at least:

    1. Sixteen semester credits in professional educator preparation program, including student teaching or appropriate college waiver, and 30 semester credits in approved major and 20 semester credits in approved minor,
or

    2. Forty semester credits in an extended major.

E. Both elementary and secondary preparation, including student teaching or university-supervised teaching experience, are required for endorsement in any approved K–12 endorsement area.

    1. The K–12 endorsement areas outlined in III, A, directly above, may also be endorsed at elementary or secondary level depending on verified level of preparation.

F. Class 1 or 2 license may be endorsed in special education P–12 with program preparation at elementary or secondary levels, or balanced K–12 program of comparable preparation.

G. Balanced K–12 license level option is available through Montana Board of Public Education–approved special education programs for those individuals with:

    1. Minimum of completed bachelor's degree,
and

    2. Verified completion of out-of-state approved special education program that includes student teaching or university supervised teaching experience.

H. Completion of accredited professional educator preparation program in any disability area shall result in a special education endorsement.

I. Applicants with graduate degrees in endorsable field of specialization may use experience instructing in relevant higher education courses as credit in that endorsement area for licensure.

Administrative Licenses

I. Class 3 Administrative License (valid 5 years)

A. Appropriate administrative areas acceptable for license endorsement are the following: elementary principal, secondary principal, K–12 principal, K–12 superintendent, and supervisor

B. To obtain Class 3 administrative license, applicant must hold at least the appropriate master's degree and qualify for 1 of the endorsements set forth directly below; see Administrative Licenses, II–VII.

C. Lapsed Class 3 administrative license may be reinstated by showing verification of 60 renewal units earned during 5-year period preceding validation date of new license.

II. Class 3 Administrative License—Superintendent Endorsement

A. Applicant must provide verification of all of the following:

1. Minimum of 3 years of successful teaching experience as appropriately licensed and assigned Class 1 or 2 teacher or Class 6 school counselor, *and*

2. Minimum of 18 semester graduate credits in school administrator preparation program, of which 12 must be beyond the master's degree, in each of the following content areas: organizational leadership; instructional leadership; facilities planning and policy; personnel and labor relations; community and board relations; policy development; and 3 semester credits of college course work each in Montana school law and in Montana school finance.

B. In addition to the requirements in A, 1 and 2, directly above, every applicant must provide verification of either:

1. Education specialist degree or doctoral degree in education leadership from professional educator preparation program accredited by either the National Council for the Accreditation of Teacher Education (NCATE) or by a Montana Board of Public Education (BPE)–approved organization, *and*

    Minimum of 1 year of administrative experience as appropriately licensed principal or 1 year of supervised Montana BPE-approved administrative internship as a superintendent;
    or

2. Master's degree in educational leadership from accredited professional educator preparation program or master's degree in education from accredited program, *and*

    Licensure and endorsement as a K–12 principal,

and

Minimum of 1 year of employment in accredited school during school fiscal year as licensed member of supervisory or administrative staff in school organization consistent with Montana's K–12 pattern,
or

3. Minimum of 1 year of supervised Board of Public Education–approved administrative internship as superintendent.

C. Class 3 administrative license endorsed as superintendent shall be renewed as follows:

1. For applicants meeting all licensure requirements at time of initial application, verification of 60 renewal units earned during valid term of license,
or

2. For applicants not meeting the requirement of 3 semester credits of college course work each in Montana school law and in Montana school finance, verification of those 6 semester credits earned during valid term of initial Class 3 license.

III. Class 3 Administrative License—Elementary Principal Endorsement

A. Applicant must provide verification of:

1. Minimum of 3 years of successful experience as appropriately licensed and assigned Class 1 or 2 teacher or Class 6 school counselor at elementary level,
and

Master's degree in educational leadership from professional educator preparation program accredited by either NCATE or by a Montana BPE-approved organization,
or

2. Master's degree from any accredited professional educator preparation program and minimum of 24 graduate semester credits from school administrator preparation program in following content areas: school leadership; instructional leadership to include supervision and elementary curriculum; successful completion of 3 semester credits of college course work in Montana school law; and school and community relations.

IV. Class 3 Administrative License—Secondary Principal Endorsement

A. Applicant must provide verification of:

1. Minimum of 3 years of successful experience as appropriately licensed and assigned Class 1 or 2 teacher or Class 6 school counselor at the secondary level,
and

Master's degree in educational leadership from professional educator preparation program accredited by either NCATE or by a Montana BPE-approved organization,
or

2. Master's degree from any accredited professional educator preparation program and minimum of 24 graduate semester credits from school administrator preparation program in following content areas: school leadership; instructional leadership to include supervision and secondary curriculum; successful

        completion of 3 semester credits of college course work in Montana school law; and school and community relations.

   B. Class 3 administrative license endorsed as a secondary principal shall be renewed upon verification of 60 renewal units earned during valid term of the license.

V. Class 3 Administrative License—K–12 Principal Endorsement

   A. Applicant must provide verification of:

      1. Master's degree in educational leadership from professional educator preparation program accredited by either NCATE or by a Montana BPE-approved organization,

      2. Full eligibility for elementary or secondary principal endorsement or current endorsement as Montana elementary or secondary principal,

      3. Minimum of 3 years of successful experience as appropriately licensed and assigned Class 1 or 2 teacher or Class 6 school counselor at any level within K–12,
        and

      4. If eligible at secondary level, at least 6 graduate semester credits in educational leadership and curriculum at elementary level; or, if eligible at elementary level, at least 6 graduate credits in educational leadership and curriculum at secondary level.

   B. Class 3 administrative license endorsed as K–12 principal shall be renewed upon verification of 60 renewal units earned during valid term of the license.

VI. Class 3 Administrative License—Supervisor Endorsement

   A. Issued in specific fields such as math, music, and school counseling, or in general areas such as elementary education, secondary education and curriculum development.

   B. Applicants must submit verification of:

      1. Successful completion, at accredited college or university, of master's degree in area requested for endorsement,

      2. Meeting eligibility requirements for Class 1 or Class 2 teaching license endorsed in field of specialization,

      3. Three years of successful experience as an appropriately licensed and assigned teacher,

      4. At least 14 graduate semester credits in education or equivalent to include: general school administration; administration in specific area to be endorsed; supervision of instruction; basic school finance; and school law,
        and

      5. Supervised practicum/internship (minimum of 4 semester credits or appropriate waiver), with recommendation of appropriate official(s) required.

   C. Class 3 administrative license endorsed as supervisor shall be renewed upon verification of 60 renewal units earned during valid term of license.

VII. Class 3 Administrative License—Special Education Supervisor Endorsement

   A. Issued in specific field of special education to applicants who submit verification of:

      1. Successful completion, at accredited college or university, of master's degree in

special education or master's degree in special education–related service field, e.g., school psychologist, speech-language pathologist, audiologist, physical therapist, occupational therapist, registered nurse, clinical social worker, or clinical professional counselor,

2. Full licensure in field of specialization,
3. Three years of successful experience in accredited school setting as appropriately licensed and assigned teacher, or 5 years of successful experience in accredited school setting as fully licensed and assigned related services provider,
4. At least 14 graduate semester credits in education or equivalent to include: general school administration; administraion in specific area to be endorsed; supervision of instruction; basic school finance; and school law, *and*
5. Supervised practicum/internship (minimum of 4 semester credits or appropriate waiver), with recommendation of appropriate official(s) required.

B. Class 3 administrative license endorsed as special education supervisor shall be renewed upon verification of 60 renewal units earned during valid term of license.

Additional Licenses

I. Class 4 Career and Technical Education License (valid 5 years)
   A. Three types of Class 4 licenses:
   1. Class 4A license issued to individuals holding valid Montana secondary level teaching license, but without appropriate career and technical education endorsement,
   2. Class 4B license issued to individuals with at least bachelor's degree, but who do not hold valid Montana secondary-level teaching license with appropriate career and technical education endorsement,
   3. Class 4C license issued to individuals who hold at least high school diploma or GED and meet minimum requirements for endorsement.
   B. Class 4 license renewal requires 60 renewal units.
   1. Class 4A licenses (with bachelor's degree) shall be renewable by earning 60 renewal units, 40 of which must be earned through college credit. Endorsement related to technical studies may be accepted with prior approval. The first renewal must show evidence of renewal units earned in the following content areas: principles and/or philosophy of career and technical education; or safety and teacher liability.
   2. Class 4A licenses (with master's degree) shall be renewable by earning 60 renewal units. The first renewal must show evidence of renewal units earned in the following content areas: principles and/or philosophy of career and technical education; or safety and teacher liability.
   3. Class 4B or 4C licenses shall be renewable by earning 60 renewal units, 40 of which must be earned through college credit. Appropriate course work to renew a Class 4B or 4C license includes the following: principles and/or philosophy

of career and technical education; curriculum and instruction in career and technical education; learning styles/teaching styles, including serving students with special needs; safety and teacher liability; classroom management; teaching methods; career guidance in career and technical education; or endorsement related technical studies, with prior approval.

C. Lapsed Class 4 license may be reinstated by showing verification of following:
1. For Class 4A licenses:
    a. If licensee does not have master's degree, 60 renewal units, 40 of which must be earned by college credit or prior approved endorsement-related technical studies, earned during 5-year period preceding validation date of new license;
      or
    b. If licensee has master's degree, 60 renewal units earned during 5-year period preceding validation date of new license.
    c. For Class 4B and 4C licenses, licensee must verify completion of 4 semester credits of course work in following areas: principles and/or philosophy of career and technical education; curriculum and instruction in career and technical education; learning styles/teaching styles, including serving students with special needs; safety and teacher liability; classroom management; teaching methods; career guidance in career and technical education; or endorsement-related technical studies, with prior approval.

II. Class 4 Endorsements
A. Recognized occupations eligible for Class 4 license shall be evaluated on annual basis by Superintendent of Public Instruction. Appropriate career and technical education areas acceptable for endorsement on Class 4 license include, but are not limited to, the following: automotive technology, welding, auto body, industrial mechanics, small engines, heavy equipment operations, electronics, horticulture, agriculture mechanics, building trades, building maintenance, culinary arts, metals, drafting, computer information systems, graphic arts, aviation, health occupations, machining, diesel mechanics, videography, and theater arts.
   1. Endorsements not on list of recognized occupations may be retained as long as holder continues to renew license.
B. To obtain an endorsement on a Class 4 license, applicant must provide the following:
   1. Verification of minimum of 10,000 hours of documented work experience, which may include apprenticeship training, documenting knowledge and skills required in specific trade in which they are to teach. Acceptable documentation is determined by the superintendent and may include, but is not limited to:
    a. Work experience completed and verified by previous employers, to include detailed description of duties performed during employment,
    b. For self-employed individuals, examples of projects completed, letters of verification from clients or customers, profit and loss statements demonstrating viability of business or self-employment,

        c. Verification of teaching experience in area requested for endorsement, accompanied by verification of substantial work experience in area requested for endorsement,

        d. Certificates of completion of appropriate technical programs or related college degrees and course work, and industry certification (e.g., ASE, AWS).

    2. For health occupations or computer information systems, an alternative to above requirement of 10,000 hours work experience may be substituted as approved by Superintendent of Public Instruction as follows:

        a. For health occupations:

            i. Hold Class 1 or 2 license with endorsement in health or any of science areas;

           ii. Verification of participation in or completion of approved internship program in medical setting,
               and

          iii. Successful completion of course work in human biology and anatomy and physiology,
               or

          iv. Hold current professional license or certificate in related health occupation field.

    3. For computer information systems, individual may provide verification of completion of approved technical program in recognized training institution and hold professional license or recognized industry standard certificate.

  C. Class 4A, 4B, or 4C career and technical education license may be approved to teach traffic education if the license meets specific requirements; contact Montana Office of Public Instruction (OPI)—see Appendix 1—for full details.

III. Class 6 Specialist License (valid 5 years)

  A. Class 6 specialist licenses may be issued with following endorsements:

    1. School psychologist,
       or

    2. School counselor.

  B. Class 6 specialist license renewal requires college credit or renewal units as follows:

    1. Four graduate semester credits,

    2. Six graduate quarter credits,
       or

    3. Sixty renewal units.

  C. Lapsed Class 6 specialist license may be reinstated by showing verification of 4 graduate semester credits or equivalent renewal units earned during 5-year period preceding validation date of new license.

IV. Class 6 Specialist License—School Psychologist

  A. To obtain Class 6 specialist license with school psychologist endorsement, applicant must provide verification of:

       1.   Current credentials as nationally certified school psychologist (NCSP) from the National Association of School Psychologists (NASP),
or

       2.   Master's degree in school psychology or education specialist degree in related field from accredited institution
and
Recommendation from Montana Association of School Psychologists Competency Review Board after completion of oral examination.

  V.   Class 6 Specialist License—School Counselor

    A.   To obtain Class 6 specialist license with a school counselor endorsement, applicant must provide verification of:

       1.   Master's degree in school counseling (K–12),
or

       2.   Master's degree with equivalent graduate-level school counseling content,
and
Supervised internship of at least 600 hours in school or school-related setting.

    B.   Class 6 specialist license endorsed in school counseling may be approved to teach traffic education if the licensee is approved by Superintendent of Public Instruction and meets specific requirements; contact OPI (see Appendix 1) for full details.

  VI. Class 7 American Indian Language and Culture Specialist (valid 5 years)

    A.   Superintendent of Public Instruction shall issue Class 7 license based upon verification by the American Indian tribe for which the language and culture licensure is desired that the individual has met tribal standards for competency and fluency as a requisite for teaching that language and culture.

       1.   Candidates for Class 7 licensure must meet all nonacademic requirements for licensure in Montana.

    B.   The board will accept and place on file the criteria developed by each tribe for qualifying an individual as competent to be a specialist in its language and culture.

    C.   A Class 7 American Indian language and culture specialist licensee may be approved to teach traffic education if the licensee is approved by the Superintendent of Public Instruction and meets specific requirements; contact OPI (see Appendix 1) for full details.

    D.   Sixty units of renewal activities authorized and verified by the tribe will be required for renewal of a Class 7 license.

    E.   A school district may assign an individual licensed under this rule only to specialist services within the field of American Indian language and culture under such supervision as the district may deem appropriate. No teaching license or endorsement is required for duties within this prescribed field.

  VII. Class B Dual Credit-Only Postsecondary Faculty License (valid 5 years)

    A.   A faculty member of a postsecondary institution is required to hold a Class 8 dual credit license, unless already licensed Class 1, 2, or 4 and properly endorsed, whenever a faculty member is teaching a course for which one or more students will earn both high school and college credit. Contact OPI (see Appendix 1) for full details.

Nebraska

Note: Recent changes include the addition of a Dual Credit certificate for college staff providing instruction to high school students and of a career education certificate for those hired by districts to provide a specific class to students. The Nebraska Certification Office sends certificates electronically as e-mail attachments; so all applicants must have a current e-mail address.

Teaching Certificates

I. Initial Certificate (valid 5 years; renewable)
   A. Requires completion of:
      1. Bachelor's degree
         and
      2. An approved teacher education program with an endorsement recommendation from an approved institution.
         a. Six semester hours must be completed within the past 5 years.
   B. Renewable with 6 semester hours or 1 year of documented experience teaching in the past 5 years in an approved school.
II. Standard Certificate (valid 5 years; renewable)
   A. Requirements include holding a valid Initial Certificate and at least 2 consecutive years of teaching experience.
   B. Renewable with 6 semester hours or 1 year of teaching experience within the past 5 years.
III. Professional Certificate (valid 10 years; renewable)
   A. Issued with completion of master's degree in curriculum and instruction, educational technology, or in the applicant's content field.
   B. Renewable with 6 approved semester hours or 1 year of teaching experience within the past 5 years.

Requirements for Teaching Certificates

I. Professional, Standard and Initial Certificates. Requirements for all include:
   A. Completion of a bachelor's degree;
      1. Originals of all college transcripts required
   B. Recommendation by college for teacher training program completed;
   C. Completion of at least 6 hours of college course work in the past 5 years;
   D. Complete Praxis Series—CORE test, a human relations course addressing the 6 competencies found in statute, and a general special education course;
      1. The CORE requirement is waived for persons who have 3 years of teaching experience in another state while holding a valid certificate with no deficiencies.

and

E.   Fingerprinting required for applicants who have not lived in Nebraska for 5 consecutive years prior to the date of application.

   1.   Applicant must have no felony convictions.

II.   Standard and Professional Certificates Additional Requirements:

A.   Both require 2 years of teaching experience during the previous 5 years.

B.   Professional certificate also requires a master's degree in curriculum and instruction, educational technology, or in the person's content area.

III.   Certificates with deficiencies. Consult the website for more detailed information at www.education.ne.gov/TCERT

A.   Provisional Teaching Certificates

   1.   Provisional Teaching Certificate (valid 1 year; renewable with provisions)

      a.   Issued to persons reentering the profession who do not have recent teaching experience but otherwise meet all requirements

      b.   Renewable with completion of 6 hours of course work

   2.   Provisional Commitment certificate

      a.   Issued at the request of a school district to employ a person who has completed 50 percent of their pre–student teaching requirements and 75 percent of their content courses to take a difficult-to-fill position

B.   Substitute Teaching Certificates

   1.   State Substitute Certificate (valid 5 years)

      a.   Issued to applicants with a bachelor's degree who have completed an education program

      b.   Allows holder unlimited days per year to substitute provided no one position is longer than 90 days

   2.   Local Substitute Certificate (valid 3 years)

      a.   Issued to applicants with at least 60 college hours including 1 education class

      b.   Allows holder to substitute only in 1 district for no more than 40 days per year

C.   Temporary Teaching Certificate

   1.   Issued to those persons who have not completed the human relations training but have met all other requirements for a regular certificate

D.   Conditional Teaching Certificate (valid for up to 1 year)

   1.   Allows teaching while fingerprints are being processed or at the direction of the Commissioner when existing deficiencies prevent the issuance of a regular certificate in a timely manner

E.   Transitional Teaching Certificate (valid 1 year in 1 district only)

F.   Career Education Certificate (valid 5 years)

   1.   Issued to a person with a particular area of expertise who is offering a program to students in 1 school district

G.   Dual Credit Certificate (valid 5 years)

   1.   Issued to college employees who are teaching high school classes for both college and high school credit

Administrative Certificates

I.   Professional Administrative Certificate (valid 10 years). Requirements include:
    A.   Two years of teaching experience;
    B.   Completion of a specialist or doctorate degree in educational administration;
    C.   Six semester hours of graduate work in educational administration within 5 years of the date of application,
         or
         Have been serving as a school administrator for 2 or more years within the past 5;
         and
    D.   Successful completion of Praxis CORE Test, human relations and special education (SPED) training.
II. Standard Administrative Certificate (valid 5 years). Requirements include:
    A.   Two years of teaching experience;
    B.   Completion of a master's degree in educational administration;
    C.   Six semester hours of graduate work in educational administration within 5 years of the date of application,
         or
         Have been serving as a school administrator for 2 or more years within the past 5;
         and
    D.   Human relations, CORE, and SPED training completed.
III. Provisional Administrative Certificate (valid 1 year; renewable with provisions)
    A.   Candidate must have at least 75 percent of a superintendents program completed or 50 percent of a principal's program completed.
        1.   Candidate must complete at least 15 hours in the first 3 years.
    B.   Renewable by completing 6 hours of course work as identified by a plan drafted by a Nebraska college.
IV. Temporary Administrative Certificate
    A.   Issued to applicant to complete human relations training

Support Services Certificates

I.   School Nurse, Educational Audiologist, Speech Technician and Coaching
    A.   Standard Special Services Certificate (valid 5 years). Requirements include:
        1.   Human relations training;
        2.   Additional subject-specific required training or course work;
        3.   Completion of an approved program in candidate's specialty;
             and
        4.   Six hours of college credit within the past 5 years or one year of valid experience.
    B.   Provisional Special Services Certificate (valid 1 year). Requirements include:
        1.   Human relations training;
        2.   Completed 75 percent of the course requirements;
             and

3.   Submit a signed statement of intent to fulfill the remaining requirements.
C.   Temporary Special Services Certificate
1.   Issued to applicants who have met all other requirements for a Special Services Certificate to complete human relations training

Nevada

Fingerprinting is required for all licensure renewals.

Teaching Certificates and Requirements

I. Standard License (valid for 5 years)
   A. Bachelor's degree from a regionally accredited college/university and completion of a program that meets approved program standards.
   B. Renewal is based on 6 semester hours of college/university credit, or 6 Nevada approved in-service credits, or a combination of both to equal a total of 6 renewal credits.
II. Non-Renewable Three-year License
   A. Same requirements as the Renewable License except with provisions for testing and course work.
   B. All provisions must be met prior to the expiration date. Once all provisions are satisfied prior to expiration date, license may be changed to Standard or Professional.
III. Professional License
   A. Meet requirements for the renewable license, submit master's degree from a regionally accredited college/university, and verify 3 years of successful teaching experience at the K–12 grade level.
   B. Renewal is based on 6 semester hours of college/university credit, or 6 Nevada approved in-service credits, or a combination of both to equal a total of 6 renewal credits.
IV. Specialist License (valid for 8 years)
   A. Meet requirements for the Renewable License, complete an educational specialist degree program from a regionally accredited college/university, and verify 3 years of successful teaching experience at the appropriate K–12 grade level. Renewal requirement is submission of professional development credit.

Basic Qualifications for Licensure

I. An applicant must be a citizen or a lawful permanent resident of the United States.
II. Degree(s) and credits for courses must have been earned from a regionally accredited college or university.
III. Foreign transcripts must be accompanied by a course-by-course and degree equivalency evaluation done by an approved evaluator service (list available on website; see Appendix 1) before applicant applies for licensure.
IV. A license is issued based on the evaluation of the applicant's official transcript(s).
V. Within 3 years from date the license is issued, all applicants will be required to submit verification of completion of course work, or pass the Education Commission–approved examination(s) in Nevada School Law, Nevada Constitution, and the U.S. Constitution, as well as competency testing examinations with the passing score established by the Department of Education.

Elementary School
(Kindergarten–8th Grade)

I. Elementary License Requirements
  A. Bachelor's degree from accredited college or university and completion of a State Board of Education–approved program of preparation for teaching in elementary grades
  B. Completion of the following:
    1. Elementary professional education, semester hours 50
      a. Supervised student teaching... 8
      b. Teaching methods of teaching basic elementary subjects, including, but not limited to, mathematics, science, and social studies 9
      c. Teaching of literacy or language arts.. 9
      d. Professional education course work.. 6
    These must include: special education and parental involvement/family engagement
II. Professional Elementary License Requirements
  A. Meet all requirements for Elementary License
  B. Hold a master's degree in education
  C. Have 3 years of verifiable elementary teaching experience in state-approved schools
III. Elementary License Endorsement
  A. Credit within the area of endorsement, semester hours... 12
    1. Recognized endorsement areas are art; computers and technology; English; health; mathematics; literacy; science; social studies; physical education; bilingual education; and music.
      a. Endorsement for English requires 3 semester hours of credit in each of the following: advanced composition, descriptive grammar, and speech.
      b. Endorsement to teach pupils enrolled in bilingual education program requires applicant to pass appropriate examination (see website in Appendix 1 for details).
  B. Endorsement on an elementary license is not required by the Department of Education to teach kindergarten through 8th grade, although a school district may require such.

Middle School
(7th–9th Grades)

I. Requirements to teach in designated middle school or junior high school
  A. Hold bachelor's or higher degree from accredited college or university,
    and
    1. Complete Board-approved preparation program for teaching at this level
      or
    Complete professional education course work, semester hours 24

Hours to include:

    a.   Supervised student teaching in designated middle or junior high school, semester hours 8

    b.   A course in methods and materials for teaching major or minor field of specialization at middle school, junior high school, or secondary grade level, or a middle or junior high school level integrated methods course

    c.   Course of study regarding education or curricular adaptation for pupils with disabilities and/or a course or study regarding educational foundation or methods in teaching English language learners, semester hours 3

    d.   Course work in at least 2 of following areas:
Middle school foundations, history, theory or philosophy; middle school curriculum, pedagogy, or assessment; adolescent growth and development; nature and needs of the adolescent including social, emotional, and cultural concerns; classroom management strategies; school/family/community collaboration; or supervision and evaluation of programs and pupils in a middle school, semester hours in each of 2 areas.................................. 6
and

    e.   Course work in any of the following subjects: English as a second language/bilingualism or biculturalism; educational technology; tests and measurement; educational psychology; education of the exceptional child; multicultural education; or educational research, semester hours 6
and

  2. Credits in a major field of endorsement or area of concentration, semester hours.. 24

  B. Subsequent minor fields of endorsement may be added to the license upon verification of 14 semester hours of credit.

II. Endorsement areas: Art; English/language arts; foreign language (see Department of Education in Appendix 1 for specifics); mathematics; music; science; and social science

  A. Mathematics endorsement requires completion of 3 semester credits, to include a course in college algebra or concepts of calculus, including an introduction to limits, derivatives and integrals, precalculus, or differential calculus.

  B. Major or minor fields of endorsement or area of concentration shall be deemed to be met if applicant holds bachelor's degree or a higher degree with a major, minor, or area of concentration identified on official transcript of record conferred by regionally accredited college or university.

Secondary School

I. Authorization

  A. A license endorsed in a recognized teaching field is required for teaching in departmentalized seventh and eighth grades, junior high schools, senior high schools, and designated and approved middle schools. Endorsements are dependent upon the applicant's field of specialization or concentration, usually designated as majors or minors or areas of concentration.

II. Initial Secondary License Requirements
   A. Bachelor's degree and completion of an approved program of preparation for secondary school teaching,
     or
   B. Bachelor's degree and completion of the following:
     1. A teaching field major from a regionally accredited institution
     2. Secondary professional education, semester hours...................................... 22
       a. Supervised teaching and/or teaching internship....................................... 8
       b. A course in methods and materials of teaching in field of specialization.
       c. Check with Department of Education (see Appendix 1) for specific requirements in occupational education

III. Professional Secondary License Requirements
   A. Meet all requirements for Initial Secondary License
   B. Hold a master's degree
   C. Have 3 years of verified teaching experience in state-approved secondary schools

IV. Teaching Endorsements
   A. Academic endorsements: art, biological science, business, English as a second language, English, general science, mathematics (major/minor), music (major/minor in instrumental or instrumental and choral; major only in choral and vocal), physical education, physical education and health, physical science, recreational physical education, social studies, and speech and drama
   B. Occupational endorsements: agricultural education, automotive technology, business education, child care, commercial housekeeping, communications and media, construction technology, drafting and design, electronic technology, food services, health occupations, home economics, hospitality and recreation, housing and home furnishing, human services, industrial arts, manufacturing technology, marketing education, stage and theater technology, technology education
   C. Comprehensive fields of concentration
     1. Majors, semester hours 36
       a. Music major, semester hours... 36
     2. Minors, semester hours 24
   D. Single-subject majors and minors
     1. Majors, semester hours 30
     2. Minors, semester hours 16
     3. For complete list of academic and occupational single-subject majors or minors, see Department of Education Teacher Licensing website (see Appendix 1).

Special Education

Available endorsements include: adaptive physical education, audiology, autism, traumatic brain injury, early childhood developmentally delayed, serious emotional disturbances, generalist, gifted and talented, health impairments, hearing impaired, specific learning disabilities, mental retardation, orthopedic impairments, speech and language impairments, and visual impairments. Contact the Teacher Licensing Office (see Appendix 1) for more detailed information in this area.

Administration

I. Authorization
    A. A Professional Administrator of a School endorsement is required for the following: superintendent, associate superintendent, assistant superintendent, principal, vice principal, supervisor, administrative assistant, and program supervisor or coordinator
    B. A Professional Administrator of a Program endorsement is required for an individual who supervises or coordinates a program of nursing, school psychology, speech therapy, physical therapy, occupational therapy, or any other program area unless that person holds a Professional Administrator of a School endorsement.
    C. A Supervisor of Curriculum and Instruction endorsement is also issued.
II. Professional Administrator of a School Endorsement: meet requirements A or B below
    A. Complete the following:
        1. Master's degree
        2. Valid teaching license for elementary, secondary, or K–12 special
        3. Three years of verified teaching experience at the K–12 level in state-approved schools
        4. Thirty-six semester hours of graduate courses in school administration, to include: administration and organization of schools; supervision of instruction; development of personnel; school finance; school law; curriculum; educational research; internship or field experience in school administration; and other courses considered to be part of an administrative program for educators;
            or
    B. Hold a qualifying valid teaching license with the appropriate teaching experience (see II, A, directly above) and have a master's degree or higher in educational administration from an accredited institution
III. Professional Administrator of a Program Endorsement
    A. Hold a master's degree
    B. Hold a valid license in program for which endorsement is requested
    C. Have and submit to Department evidence of 3 years of experience as licensed employee in kindergarten or grades 1–12
    D. Have completed at least 27 semester hours in administration courses (which may not be taken as independent study), to include:
        1. Administration and organization of a school or the role of a program administrator in the applicant's endorsement area,
        2. General principles of supervision of personnel or supervision of personnel for a program in the applicant's endorsement area,
        3. Finances of a school or finances of a program in the applicant's endorsement area,
        4. The laws that apply to schools,
        5. The evaluation and development of personnel for a school or for a program in the applicant's endorsement area,
            and

6. Any other courses that are required for a degree in the administration of a program in the applicant's endorsement area.

School Counselor

I. Endorsement as a School Counselor
   A. Hold a master's degree or higher in school counseling from a regionally accredited college and/or university,
      or
   B. Hold a master's degree or higher from a regionally accredited college and/or university and a specialty credential as a national certified school counselor issued by the National Board for Certified Counselors,
      or
   C. Hold a master's degree or higher with a major in counseling from a regionally accredited college or university and fulfill requirements in I, E, 1 and 2, directly below,
      or
   D. Hold a master's degree or higher from a regionally accredited college or university and have at least 2 years of teaching experience, or at least 2 years of school counseling experience, and fulfill requirements in I, E, 1 and 2, directly below
   E. Complete the following:
      1. At least 600 hours of a practicum, internship, or field experience in school counseling at any grade level in grades K–12,
         and
      2. At least 36 semester hours of graduate credits in school guidance and counseling in the following areas of study
         a. The process of individual counseling
         b. The process of group counseling
         c. Testing and educational assessments
         d. Legal and ethical issues in counseling
         e. Career counseling
         f. Organization and administration of school counseling programs
         g. Multicultural counseling
         h. Child and family counseling,
            and
         i. Complete 2 of the following:
            i. The use of technology in education
            ii. Exceptional children
            iii. Human growth and development
            iv. Substance abuse counseling

Library Media Specialist

I. Endorsement as School Library Media Specialist, K–12
   A. Hold a valid elementary, secondary, or special teaching license, excluding a business and industry endorsement or a special qualification,

and

B. Complete a program for school library media specialists that has been approved by the board or a regional accrediting association,
   or

C. Hold a master's degree in library science, with specialization in school librarianship, from a school accredited by the American Library Association,
   or

D. Complete 21 semester hours of course work in the following subjects
   1. Organization and administration of a school library
   2. Cataloging and classification of materials for a library
   3. Reference, bibliography, and information skills
   4. Use and selection of educational media for a library
   5. Children's and young adults' literature
   6. Computers in the library
   7. A supervised practicum in an elementary or secondary school library

II. Endorsement as Professional School Library Media Specialist
   A. Hold a master's degree in any field,
   B. See I, A–C, directly above,
   C. Complete an additional 9 semester hours in curriculum and instruction, educational technology, or information technology,
      and
   D. Have 3 years of experience in state-approved schools or accredited private schools as a librarian or school library media specialist.

New Hampshire

Alternatives for Certification

I. General Requirements for Certification Alternatives 1–5, below
   A. This basic academic skills requirement applies to all five certification alternatives.
      1. Passing score on Praxis I Pre-Professional Skills Test or Computer-Based Test,
         or
         passing score on Praxis I composite score option,
         or
         equivalent test
      2. Exemptions: Ed 513.01 (b) (July 2003)
         a. Master's degree or higher,
            or
         b. Seven or more years of educational experience under a credential issued by another state
   B. This subject area assessment applies to all five certification alternatives.
      1. Passing score on Praxis II subject-specific tests for initial certification in art, Latin, English, French, German, Spanish, social studies, middle school science, life science, biology, chemistry, earth/space science, middle school mathematics, secondary mathematics, physical science, physics, elementary education, early childhood, middle school social studies, and middle school English
      2. See I, A, 2, a and b, above
   C. Criminal record check, which is conducted at the district level upon employment
II. Alternative 1—Approved Programs in New Hampshire
   A. New Hampshire State Department of Education–approved programs of professional preparation in education
   B. Certification for teachers, education specialists, and administrators
      1. Successful completion of the approved program
      2. Written recommendation by designated official of the institution
      3. Application to New Hampshire State Department of Education, Bureau of Credentialing
      4. Praxis I and Praxis II, if applicable
III. Alternative 2 has 2 distinct sets of requirements, known as Alternatives 2A and 2B.
   A. Alternative 2A concerns applicants from other states party to the National Association of State Directors of Teacher Education and Certification (NASDTEC) Interstate Contract and shall consist of the following:
      1. Individuals shall qualify for a beginning or experienced educator credential by:
         a. Completing a program in another state party to the NASDTEC Interstate Contract that would qualify the applicant for certification as an educator in the other state. This includes, but is not limited to, an alternative

certification program consistent with the terms of the NASDTEC Interstate
Contract with New Hampshire,
or

   b. Holding an equivalent, valid credential from such a state and having 3 years
of educational experience in the last 7 years under a credential from a
participating state

  2. Applicants seeking to obtain certification under Alternative 2A shall apply to
the Bureau of Credentialing pursuant to Ed 508.

B. Alternative 2B concerns applicants from states not signatory to the NASDTEC
Interstate Contract.

  1. Individuals from a state not party to the NASDTEC Interstate Contract shall
qualify for a beginning or experienced educator credential by:

    a. Completing a program in such a state that would qualify the applicant
for certification as an educator in that state, including but not limited to an
alternative certification program approved by the department of education
in such a state,
or

    b. Holding an equivalent, valid credential from such a state and having at least
3 years of experience as an educator in the last 7 years under a credential
issued by that state.

IV. Alternative 3—Demonstrated Competencies and Equivalent Experiences—has 3 distinct
sets of requirements, known as Alternatives 3A, 3B, and 3C.

A. Alternative 3A for Educators

  1. An applicant who has acquired competencies, skills, and knowledge through
means other than Alternatives 1 or 2 may request a credential by submitting to
the Bureau:

    a. A completed official application form,

    b. Official college or university transcripts verifying that the applicant holds a
bachelor's degree,
and

    c. A letter from an employer verifying completion of at least 3 months of
full-time experience in the area of the endorsement sought

  2. The Bureau shall evaluate the materials listed above to determine whether or not
the individual qualifies under this method.

    a. If not, the Bureau shall notify the individual within 15 days of its decision,
providing reasons for the determination and recommending another
appropriate application method, if applicable

    b. If so, the applicant shall attend on oral interview with a duly appointed
review board, which shall make a written recommendation to the
administrator whether or not to certify the applicant.

    c. If denied credentialing, the applicant may appeal the administrator's
decision.

B. Alternative 3B for National or Regional Certification

  1. An applicant eligible for a credential because of national or regional
examination results may submit an official application for certification along

with his or her examination scores to the Bureau with appropriate filing fees and accompanying documentation of:

    a.   A national-level or regional certification validated by passing a national or regional examination designed to assess the individual's skills in the area of certification sought,

        or

    b.   Proof of completion of a specialized program such as, but not limited to, a bachelor's degree in social work, culminating in a bachelor's degree from an accredited college or university.

C.   Alternative 3C for Administrators

    1.   Applicants for superintendent, principal, or special education administrator shall submit an official application for certification to enable the Bureau to determine by transcript analysis whether the applicant meets the appropriate program requirements:

        a.   For superintendent applicants, Ed 614.05

        b.   For principal applicants, Ed 614.04

        c.   For special education administrator applicants, Ed 506.07(d)

V.   Alternative 4—Critical Shortage Areas, Career & Technical Education, and Business Administrator

A.   Alternative 4 is a qualifying method for certification that requires:

    1.   Bachelor's degree from an approved institution,

    2.   Completion of a professional development plan in a critical shortage teaching area, career & technical education and/or business administration. New Hampshire Department of Education, Bureau of Credentialing website has a complete list of Critical Shortage areas (see Appendix 1),

    3.   Successful teaching under a mentor teacher,

        and

    4.   Recommendation for certification from the local Superintendent of Schools.

B.   An applicant may be employed as an educator after obtaining a statement of eligibility from the Bureau of Credentialing (see Appendix 1) and while completing an approved individualized professional development plan.

C.   Applicant who holds a Statement of Eligibility may be hired by a Superintendent or agency head to pursue Alternative IV. This document is not a teaching certificate. Exemptions to the basic academic skills requirement include:

    1.   Master's degree or higher,

    2.   Seven or more years of educational experience under a credential issued by another state,

        or

    3.   New Hampshire certification in another content area.

VI.   Alternative 5—Site-Based Certification Plan

A.   Available in elementary and secondary teaching areas, excluding career technical and special education

B.   Qualifications

    1.   A bachelor's degree from an approved institution

2. The applicant shall meet one of the following criteria:
   a. For secondary education, at least 30 credit hours in the subject to be taught and an overall grade-point average of at least 2.5, or equivalent
   b. For elementary education, successful completion of courses in mathematics, English, social studies, and science with an overall grade-point average of at least 2.5, or equivalent
3. An individual who fails to meet the grade-point average requirement shall still qualify for site-based certification plan provided that:
   a. All other requirements are met,
   b. Collegiate graduation occurred more than 5 years prior to application for the site-based plan,
      and
   c. Occupational experience totaling 5 years directly related to the area to be taught is documented by letter from previous employers; employment contracts; or letters of commendation and recommendations from parties knowledgeable about the applicant's backround and experience.
C. Candidates must complete a specifically designed site-based educational plan, normally during the first 1 to 2 years of service.

Levels of Professional Certification

I. Beginning Educator Certificate (valid 3 years)
   A. Successful completion of an approved program of professional preparation in education
   B. Recommendation by designated official of preparatory institution
   C. Upon recommendation of Superintendent of Schools, a beginning educator may be eligible for Experienced Educator Certificate at the close of the 3-year period.
II. Experienced Educator Certificate (valid 3 years)
   A. Has met all requirements for previous levels of certification
III. Educator Recertification
   A. Every educator applying for credential renewal must acquire all of the following:
      1. A minimum of 75 hours of approved professional development activity every 3 years
      2. A minimum of 45 hours of the total hours required shall be devoted to approved professional development activities meeting district needs, school goals, and/or school improvement plans.
      3. A minimum of 30 hours of the total hours required shall be devoted to approved professional development activity in each subject area and/or field of specialization for which recertification is sought.
      4. For each endorsement, an additional 30 hours shall be devoted to approved professional development activity in each subject area and/or field of specialization.

New Jersey

Applicants are strongly advised to consult the New Jersey Licensing Code, available at http://www.state.nj.us/education/educators/license/, for specific eligibility requirements for obtaining certificates.

Certification Overview

I. New Jersey certificates are issued under 4 categories; for detailed listings of the many certificates and specific requirements for them, go to http://www.state.nj.us/education/educators/license/
    A. Teacher certificates for classroom teachers
    B. Educational Services Personnel certificates for such positions as school social worker, school psychologist, learning disabilities teacher-consultant, substance awareness coordinator, etc.
    C. School Leaders certificates for school administrator, principal, supervisor, and school business administrator
    D. Career and Technical Education certificates for positions such as automotive technology, carpentry, cosmetology/hair styling, plumbing, etc.
    E. In addition, the following certificates may be issued when the appropriate requirements have been satisfied:
        1. Emergency Certificate: a substandard 1-year license issued only in limited fields of educational services
        2. County Substitute Credential: a temporary certificate issued by the county office which allows the holder to temporarily perform the duties of a fully licensed and regularly employed teacher when none is available
II. Endorsement and Highly Qualified Status
    A. An endorsement is an area of certification with distinct grade-level and subject matter authorizations in which a certificate holder is authorized to serve.
    B. Although an endorsement authorizes the holder to teach in the area of their endorsement, the individual must also meet the highly qualified requirements required by the federal government. For further information on meeting the highly qualified requirements, go to http://www.nj.gov/education/profdev/nclb/
III. Certification Process for Novice Educators
    A. Certificate of Eligibility (CE): for applicants who did not complete a teacher preparation program. Requirements:
        1. Hold bachelor's or advanced degree from regionally accredited college or university
        2. Students graduating on or after September 1, 2004, must achieve cumulative minimum GPA of 2.75 (when 4.00 GPA equals an A grade) in baccalaureate, higher degree, or state-approved post-baccalaureate certification program with at least 13 semester-hour credits

      a.   For students graduating before September 1, 2004, same requirements apply except minimum GPA is 2.50

3.   For subject area endorsements, complete at least 30 credits in coherent course sequence appropriate to instructional area (at least 12 of such semester-hour credits must be at advanced level, including junior-, senior-, or graduate-level study)

      a.   For elementary school endorsement, complete liberal arts, science, dual content, or interdisciplinary academic major, or minimum of 60 semester hour credits in liberal arts and/or science

4.   All course work must appear on transcript of regionally accredited 2- or 4-year college or university

5.   Pass appropriate state test of subject matter knowledge; and

6.   Pass examination in physiology, hygiene, and substance abuse issues

7.   Elementary school (K–5) CE, Instructional Area CE, or Preschool through Grade Three CE

      a.   Effective October 31, 2009, candidates for the Elementary school (K–5) CE or Instructional Area CE must demonstrate knowledge of basic pedagogical skills appropriate to the area of endorsement through transcripts showing successful completion of a minimum of 24 hours of study offered through a state-approved provider or through approved course work at a New Jersey state-approved college.

          i.   Exceptions: Holders of a CEAS, provisional, or standard certificate in another instructional area are exempt from this requirement.

      b.   Effective September 1, 2009, candidates for the Preschool through Grade Three CE must also follow procedures described directly above in 7, a, i.

B.   Certificate of Eligibility with Advanced Standing (CEAS): for applicants who did complete a teacher preparation program. Requirement:

1.   The candidate shall meet the requirements in I, A, 1–7, directly above and complete one of the following programs of teacher preparation:

      a.   A New Jersey college program, graduate or undergraduate, approved by the Department for the preparation of teachers;

      b.   A college preparation program included in the interstate certification reciprocity system of the National Association of State Directors of Teacher Education and Certification (NASDTEC);

      c.   An out-of-state teacher education program approved by the National Council for the Accreditation of Teacher Education (NCATE), Teacher Education Accreditation Council (TEAC), or any other national professional education accreditation body recognized by the Council on Higher Education Accreditation approved by the Commissioner;

      d.   A teacher education program approved for certification by the Department in one of the states party to the NASDTEC Interstate Contract, provided the program was completed on or after January 1, 1964, and the state in which the program is located would issue the candidate a comparable endorsement;

      or

        e.   An out-of-state college teacher education program approved by the state department of education in which the program is located.

    2.   The teacher preparation programs listed in I, B, 1, a–e, directly above must culminate in college supervised student teaching.

    3.   A candidate who graduates on or after September 1, 2004, will meet the requirements in I, B, 1, a–e directly above if they fall within the parameters in 3, a and b, directly below. For details, consult http://www.state.nj.us/education/educators/license/gpa.htm

        a.   A GPA that is below 2.75, but at least 2.50 and whose score in the appropriate state test of subject matter knowledge exceeds the passing score by 10 percent or more;

            or

        b.   A GPA that is 3.50 or higher, but whose score in the appropriate State test of subject matter knowledge falls below the passing score by no more than five percent.

C.   Standard Certificate: for applicants who have at least 1 year of full-time teaching experience under a valid out-of-state license and have completed a full-time teacher preparation program that included student teaching. Requirements:

    1.   Possess a provisional certificate;

        and

    2.   Successfully complete a state-approved district training program while employed provisionally in a position requiring the appropriate instructional certificate.

    3.   Further eligibilities and their restrictions are available at http://www.state.nj.us/education/educators/license/

    4.   A candidate who holds National Board professional Teacher Standards (NBPTS) certification and the corresponding out-of-state license or out-of-state certificate shall be eligible for the standard certificate in the NBPTS certificate field without additional requirements.

    5.   Completion of an out-of-state non-traditional or alternate route teacher preparation program that is determined by the Department to be comparable to the state's school-based training and evaluation program provided to all New Jersey novice teachers;

        and

    A valid standard certificate from the state in which the above was completed.

IV. Provisional Teacher Program

A.   School-based training and evaluation program provided to all novice teachers during first year of New Jersey teaching

B.   Building principal recommends standard certification at completion of program requirements

C.   Both alternatively and traditionally prepared teacher candidates participate and receive support by veteran teachers in their school. Contact Department of Education (see Appendix 1) for full details.

D.   Alternate route candidates complete 200 hours of formal instruction in professional education aligned with New Jersey Professional Standards for Teachers.

V.   Interstate Reciprocity
   A.   Any applicant who presents a valid instructional certificate issued by any other state shall, upon payment of the appropriate fee, be issued a New Jersey instructional certificate for the equivalent and currently issued New Jersey grade level or subject endorsement and certificate level; i.e., certificate of eligibility, certificate of eligibility with advanced standing, or standard certificate.
   B.   If there is no equivalent current New Jersey endorsement, then the provisions of the New Jersey Administrative Code 6A:9-8.1 through 8.8 shall apply to the applicant (see website for details), with two limitations:
      1.   For equivalent endorsements with required subject matter tests, if the applicant has not passed a state subject matter test to receive the other state's endorsement, the applicant must pass the appropriate New Jersey subject matter test;
         and
      2.   Candidates who have not taught successfully for 3 years under their out-of-state certificate shall be required to meet the New Jersey grade-point average requirement.
         a.   Successful teaching experience shall be documented by a letter of experience from the applicant's supervisor or authorized district representative.

Educational Services Certification

New Jersey issues 21 educational service endorsements, including school psychologist, school nurse, school social worker, and speech-language specialist. For a full listing of available endorsements, authorizations, and related requirements, see the New, Jersey Department of Education website: http://www.nj.gov/njded/code/current/title6a/chap9.pdf, beginning on page 79.

Administrator Certification

I.   Standard Certificate for Principal, School Administrator, or School Business Administrator
   A.   Candidate must:
      1.   Complete advanced degree in one of recognized fields of leadership or management, or in curriculum and instruction, including study area requirements
         a.   School business administrator certificate requires either a master's degree or a certified public accountant license.
      2.   Pass written examination
         a.   School Leaders Licensure Assessment for principal; and School Superintendent Assessment for school administrator
      3.   Apply for Certificate of Eligibility (CE)
   B.   When candidate obtains position requiring principal, school administrator, or school business administrator certification, school district must
      1.   Register candidate into Administrator Training Program (2 years in length)

        2.   Send Statement of Assurance of Position and Standard Residency Agreement to initiate residency period

  C. When mentor is assigned to candidate, a training program is developed by district, mentor, and candidate, subject to Department of Education approval. A provisional certificate (valid 2 years) is then issued to candidate.

  D. Upon satisfactory completion of residency (candidate is evaluated 3 times) and recommendation of mentor, State Board of Examiners may issue standard certificate.

II.   Standard Certificate for Supervisor

  A. Three years of full-time teaching or educational services experience

  B. Valid New Jersey instructional or educational services certificate or out-of-state equivalent

  C. Master's degree from regionally accredited college or university

  D. Twelve graduate credits in supervision and curriculum development, to include the following:

      1.   A course in general staff supervision for grades PK–12

      2.   A course in general curriculum development for grades PK–12

      3.   An elective course in curriculum development

      4.   An elective course in either curriculum development or staff supervision

III. For more detailed information on available administrative endorsements, authorizations, and related requirements, see the New Jersey Department of Education website: http://www.nj.gov/njded/code/current/title6a/chap9.pdf, beginning on page 67

IV. For administrative certification application information, see Certification Application Process, I–III, above

New Mexico

Licensure Levels and Requirements for Advancement

I. Level 1 License (valid 5 years; nonrenewable)
   A. Issued to applicants meeting all requirements with less than 3 years of verifiable teaching experience.
      1. To teach in a core academic area (fine arts, language arts, mathematics, modern and classical languages, reading, sciences, social studies), applicants must hold a bachelor's degree, pass all required licensure tests, and earn full state licensure; no waivers are permitted.
      2. To teach in a noncore area, applicants must hold a bachelor's degree and pass all required licensure tests—waivers may be permitted.
      3. To teach in a career and technical area, applicants must hold a bachelor's degree or have relevant work experience. Tests are not required, and waivers may be permitted.
   B. During the period of Level 1 licensure, educators will receive mentorship services; they also must:
      1. With principal at the beginning of each school year, develop a Professional Development Plan (PDP) based on New Mexico's 9 teacher competencies and differentiated indicators for Level 1 licensure
      2. Be assessed annually on PDP and 9 teacher competencies by principal
      3. For those teaching in core academic areas, be "highly qualified" (programs/no-child-left-behind.html) for their teaching assignment(s) each year.
   C. To remain in the teaching profession in New Mexico, a Level 1 teacher must advance to Level 2 at a time after the third year of experience and before the end of the fifth year of experience at Level 1. Requirements include:
      1. Complete an approved mentoring program;
      2. Complete 3 complete academic years of teaching at Level l; *and*
      3. Demonstrate increased teaching competencies required for Level 2 by submitting Professional Development Dossier (PDD) to the Publication Education Department. Consult http://teachnm.org/programs/3-tiered-licensure-system/3-tls-overview.html for required components of the PDD.
II. Level 2 License (valid 9 years)
   A. Issued to applicants meeting all requirements with 3 to 5 years of verifiable teaching experience.
   B. As a Level 2 educator, a teacher must:
      1. See I, B, 1–3, except for differentiated indicators for Level 2 licensure
      2. Teachers may choose to remain at Level 2 for the remainder of their teaching careers by renewing this license every 9 years: advancement to Level 3A is optional.

a.   Superintendent must verify that teacher meets the competencies and indicators for Level 2 and recommend that license be renewed.

C.   To advance to Level 3A (Instructional Leader), teacher must:

1.   Earn a master's degree; or earn National Board for Professional Teaching Standards (NBPTS) certification (experienced-teachers/national-board-certification.html);

2.   Complete at least 3 academic years of teaching at Level 2;

3.   Demonstrate the 9 teacher competencies and differentiated indicators required for Level 3A by submitting PDD to the Public Education Department. Consult http://teachnm.org/programs/3-tiered-licensure-system/3-tls-overview.html for required components of the PDD;
     and

4.   Level 3A teachers who teach in core academic areas must be "highly qualified" (programs/no-child-left-behind.html) for their teaching assignment(s) each year.

5.   See B, 2, a, directly above, except for Level 3A.

III.   Level 3A License (valid 9 years)

A.   Issued to applicants meeting all requirements with 6 or more years of verifiable experience and a master's degree.

IV.   Level 3B Administrative License (valid 9 years)

A.   Hold a bachelor's or master's degree;

B.   Complete an approved educational administration program;

C.   Hold a Level 3A teaching license;
     and

D.   Pass the Education Administrator Assessment.

Licenses

I.   Level 1 Elementary License (valid 5 years)

A.   Requirements

1.   Bachelor's degree from a regionally accredited college or university;
     and

2.   Minimum of 30–36 semester hours in an elementary education program including student teaching;
     and

3.   6 semester hours of credit in the teaching of reading for those who first entered any college or university on or after August 1, 2001;
     and

4.   Minimum of 24 semester hours in one teaching field, such as mathematics, science, language arts, etc.;
     and

5.   Passage of the New Mexico Teacher Assessments (NMTA)

a.   Basic Skills

b.   Teacher Competency, Elementary

c.   Content Knowledge Assessment in Elementary Education;

6. Pass the National Evaluation Systems assessment in Essential Components of Elementary Reading Instruction
   or
7. Possess a certificate issued by the National Board for Professional Teaching Standards.

II. Level 1 Middle Level Education, Grades 5–9 (valid 5 years)
   A. This license authorizes individuals to teach in a departmentalized setting.
      1. Individuals must be endorsed in the subject they are teaching.
   B. Requirements for Option I:
      1. Bachelor's degree from a regionally accredited college or university;
         and
      2. Minimum of 30–36 semester hours in a middle level education program, including student teaching
         and
      3. 3 semester hours of credit in teaching reading for those who first entered any college or university on or after August 1, 2001;
         and
      4. Minimum of 24 semester hours in at least one teaching field such as mathematics, science, language arts, etc., with 12 of those hours earned at the upper division level (300 and above);
         and
      5. Passage of the New Mexico Teacher Assessments;
         a. Basic Skills
         b. Teacher Competency, Elementary or Secondary
         c. Content Knowledge Assessment in the teaching field
   C. Requirements for Option II:
      1. Possess a New Mexico elementary, secondary, preK–12 specialty, or special education license;
         and
      2. Provide verification of 5 years of successful teaching experience at the middle school level;
         and
      3. Complete a minimum of 24 semester hours of credit in each subject the teacher teaches, 6 of which must be upper-division credit;
         and
      4. Pass the NMTA in each subject the teacher teaches
         or
      5. Possess a certificate issued by the National Board for Professional Teaching Standards.

III. Level 1 Secondary Education, Grades 7–12 (valid 5 years)
   A. This license authorizes individuals to teach in a departmentalized setting.
      1. Individuals must be endorsed in the subject they are teaching.
   B. Requirements
      1. Bachelor's degree from a regionally accredited college or university;
         and

2. Minimum of 24 semester hours in a secondary education program, to include student teaching;
    and

3. Three semester hours of credit in teaching reading for those who first entered college or university on or after August 1, 2001;
    and

4. Minimum of 24 semester hours in at least one teaching field, such as mathematics, science, language arts, etc., with 12 of those hours earned at the upper division level (300 and above);
    and

5. Passage of the New Mexico Teacher Assessments;
    a. Basic Skills
    b. Teacher Competency, Secondary
    c. Content Knowledge Assessment in the teaching field
        or

6. Possess a certificate issued by the National Board for Professional Teaching Standards.

IV. Level 3B Educational Administration, PreK–12 Program (valid 9 years)

A. Bachelor's and master's degree from a regionally accredited college or university;
    and

B. Minimum of 18 semester hours of graduate credit in an educational administration program;
    and

C. Completion of an administrative apprenticeship/internship at a college/university, or under the supervision of a local superintendent;
    and

D. Hold a Level 3A New Mexico teaching license;
    and

E. Passage of the New Mexico Teacher Assessment
    1. Content Knowledge Assessment in Educational Administration.

V. Approved licenses. For comprehensive requirements for each license not detailed above, consult http://www.ped.state.nm.us/licensure

A. Administrators
    1. Education administration, PreK–12

B. Teachers
    1. Blind and visually impaired, B–12; early childhood, birth–grade 3; elementary, K–8; middle level, 5–9; PreK–12 specialty; secondary, 7–12; secondary vocational-technical, 7–12; special education, PreK–12

C. Instructional Support Providers (PreK–12 unless otherwise noted)
    1. Alcohol, drug, and substance abuse counselor; certified occupational therapy assistant; educational diagnostician; interpreter for the deaf; licensed practical nurse; occupational therapist; orientation and mobility specialist; physical therapist; physical therapist assistant; recreational therapist; rehabilitation counselor; school counselor; school nurse; school psychologist; school social worker; speech language pathologist

    D.   Support providers (PreK–12 unless otherwise noted)
        1.   Athletic coaching, 7–12; educational assistant; health assistant; substitute teacher

VI. Alternative Licenses. For comprehensive requirements, consult http://www.ped.state .nm.us/licensure
    A.   Administrators
        1.   Post-secondary experienced alternative administrator, PreK–12
    B.   Teachers
        1.   Early childhood, Birth–Grade 3
        2.   Elementary, K–8
        3.   Middle level, 5–9
        4.   PreK–12 specialty
        5.   Secondary, 7–12
        6.   Special education

Reciprocity for Teaching Licenses

I. Reciprocity Requirements
    A.   Possess a bachelor's and/or a master's degree from a regionally accredited college or university;
    B.   Possess a current valid and standard certificate/license from another state/country;
    C.   Provide proof of having completed an approved teacher education program for that state/country;
    D.   Provide proof of passage of a teacher competency examination for the out-of-state/country certificate/license;
        and
    E.   Provide evidence of having satisfactorily taught under that out-of-state certificate/license.

New York

Recent Certification Requirements Changes and Updates

I. Certification Examinations
 A. New examinations are required for all candidates who apply for certification on or after May 1, 2014; or for candidates who apply for certification on or before April 30, 2014, but do not meet all the requirements for an initial certificate on or before April 30, 2014.
  1. New examinations include the Academic Literacy Skills Test (ALST), the Educating All Students (EAS) test, the Teacher Performance Assessment (edTPA), and the School Building Leader (SBL) performance assessment, as well as revisions to the Content Specialty Tests (CSTs).
 B. Requirements changes for Initial Certificates in Career and Technical Education (CTE) Fields—Option A and B Pathways
  1. The Board eliminated the requirement for candidates to complete the edTPA for initial certification and instead requires a performance assessment for CTE teachers seeking their professional certification when it becomes available.
 C. Professional School District Leader Certificate Requirements Changes
  1. The Board now requires a candidate who applies for a professional School District Leader certificate on or after May 1, 2015, to pass the Educating All Students examination.
   a. In addition, any candidate applying for a School District Leader certificate under the endorsement pathway on or after October 2, 2013, shall achieve a satisfactory level of performance on the School District Leader examination.
   b. Candidates applying for a School District Leader certificate on or after May 1, 2014, or candidates applying for certification on or before April 30, 2014, but who do not meet all the requirements for a professional certificate on April 30, 2014, shall submit evidence of having achieved a satisfactory level of performance on the Educating All Students examination.
 D. Requirements Changes for Initial Certification in Education Technology Specialist
  1. Candidates for the Education Technology Specialist must complete a practicum, rather than student teaching. The proposed amendment removes the edTPA requirement for these candidates.
 E. Requirements Changes for Initial certification of Speech and Language Disabilities
  1. Candidates applying for certification on or after May 1, 2014, or candidates who applied for certification on or before April 30, 2014, but who did not meet all of the requirements for an initial certificate on or before April 30, 2014, no longer must pass the edTPA. These candidates are still required to pass the Speech and Language Pathology (PRAXIS) examination, which is also required for a professional license as a Speech and Language Pathologist.

II. Dignity for All Students Act (DASA) Training Information for Applicants for Certification
   A. Effective December 31, 2013, all applicants for certification are required to complete 6 clock hours of course work or training in accordance with Article 2 Sections 10–18 of the Education Law.

Types of Certificates

I. Initial Certificate (valid 5 years; nonrenewable; leads to Professional Certificate)
   A. Entry-level certificate issued in specific subject/grade titles for classroom teaching and school building leaders
II. Professional Certificate (valid continuously with completion of required professional development hours every 5 years)
   A. Advanced-level certificate issued in specific subject/grade titles for classroom teaching and school building leaders.
III. Provisional Certificate (valid 5 years; nonrenewable)
   A. Entry-level certificate for pupil personnel professionals, issued in specific subject/grade titles
IV. Permanent Certificate (valid for life, unless revoked for cause)
   A. Advanced-level certificate for pupil personnel professionals, as well as for classroom teachers and school administrators who hold a valid Provisional certificate

Preparation Pathways

This overview is a general description only; for information on requirements for specific areas of interest; subject areas; grade levels; titles; and types of certificate, consult http://eservices.nysed .gov/teach/certhelp/CertRequirementHelp.do

I. High School Graduates
   A. General Requirements
      1. Approved Teacher Preparation Program
         a. Earn a bachelor's degree and complete a traditional teacher preparation program at a college or university in New York State; upon graduation, the institution of higher education recommends candidates for certification;
            or
            Earn a bachelor's degree and complete a traditional teacher preparation program at a college or university in another state with a reciprocity agreement with New York State; upon graduation, candidates apply directly to the State Education Department under the Interstate Reciprocity pathway;
            and
      2. Pass the New York State Liberal Arts and Sciences Test (LAST), the Assessment of Teaching Skills-Written (ATS-W), and the appropriate Content Specialty Test(s) (CST).
II. College Graduates
   A. General Requirements

    1.   Approved Teacher Preparation Program

        a.   Possess a bachelor's degree and complete a graduate program at a college or university in New York State leading to a first teaching certificate, usually including an internship in a K–12 school; upon graduation, the institution recommends candidates for certification;
and

        b.   Pass the New York State Liberal Arts and Sciences Test (LAST), the Assessment of Teaching Skills-Written (ATS-W), and the appropriate Content Specialty Test(s) (CST).

III.   Career Changers, Persons Educated Outside the United States, and Persons Not Graduated from a Teaching Program

    A. General Requirements

        1.   Earn a bachelor's degree with a grade-point average (GPA) of at least 2.5;

        2.   Satisfy semester hour requirements and meet specific liberal arts and sciences general core, content core, and pedagogical core competencies for the certificate title sought;

        3.   Pass the New York State Liberal Arts and Sciences Test (LAST), the Assessment of Teaching Skills-Written (ATS-W), and the appropriate Content Specialty Test(s) (CST); and

        4.   Apply for a certificate to the New York State Education Department (NYSED) Office of Teaching Initiatives.

IV.   Career Changers, College Graduates

    A. General Requirements

        1.   Approved Teacher Preparation Program, (Alternative Certification "Transitional B" Program)

          a.   Possess a bachelor's degree (minimum 3.0 GPA) with a major in the subject to be taught, or 18 semester hours in the subject to be taught with 12 semester hours in a related subject;

          b.   Enroll in one of the Alternative Teacher Certification (ATC) Programs offered by college-school partnerships in various locations throughout New York State to complete teacher education study; upon completion of the alternative program, candidates are recommended for certification by the college or university;

          c.   Pass the New York State Liberal Arts and Sciences Test (LAST) and the appropriate Content Specialty Test(s) (CST);
and

          d.   Once the program and additional required course work are completed, and the candidate passes the Assessment of Teaching Skills-Written (ATS-W), the college will recommend candidate for a certificate.

V.   National Board Certified Teachers

    A. General Requirements

        1.   Apply to the NYSED Office of Teaching Initiatives for a certificate in a title comparable to National Board certificate.

VI.   Certified Teachers from Other States

    A. General Requirements

1. Apply for a certificate to the NYSED Office of Teaching Initiatives through Interstate Reciprocity;
   and
2. Pass the New York State Liberal Arts and Sciences Test (LAST), the Assessment of Teaching Skills-Written (ATS-W), and the appropriate Content Specialty Test (CST).
   a. Candidates may receive a conditional certificate, which allows them 2 years to satisfy the testing requirement.

VII. New York State Teachers Seeking Additional Certificate
   A. General Requirements
      1. Possess a valid New York State classroom teaching certificate;
      2. Satisfy the 30 semester hour content core requirements for the certificate title sought;
         a. Some certificates require additional pedagogy as well.
      3. Apply for a Certificate to the NYSED Office of Teaching Initiatives through Individual Evaluation for Additional Certificate;
         and
      4. Pass the appropriate New York State Content Specialty Test(s) (CST).
         a. If candidate's first certificate was issued as the result of completing an approved program or a professional license, candidate must submit official transcripts of all completed course work from all colleges attended.

VIII. New York State Certified Teachers Seeking to Teach Another Subject While Completing Requirements for the Certificate
   A. General Requirements
      1. Possess a valid New York State classroom teaching certificate;
      2. Satisfy the 12 semester hour content core requirements for the certificate title sought;
      3. Obtain a recommendation from the employing school district;
      4. Apply for a Certificate to the NYSED Office of Teaching Initiatives through Individual Evaluation for Supplementary Certificate;
         and
      5. Pass the appropriate New York State Content Specialty Test(s) (CST).

IX. New York State Licensed Speech Language Pathologists
   A. General Requirements
      1. Hold a New York State speech language pathology license;
         and
      2. Apply for a certificate to the NYSED Office of Teaching Initiatives.

X. College Professors with a Master's or Higher Degree and Two Years of Teaching Experience in Mathematics or One of the Sciences at the College Level
   A. General Requirements for science, technology, engineering, and mathematics (STEM)
      1. Possess a master's or higher degree in mathematics or one of the sciences;
      2. Two years of satisfactory teaching experience at the college level;
         and
      3. Pass the appropriate New York State Teacher Certification exam(s) to become certified as a secondary classroom teacher.

North Carolina

Licensure Categories

I. Standard Professional 1 (SP1) [intended for teachers with 0–2 years of teaching experience; valid 3 years]. Applicant must have:
- A. Completed a state-approved teacher education program from a regionally accredited college or university

  or

  Completed another state's approved alternative route to licensure,

  and
- B. Met the federal requirements to be designated as "Highly Qualified" and earned a bachelor's degree from a regionally accredited college.

II. Standard Professional 2 (SP2) [intended for teachers with 3 or more years of teaching experience; valid 5 years]
- A. License is issued to teachers who have 3 or more years of teaching experience in another state and who are fully licensed and "Highly Qualified" in another state,

  and
  1. Who meet North Carolina's Praxis testing requirements (consult http://www.NCPublicSchools.org/licensure)

     or
  2. Who have certification from the National Board for Professional Teaching Standards (NBPTS).

III. Lateral Entry Provisional Licenses (valid 3 years)
- A. Issued to an individual who is employed in a North Carolina public school system and who affiliates with a college or university with an approved teacher education program in the license area or with one of the Regional Alternative Licensing Centers in North Carolina.
  1. An individual plan of study is prescribed for the lateral entry teacher
- B. Applicants must hold at least a bachelor's degree from a regionally accredited institution,

  and
  1. One of the following:
     - a. Bachelor's degree or higher that is relevant to the subject being taught;

       or
     - b. 24 semester hours of course work in core area with the following exceptions:
       - i. Elementary Education or Exceptional Children (Teacher of Record) requires prior to employment a passing score on the Praxis II subject assessment; and at least a bachelor's degree
       - ii. English as a Second Language requires a degree in English, *or* 24 semester hours in English, *or* linguistics, *or* a passing score on the Praxis II subject assessment

or

    c. Passing score on the Praxis II subject assessment test(s) for the area of license;

        or

    d. For world languages except English, passing score on the American Council on the Teaching of Foreign Languages (ACTFL) examination;

        and

  2. One of the following:

    a. 2.5 GPA or above;

        or

    b. At least 5 years of experience considered relevant by the employing Local Education Agency (LEA);

        or

    c. Passing score on the Praxis I, *or* a total SAT score of 1100, *or* a total ACT score of 24, *plus* 1 of the following:

        i. GPA of 3.0 in the major field of study,

           or

        ii. GPA of 3.0 in all courses in senior year,

           or

        iii. GPA of 3.0 on a minimum of 15 semester hours of courses completed within the last 5 years after the bachelor's degree or higher.

C. Lateral Entry License holders must complete at least 6 semester hours of course work each year and satisfy Praxis II testing requirements.

Licensure Renewal

I. Standard Professional 2 (SP2) licenses must be renewed every 5 years.

II. Requirements to renew the Standard Professional 2 (SP2) license:

  A. Professional Educators

    1. 1 renewal credit each for literacy and in the specific academic subject area; and 5.5 general credits (as determined by the LEA, if employed), not to include years of experience

  B. Administrators

    1. 3 credits focused on the school executive's role as instructional, human resources, and managerial leader; and 4.5 general credits (as determined by the LEA, if employed), not to include years of experience

  C. National Board for Professional Teaching Standards (NBPTS) Certification

    1. 7.5 credits for completion; and 2 credits (1 for literacy and 1 for content) for 10-year renewal

III. Renewal Credits

  A. Definition and equivalencies

    1. 1 unit of renewal credit is equivalent to one quarter hour or one in-service credit from a North Carolina public school system.

    2. Generally, a unit reflects ten contact hours.

    3. 1 semester hour is equivalent to 1.5 units of credit.

B. Exclusions and Restrictions
1. The Department of Public Instruction (DPI) Licensure Section does not accept renewal credits of less than one unit.
2. For a professional educator's license to remain current, all credit must be earned by the expiration date of the existing professional educator's license.
3. To renew an expired professional educator's license, 10 semester hours or 15 units of renewal credit must be earned within the most recent 5-year period.

III. Activities accepted for renewal credit
A. College or university courses
1. Transcripts are required as documentation; grade reports are not accepted.
B. Local in-service courses or workshops
1. The administrative unit certifies credits
C. Classes and workshops approved by a Local Education Agency (LEA)
1. Documentation of completion is provided by the agency sponsoring the activity.

Administrators/Special Service Personnel

I. Requirements for administrators, special services, and instructional support personnel
A. Obtain a valid Standard Professional 2 (SP2) License
B. Student services personnel who have completed an approved preparation program *and*
1. Have satisfied North Carolina's testing requirements are issued an SP2 license
2. Have not satisfied North Carolina's testing requirements are issued an SP1 license
a. When North Carolina's testing requirements are satisfied, the license is converted to an SP2.
C. Student services personnel who are fully licensed in another state will be issued the SP2 license when they:
1. Meet North Carolina's Praxis testing requirements,
or
Earn National Board certification;
or
2. After 1 year of satisfactory student services experience in North Carolina and with 3 or more years of student services school experience in another state, the employing LEA recommends licensure and verifies an offer of reemployment, which the individual is not required to accept.

License Areas and Requirements

I. School Administrator—Superintendent
A. Eligibility to serve as a superintendent must be verified by the State Board of Education prior to election by a local board of education
B. Minimum of 1 year of experience (or the equivalent) as a principal
C. Advanced graduate level (6th-year degree) in school administration
or

    D.   At least a bachelor's degree from a regionally accredited college or university and 5 years of leadership or managerial experience considered relevant by the employing local board of education.

  II.   School Administrator—Principal

    A.   Completion of an approved program in school administration at the master's level or above

    B.   No provisional principal license is issued for service as a principal

  III.   School Administrator—Assistant Principal

    A.   Completion of an approved program in school administration at the master's level or above

    B.   Provisional principal license is issued for service as an assistant principal if the local board determines there is a shortage of individuals with principal licensure

    C.   Affiliation with a master's school administrator program must occur before the expiration of the provisional license. Provisional principal licenses can be extended for up to 2 additional school years, during which time program requirements must be completed.

  IV.   Curriculum Instructional Specialist

    A.   Completion of an approved program for a curriculum instructional specialist at the master's degree level or above

    B.   NTE/Praxis Educational Leadership: Administrative and Supervision required score

  V.   Career-Technical Director

    A.   Completion of an approved program for a career-technical education director at the master's level or above

  VI.   Exceptional Children Program Administrator (licensure is a supervisory classification)

    A.   Master's degree in an exceptional children area or an advanced (6th-year) degree in school psychology,
and
Three graduate semester hours of credit in each of the following:

      1.   Administration

      2.   Curriculum development

      3.   Supervision,
and
NTE/Praxis Educational Leadership: Administrative and Supervision required score;
or

    B.   A master's degree in administration and/or curriculum instruction,
and
Nine semester hours of course work in exceptional children,
and
NTE/Praxis Educational Leadership: Administrative and Supervision required score.

  VII.   Instructional Technology Specialist — Computers

    A.   Completion of a college or university program at the master's level or above

  VIII.   Instructional Technology Specialist — Telecommunications

    A.   Completion of a college or university program at the master's level or above

IX. Media Supervisor
    A. Master's degree in school media
    B. Three graduate semester hours in each of the following:
        1. Administration
        2. Curriculum development
        3. Supervision

X. Media Coordinator
    A. One of the following:
        1. Completion of an approved program for a media coordinator at the master's degree level or above
        2. Completion of an approved program after July 1, 1984, allows a provisional license upon employment with requirement to update to master's degree level
        3. Obtain a provisional media coordinator license; consult www.ncpublicschools .org/licensure/administrator

XI. School Counselor
    A. Completion of an approved program in school counseling at the master's level or above
    B. NTE/Praxis Professional School Counselor test required score

XII. School Social Worker
    A. Completion of an approved program in school social work at the bachelor's level or above

XIII. School Psychologist
    A. Completion of an approved program in school psychology at the sixth-year level
    B. NTE/Praxis School Psychology required score

XIV. School Speech-Language Pathologist
    A. Current valid North Carolina Board of Examiners for Speech and Language Pathologists and Audiologists (NCBOESLPA) license

XV. School Audiologist
    A. One of the following:
        1. Audiology Certificate of Clinical Competence (CCC-A) from the American Speech-Language-Hearing Association
            or
        2. License from the North Carolina Board of Examiners for Speech and Language Pathologist and Audiologist
            or
        3. Completion of an approved program in audiology at the master's level or above.
    B. NTE/Praxis Audiology required score

North Dakota

Types of Licenses

I. North Dakota Century Code Authority
   A. Individual must hold valid North Dakota license issued by the North Dakota Education Standards and Practices Board (ESPB) in order to be permitted or employed to teach in any state public school.
   B. Nonpublic schools must employ licensed teachers to be approved and in compliance with compulsory attendance laws.

II. Licensure Level
   A. Level I indicates that individual still has educational or employment requirements to meet before receiving regular Level II license, or that they are not currently maintaining contracted employment.
   B. Level II indicates that individual has met all basic requirements for regular North Dakota Educators' Professional License.
   C. Level III indicates that individual has earned advanced degrees beyond bachelor's level (master's, specialist, or doctoral) or National Board for Professional Teaching Standards (NBPTS) advanced licensure.

III. Types of Educator's Licenses and Procedures
   A. 40-Day Provisional: Issued to applicants who have been offered a job and have completed entire application process with exception of background investigation. Letter from school administrator indicating desire to issue contract without background investigation being complete and letter from applicant indicating any criminal background history are needed by ESPB prior to issuing this license.
   B. Initial License (valid 2 years): Issued to first-time applicants who have met all state requirements for licensure
   C. Regular (valid 5 years): Issued to individuals who have met all requirements for a state Educator's Professional License and have successfully taught for 18 months (full-time equivalent) in state
   D. Alternate License (valid 1 year): Issued in documented shortage area. License is initiated by letter from local school administrator indicating search for qualified applicant and desire for this license to be issued. Requirements include:
      1. Initial License
      2. Bachelor's degree in appropriate content area
      3. Plan of study from college of education where applicant will complete 8 semester hours each year toward teaching degree.
   E. Out-of-State Reciprocal (valid 2 years): Issued to individuals who hold valid license from another state but have not met this state's standards and rules. Plan of study is developed for each individual indicating course work needed. Individual has 4 years to complete all requirements.

F. Additional types of educator's licenses and procedures. For full details, consult http://www.nd.gov/espb/licensure/types.html?print=y
    1. Two-Year Renewal
    2. Interim/Substitute (One Year)
    3. Re-Entry (Two Years)
    4. Probationary (Two Years)
    5. Minor Equivalency Endorsement
    6. Middle School Endorsement
    7. Elementary Reeducation Endorsement
    8. Kindergarten Endorsement
    9. Other State Educator License (OSEL) (Either Two Years or Five Years)
    10. Waivers

Elementary School

I. North Dakota Educator's Professional License
    A. Bachelor's degree from an accredited college approved to offer teacher education
    B. Professional requirements, credits in professional education, including student teaching, overall grade-point average 2.5, semester hours 34
    C. Valid for 2 years for teaching in the level of preparation
    D. A 5-year renewal may be issued with 2 years of successful full-time teaching experience in the state. Each renewal of the 5-year license requires 6 semester hours of work.
    E. Submission of PPST/Praxis I scores in reading, writing, and mathematics that meet or exceed North Dakota cut scores
    F. Submission of Praxis II content and pedagogy test scores that meet or exceed North Dakota cut scores
    G. Background investigation, including Bureau of Criminal Investigation and the F.B.I.

Secondary School

I. North Dakota Educator's Professional License
    A. Same as Elementary School, I, A–G
    B. Semester hours 32
    C. Submission in core academic areas only of Praxis II test scores that meet or exceed North Dakota cut scores

Superintendent

I. Provisional Credential
    A. Valid until the end of the second school year following the year in which the provisional credential is issued; not renewable
    B. Issued as the initial credential to an individual who does not meet the qualifications for a professional credential

    C.   Issued to those who have a level I principal's credential but lack the course work, the experience, or both that are necessary for the professional credential

    D.   Applicant must fulfill all the following standards:

        1.   Hold a valid North Dakota teaching license during the life of the credential

        2.   Have at least 3 years of teaching experience, verified in a letter of recommendation by a supervisor or employer who has firsthand knowledge of the individual's professional work

        3.   Have at least 2 years of administrative experience comprising at least half time as an elementary or secondary principal, a central office administrator, or an administrator of an approved school with a 12-year program. This experience is to be verified by a supervisor or employer who has firsthand knowledge of the individual's professional work.

        4.   Complete the requirements for the level I elementary or secondary principal credential and 8 additional hours of designated course work specific to the superintendency; see state Department of Public Instruction (DPI), Appendix 1

  II. Professional Credential

    A.   Issued to coincide with the period for which the individual is licensed to teach by the ESPB and may be renewed; an individual holding a lifetime educator's professional license must renew the credential every 5 years,
and

    B.   Issued upon satisfying credential standards; see I, D, 1–4, directly above

 III. Renewal Requirements

    A.   Applicant must fulfill one of the following:

        1.   Provide a copy of official transcripts showing satisfactory completion of at least 8 semester hours of graduate work in education, of which 4 semester hours are in the area of educational administration,
or

        2.   Provide a copy of official transcripts showing satisfactory completion of at least 4 semester hours of graduate work and verification of attendance or participation in at least 6 administrative educational conferences or workshops from a state-approved list with specific verification.

Secondary Principal

  I. Provisional Credential

    A.   Issued as the initial credential to an individual who does not meet the qualifications for a level I or level II professional credential and is employed as a secondary principal; valid until the end of the second school year following the year in which the provisional credential is issued; not renewable

    B.   Issued to a person enrolled in a state-approved program in educational leadership who has completed 8 semester hours of course work in that area

    C.   Issued upon satisfying the following credentials standards with specific verification of each:

     1. Valid North Dakota educator's professional license issued by the ESPB allowing the individual to teach at the secondary level

     2. At least 3 years of teaching or administrative experience (as defined by DPI) or a combination thereof in secondary schools:

       a. Equal to full-time equivalency: at least 6 hours for a 180-day school term

       b. Positions must have been stated on a professional contract

II. Level I Professional Credential

    A. Issued to coincide with the period for which the individual is licensed to teach by the ESPB and may be renewed at the end of that period; an individual holding a lifetime educator's professional license must renew their credential every 5 years, *and*

    B. Issued upon satisfying the following credentials standards:

     1. See I, C, 1 and 2, directly above

     2. The level I credential requires 1 of the following:

       a. Master's degree in educational administration from a state-approved program with designated subjects, *or*

       b. Master's degree with a major certifiable by the ESPB in addition to 20 semester hours of credit that include designated courses specific to the secondary level contained within a master's degree in educational administration from a state-approved program

III. Level II Professional Credential

    A. Issued to coincide with the period for which the individual is licensed to teach by the ESPB; an individual holding a lifetime educator's professional license must renew their credential every 5 years

    B. Renewal of the level II professional credential is available only for principals serving secondary schools with 100 or fewer students, *and*

    C. Issued upon satisfying the following credentials standards:

     1. See I, C, 1 and 2, directly above

     2. The level II credential requires 20 semester hours of graduate credit taken in a master's degree program from a state-approved program with designated subjects in educational administration.

IV. Renewal Requirements

    A. To renew the level I and level II professional credentials, an individual shall submit 1 of the following:

     1. A copy of official transcripts of 8 semester hours of graduate work in education acquired after the date of the original credentialing or last renewal, of which 4 semester hours are in the area of educational administration, *or*

     2. A copy of official transcripts of 4 semester hours of graduate work in education acquired after the date of the original credentialing or last renewal and verification of attendance or participation in at least 6 educational conferences or workshops from a designated list with specific verification.

Elementary Principal

I. Provisional Credential
    A. Issued as the initial credential to an individual who does not meet the qualifications for a level I or level II professional credential and is employed as an elementary principal; valid until the end of the second school year following the year in which the provisional credential is issued; not renewable
    B. Issued upon completion of 8 semester hours of course work in educational leadership from a state-approved program in educational administration
    C. Issued upon meeting the following credential standards with specific documentation and verification of each:
        1. A valid North Dakota teaching license issued by the ESPB allowing the individual to teach at the elementary level
        2. At least 3 years of teaching or administrative experience (as defined by DPI) or a combination thereof in elementary schools:
            a. Equal to full-time equivalency: at least 5 and one-half hours daily, for a 180-day school term
            b. Positions must have been stated on a professional contract
II. Level I Professional Credential
    A. Issued to coincide with the period for which the individual is licensed to teach by the ESPB; an individual holding a lifetime educator's professional license must renew their credential every 5 years
    B. Issued upon satisfying the following credential standards:
        1. See I, C, 1 and 2, directly above
        2. The level I credential requires 1 of the following:
            a. Master's degree in educational administration that includes designated course work specific to the elementary level from a state-approved program,
                or
            b. Master's degree with a major certifiable by the ESPB. Twenty semester hours of credit that includes designated courses specific to the elementary level contained within a master's degree in educational administration from a state-approved program are required.
III. Level II Professional Credential
    A. Issued to coincide with the period for which the individual is licensed to teach by the ESPB; however, an individual holding a lifetime educator's professional license must renew their credential every 5 years
    B. Renewal of the level II professional credential is available only for principals serving elementary schools enrolling 100 or fewer students
    C. Issued upon satisfying the following credential standards:
        1. See I, C, 1 and 2, directly above
        2. Level II credential requires 20 semester hours of graduate credit in a master's degree program from a state-approved program in educational administration with designated courses.
IV. Renewal Requirements

A. To renew the level I and level II professional credentials, an individual must submit 1 of the following:
   1. A copy of official transcripts of 8 semester hours of graduate work in education acquired after the date of the original credentialing or last renewal, of which 4 semester hours are in the area of educational administration, *or*
   2. A copy of official transcripts of 4 semester hours of graduate work in education acquired after the date of the original credentialing or last renewal and verification of attendance or participation in at least 6 educational conferences or workshops from a designated list with specific verification.

School Counselor

I. School Counselor Credentials
   A. Credential designations
      1. SC03 for grades K–12
      2. Counselor Designate credential CD 16 (will not be issued after June 30, 2010)
   B. Credential is valid only while the individual holds a North Dakota educator's professional license or a professional school counseling restricted license.
      1. A credential must be renewed each time the individual's educator's professional license is renewed.
      2. Holders of a lifetime North Dakota educator's professional license must renew the credential every 5 years.
      3. To renew the credential, submit a copy of college transcripts documenting 4 semester hours of graduate course work in education, of which 2 semester hours must be in counseling.
         a. Two semester hours of required counseling course work may be replaced by 30 clock hours of continuing education hours in counseling with a signed verification of attendance or participation by the conference or workshop sponsor, the employer, or a school district business manager.
   C. SC03 credential standards – counselor must:
      1. Hold a valid educator's professional license or a professional school counseling restricted license
         and
      2. Have a master's degree in counseling, education, or a related human service field and the following graduate core counseling course work content from a state-approved school counseling program:
         a. Elementary school counseling;
         b. Secondary school counseling;
         c. Supervised school counseling internship consisting of a minimum of 450 contact hours, of which at least 150 are at both the elementary and secondary level;
         d. Counseling program management;

   e.   Counseling theories;
   f.   Assessment techniques;
   g.   Group counseling;
   h.   Career counseling and assessment;
   i.   Social and multicultural counseling;
   j.   Ethics and law;
        and
   k.   Counseling techniques.
   D.   If a school is unable to employ a credentialed counselor, the school may employ a licensed teacher to serve as the counselor on a plan of study approved by the DPI to satisfy accreditation requirements, Contact DPI for details at http://www.dpi.state.nd.us

Library Media

Contact the Department of Public Instruction (see Appendix 1) for a detailed listing of required course work, official application forms, and instructions.

   I.   Librarian (LM03)
   A.   Bachelor's degree with a licenseable major or minor or an endorsement in elementary, middle-level, or secondary education
   B.   Valid North Dakota Educator's Professional License
   C.   Complete course work in library media from a state-approved program as detailed in Subsection 1 of Section 67-11-04-05, semester hours* 15
   D.   Validity Length
        1.   Valid only while the individual holds a valid North Dakota educator's professional license
        2.   Must be renewed each time professional license is renewed; graduate semester hours in library media and information science from a state-approved program 2
             a.   Individual holding a lifetime North Dakota educator's professional license must renew the credential every 5 years
   II. Library Media Specialist (LM02)
   A.   See I, A, directly above
   B.   Valid North Dakota Educator's Professional License
   C.   Complete course work in library media from a state-approved program as detailed in Subsection 1 of Section 67-11-04-05, semester hours* 15
        Subsection 2 of Section 67-11-04-05, semester hours* 9
   D.   See I, D, directly above
   III. Library Media Director (LM01)
   A.   Master's degree in library science, media education, education, or educational administration from a state-approved program
   B.   Valid North Dakota Educator's Professional License (based on bachelor's degree with a licenseable major or minor or an endorsement in elementary, middle-level, or secondary education)

    C.   Complete course work in library media from a state-approved program as detailed in

          Subsection 1 of Section 67-11-04-05, semester hours* 15

          Subsection 2 of Section 67-11-04-05, semester hours* 9

          Subsection 3 of Section 67-11-04-05, semester hours (graduate in school library

          or school administration)... 6

IV.   Plan of Study Option to qualify for library media director, library media specialist, or librarian credentials

    A.   If school is unable to employ credentialed librarian, as required by enrollment of students served, may employ licensed teacher to serve as librarian if licensed teacher has completed at least 6 semester hours in library media course work and has submitted a written plan of study showing at least 6 graduate or undergraduate semester hours in library media course work to be completed annually until credential is earned.

    B.   Once plan is approved, licensed teacher must document a minimum of 6 semester hours of library media course work each year until qualified for required credential

V.   Renewal Requirements (LM03, LM02, LM01)

All are renewed by submitting application form and documenting completion of 2 semester hours of graduate credit in library media and information science.

*   graduate or undergraduate

Ohio

Ohio's standards are performance-based and lead to licensing based on assessments (administered under the authority of the state board of education) of the performance of teachers during their participation in the Ohio Resident Educator Program. Applicants for any license or permit must complete both an Ohio and an FBI criminal background check, conducted by the Bureau of Criminal Identification and Investigation. For full details, consult Educator Licensure at education.ohio.gov

Resident Educator

I. Resident Educator License (valid 4 years)
    A. Holds degree required by license
    B. Deemed to be of good moral character
    C. Successfully completed approved program of preparation
    D. Recommended by dean or head of teacher education at institution approved to prepare teachers
    E. Successfully completed Ohio Assessments for Educators (OAE) examination in content and professional knowledge, or equivalent out-of-state licensure exam for out-of-state applicants
        1. For world languages, the American Council on the Teaching of Foreign Languages (ACTFL) Oral Proficiency Interview and Writing Proficiency Test is also required.
    F. Demonstrated skill in integrating educational technology in instruction of children
    G. Completed course work in teaching of reading, semester hours 12
        1. For early childhood, middle childhood, and intervention specialist license, this must include at least one separate 3-semester-hour course in teaching of phonics
        2. For multiage and adolescence to young adult licenses, 3 semester hours in teaching of reading
    H. If applicant's education program completed outside Ohio
        1. Individuals who have completed licensure programs at colleges/universities outside the state of Ohio apply to the Ohio Office of Educator Licensure (see Appendix 1).
II. Resident Educator Program for Teachers
    A. Candidate holds 4-year resident educator license or alternative resident educator license
    B. Candidate completes the 4-year Ohio Resident Educator Transition Program including:
        1. Four-year program of mentoring and support;
            and
        2. Assessment of beginning teacher's acquisition of knowledge and skills through use of formative assessments and a summative performance-based assessment, the Resident Educator Summative Assessment (RESA).

Professional Licenses

I. Professional Teacher License (valid 5 years)
    A. Holds provisional license, resident educator license, or alternative resident educator license
    B. Holds baccalaureate degree
    C. See Resident Educator License, I, B, C, and E, above
    D. Successful completion of Ohio Resident Educator Program
    E. Alternative license holders complete additional course work or professional development work to obtain professional license

II. Professional Teacher License Areas
    A. Early childhood license (PreK–3)
        1. Minimum course work in teaching of reading, semester hours 12
    B. Middle childhood license (4–9)
        1. Middle childhood teacher preparation program shall include preparation in humanities (including the arts) and areas of concentration in at least 2 of the following: reading and language arts, mathematics, science, and social studies
        2. See II, A, 1, directly above
    C. Adolescence to young adult license (7–12)
        1. Preparation in teaching field shall constitute at least an academic major or its equivalent with sufficient advanced course work in all areas to be taught
        2. Licenses are issued in following teaching fields:
            a. Earth sciences, integrated language arts, integrated mathematics, integrated science, integrated social studies, life sciences, and physical sciences (including physical sciences: chemistry; physical sciences: physics; or chemistry and physics)
    D. Multiage license (PreK–12)
        1. See II, C, 1, directly above
        2. Licenses are issued in the following teaching fields:
            a. Computer information science, dance, drama/theater, foreign language, health, library/media, music, physical education, teaching English to speakers of other languages (TESOL), and visual arts
    E. Other professional teacher license areas include intervention specialist, early childhood intervention specialist, and a variety of career–technical areas. Please consult Educator Licensure at education.ohio.gov for details.

Professional Pupil Services Licenses

I. Professional Pupil Services License (valid 5 years)
    A. Deemed to be of good moral character
    B. Completed approved program of preparation
    C. Recommended by dean or head of teacher education
    D. Completed examination prescribed by state board of education

II. License Areas
    A. School audiologist

    1.   Master's degree and current license to practice audiology

    2.   See I, A–D, directly above

  B. School counselor

    1.   Master's degree

    2.   See I, A–D, directly above

  C. School psychologist

    1.   Master's degree and approved program of preparation, successful completion of Praxis II or Ohio Assessments for Educators (OAE) examination, successful completion of 9-month, full-time internship in approved school setting

    2.   See I, A–D, directly above

  D. Other professional pupil personnel license areas include school social worker; school speech-language pathologist; school nurse; and orientation and mobility specialist. Please consult Educator Licensure at education.ohio.gov for details.

Professional Administrator Licenses

I. Professional Administrator License

  A. Deemed to be of good moral character

  B. Holds master's degree

  C. Recommended by dean or head of teacher education at institution approved to prepare teachers

  D. Successfully completed examination prescribed by state board of education

II. License Areas

  A. Principal License

    1.   Successful completion of an approved program of preparation for principal licensure and the prescribed examination.

    2.   Valid for working with

      a.   Ages 3–12 and grades PK–6

      b.   Ages 8–14 and grades 4–9

      c.   Ages 10–21 and grades 5–12

  B. Administrative Specialist License

    1.   Valid for working in central office or supervisory capacity

    2.   Prior to issuance, applicant must have completed 2 years of successful teaching experience under professional teacher's license and must have successfully completed approved program of preparation.

  C. Superintendent License

    1.   Prior to issuance, applicant must have completed 3 years of successful experience in position requiring principal or administrative specialist license and must have successfully completed approved preparation program for superintendents.

Oklahoma

Note: Oklahoma Senate Bill #1443 waives requirements of educator residency for fiscal year 2013–14, thus exempting school districts from participation in a residency program during that time frame. Accordingly, resident teacher programs and committees mentioned in the text below are currently on hold. Refer to the Oklahoma State Department of Education website for the most current information at http://sde.state.ok.us/Teacher/ProfStand/CertGuide

Traditional Licensure and Certification

I. Traditional Teaching License (valid 5 years)
   A. License is a credential initially issued to educators who have completed a teacher education program after February 1, 1982, and who have zero years of teaching experience in an accredited school.
   B. Requirements for licensure
      1. Holds a bachelor's degree from an accredited institution of higher education (IHE) that has approval or accreditation for teaching education,
      2. Successfully completed a higher education teacher education program approved by the Oklahoma Commission for Teacher Preparation (OCTP)—see Appendix 1 for contact information,
      3. Has met all other requirements as may be established by the Oklahoma State Board of Education (OSBE),
      4. Has made necessary application and paid competency examination fees in amount and as prescribed by OCTP,
      5. Successfully completed 3 competency examinations, including:
         a. Oklahoma General Education Test (OGET)
         b. Oklahoma Subject Area Test(s) (OSAT)
         c. Oklahoma Professional Teaching Examination (OPTE),
            and
      6. Has on file with the OSBE both a current Oklahoma and national criminal history record search from the Oklahoma State Bureau of Investigation (OSBI) and Federal Bureau of Investigation (FBI), respectively.
   C. A licensed teacher will participate in the Resident Teacher Program during the initial year of teaching in Oklahoma. See Oklahoma State Department of Education website for the most current information on resident teacher programs and committees at http://sde.state.ok.us/Teacher/ProfStand/CertGuide
      1. Employing school district shall establish a resident teacher committee consisting of a mentor teacher, an administrator, and a faculty member from an IHE to provide guidance and assistance to the beginning teacher, ultimately making a recommendation regarding certification.
II. Traditional Teaching Certificate (valid 5 years, renewable).
   A. Certificate is a credential issued to educators who have completed the Resident

Teacher Program of verified teaching experience under a valid teaching credential in a state- or regionally accredited school. See Oklahoma State Department of Education website for the most current information on resident teacher programs and committees at http://sde.state.ok.us/Teacher/ProfStand/CertGuide

B. Requirements for certification
1. Holds a license to teach,
2. Has served a minimum of 1 school year as a resident teacher;
3. Has been recommended for certification by a Resident Teacher Committee; *and*
4. Has made the necessary application and paid the certification fee; *or*
5. Holds an out-of-state certificate and meets standards set by the Oklahoma State Board of Education (OSBE); *or*
6. Holds certification from the National Board for Professional Teaching Standards.
7. For those who do not have a teacher education degree, see alternative routes to teaching below.

C. Additional subjects may be added to certificate by testing: contact Teacher Certification for details.

D. Special Education teachers new to the profession after December 3, 2004, are required to have a Special Education certificate as well as an appropriate certificate in 1 of the following areas: early childhood, elementary education, middle or secondary education in math, science, or language arts.

E. Credentialing for Educators with Out-of-State Licensure
1. Applicants who hold a full teaching credential in any state are eligible for Oklahoma certification in equivalent subject areas with the possibility of having to take Oklahoma tests.
   a. Applicants who completed a teacher education program after February 1, 1982, and do not have at least 1 year of teaching experience will be required to participate in the Resident Teacher Program. See Oklahoma State Department of Education website for the most current information on resident teacher programs and committees at http://sde.state.ok.us/Teacher/ProfStand/CertGuide
   b. Applicants who completed a teacher education program after February 1, 1982, and have at least 1 year of teaching experience, will be issued a 5-year provisional certificate in order to complete the Oklahoma testing requirements (OGET, OSAT[s], and OPTE) and to complete 1 year of successful employment in an Oklahoma accredited school.
      i. Applicants who have passed teacher test(s) in another state may request a review of these test(s) for comparability to Oklahoma test(s) by the OCTP to determine if any of the out-of-state tests are comparable and acceptable. Contact the OCTP (see Appendix 1) for full details.
   c. Applicants who graduated after February 1, 1982, and have zero years

of teaching experience will be issued an Oklahoma license in order to complete the Resident Teacher Program required of beginning teachers. No 5-year standard license will be issued until all tests have been completed and the Resident Teacher Committee has made its recommendation for certification to the OSBE. See Oklahoma State Department of Education website for the most current information on resident teacher programs and committees at http://sde.state.ok.us/Teacher/ProfStand/CertGuide

2. Oklahoma does have certification agreements limited to educator preparation program requirements with certain participating states/jurisdictions; see Appendix 3 for full listing.

   a. Contact individual states regarding ancillary requirements such as minimum grade-point average, standardized testing, mentoring experience, or graduation from an accredited institution.

3. If applicants hold a full credential in any state, they are eligible for Oklahoma certification in equivalent subject areas, once Oklahoma testing requirements are met.

III. Specialist Certificate (valid 5 years, renewable)

   A. Specialist certification is awarded for library-media specialist, school counselor, school psychometrist, school psychologist, speech-language pathologist, and reading specialist.

   B. In addition to meeting initial licensure requirements (see I, A–C, directly above), specialist certification requires completion of a graduate degree program meeting the professional education association standards specific to the profession.

      1. Specialist certification may not be added through testing alone.

   C. Application for certification in the specialist areas listed above should be initiated through the director of teacher education at the recommending IHE.

IV. Administrator Certificate

   A. Principal Standard Certificate (valid 5 years, renewable)

      1. Holds a standard master's degree,

      2. Completed an Oklahoma-approved building-level leadership skills program in educational administration,

      3. Achieved a passing score on common core and principal specialty areas of the principal OSATs,
         and

      4. Completed 2 years of successful teaching experience in an OSBE-accredited Oklahoma public or private school.

   B. Superintendent Standard Certificate (valid 5 years, renewable)

      1. Holds principal certification
         or
         Completed an Oklahoma-approved building-level leadership skills program in educational administration that includes a standard master's degree,

      2. Achieved a passing score on superintendent OSAT,

      3. Completed an Oklahoma-approved district-level leadership skills program in educational administration,

and

4. Completed 2 years of administrative experience in an OSBE-accredited Oklahoma public or private school.

C. For alternative administrator certification for principal or superintendent (valid 3 years, nonrenewable)

1. Holds a standard master's degree,
2. Completed 2 years of relevant work experience in a supervisory or administrative capacity,
3. Achieved passing scores on the required administrator OSAT(s), *and*
4. Has on file with the director of teacher education at an Oklahoma-accredited IHE a declaration of intent to earn standard certification through completion of an approved alternative administrative preparation program within 3 years.

Alternative Routes to Teaching

I. Alternative Placement Program

A. Provides an opportunity for individuals with nonteaching degrees to teach in Oklahoma accredited schools.

B. Eligibility requirements:

1. Minimum of a baccalaureate degree from an accredited college/university,
2. Major in a field of study corresponding to an area of Oklahoma certification for secondary, elementary/secondary, or career and technology education certificate (see OSDE, Appendix 1, for full listing),
3. At least a 2.5 grade-point average, *and*
4. Document 2 years of post-baccalaureate work experience if no post-baccalaureate course work.

C. Once approved to seek an alternative license, applicant must:

1. Complete the OGET and desired OSAT tests; contact OCTP (see Appendix 1) for details,
2. Have on file with the OSBE a current approved OSBI/FBI criminal history fingerprint check, *and*
3. Receive a recommendation for certification from the Oklahoma Teacher Competency Review Panel, as well as receive OSBE approval.

D. Once the OSDE issues license, applicant must:

1. Complete the Oklahoma Resident Teacher Program. See Oklahoma State Department of Education website for the most current information on resident teacher programs and committees at http://sde.state.ok.us/Teacher/ProfStand/CertGuide
2. Within 3 years, pass the OPTE and complete a professional education component as follows:
   a. With a bachelor's degree, 18 college credit hours or 270 clock hours

   b. With a post-baccalaureate degree, 12 college credit hours or 180 clock hours
    and
  3. Apply for a standard certificate.

II. American Board for Certification of Teacher Excellence (ABCTE)

  A. Funded with a U.S. Department of Education grant, ABCTE offers a flexible and cost-effective certification program designed to inspire career changers to enter teaching.

  B. Requirements

   1. Bachelor's degree from accredited IHE,
   2. Accepted by the ABCTE,
   3. Pass ABCTE desired middle-level or secondary-level subject test and professional teacher test,
    and
   4. Have on file with the OSBE a current approved OSBI/FBI criminal history fingerprint check.

  C. When requirements are completed, OSDE issues middle-level or secondary-level license (valid 1 year)

   1. Licensee must participate in 1-year mentoring program and apply for a standard certificate. See Oklahoma State Department of Education website for the most current information on resident teacher programs and committees at http://sde.state.ok.us/Teacher/ProfStand/CertGuide

III. Teach for America

  A. This is a national corps of outstanding recent college graduates and professionals of all academic major and career interests who commit 2 years to teach in urban and rural public schools and become leaders in the effort to expand educational opportunity. For full details, go to: http://www.teachforamerica/org.

  B. Once accepted into the program, applicant could be assigned to teach in Oklahoma.

IV. Additional Alternative Certificates

Oklahoma also offers alternative certificates in the following programs; contact the OSDE (see Appendix 1) for full details.

  A. Four-Year-Olds and Younger Certificate
  B. Career Development Program for Paraprofessionals to be Certified Teachers
  C. Troops to Teachers Defense Authorization Act
  D. Non-Traditional Special Education Provisional

Oregon

Teaching Licenses

I. Initial Teaching License (valid 18 months, by which time individual must qualify for Initial I Teaching License; not renewable). Note: Initial Teaching License is usually first license issued to out-of-state applicants who need time to complete requirements for Initial I Teaching License.

   A. Initial Teaching License—Unrestricted
      1. Baccalaureate degree from regionally accredited U.S. institution or approved foreign equivalent related to teaching at 1 or more levels in 1 or more specialties
      2. Completion of approved teacher-education program in endorsement area(s) requested
      3. Furnish fingerprints and provide satisfactory responses to character question contained in licensure application

   B. Restricted Transitional Teaching License (valid 3 years; nonrenewable)
      1. Issued to applicants who have not held unrestricted license for full-time teaching in any state or have not completed approved teacher-education program but do hold baccalaureate degree in subject matter relevant to position being sought; see I, A, 1, above
      2. Restricted to district and requires coapplication with district
      3. Furnish fingerprints and provide satisfactory responses to character question contained in licensure application
      4. Completion of civil rights examination approved by Oregon Teacher Standards and Practices Commission (TSPC)

II. Initial I Teaching License (valid 3 years, renewable twice under conditions described below)

   A. Baccalaureate degree from regionally accredited U.S. institution or an approved foreign equivalent of such degree

   B. Completion of approved Oregon teacher-education program in endorsement area(s) requested,
      or
      Current license issued by another state, not limited due to course work, and valid for endorsement(s) requested on Oregon license

   C. See I, B, 4, directly above

   D. Professional knowledge
      1. Passing score on each required test of subject mastery for license endorsement, except for tests waived due to approved special academic preparation, together with 5 years of experience teaching specialty in U.S. public or regionally accredited private school before holding any Oregon license
         a. Transcript review required for academic preparation in lieu of testing.
      2. Passing scores on Praxis I Series: PPST Mathematics (175); PPST Reading (174); and PPST Writing (171),

or

California Basic Educational Skills Test (CBEST) (123),

or

Washington Educator Skills Test-Basic skills (WEST-B),

or

Hold regionally accredited doctoral degree.

   E.   Renewable under following conditions only:
- 1. First renewal (at 3 years)
  - a. All candidates must show progress of at least 3 semester hours or 4.5 quarter graduate hours germane to license, which must be completed within 10 years from date Initial License was first granted.
  - b. Educator must qualify for Initial II license upon expiration of 9 years following first Initial I license issue date. Candidate may apply for 1-year unconditional extension if unable to meet all requirements within 9-year period.
  - c. Teacher may choose to become eligible for Continuing Teaching License in lieu of obtaining Initial II license.

   F.   Furnish fingerprints and provide statisfactory responses to character question contained in licensure application.

III.   Initial II Teaching License (valid 3 years; renewable repeatedly under requirements below)

   A.   Requirements if Initial I teaching license granted on basis of baccalaureate degree from teacher preparation program
- 1. Complete master's or higher degree in arts and sciences, or advanced degree in the professions, from regionally accredited U.S. institution or approved foreign equivalent of such

  or

  Complete specified graduate course work germane to license or to public school employment, including at least 10 semester hours or 15 quarter hours each of subject matter course work; of graduate educational-related course work; and of graduate electives

   B.   Requirements if Initial I teaching license granted on basis of post-baccalaureate degree from teacher-preparation program; complete one of the following:
- 1. Six semester hours or 9 quarter hours graduate academic credit from regionally accredited college or university. Graduate credit must be completed after Initial I teaching license is first issued and be germane to license or to public school employment; may include pedagogy, or content related to existing endorsement or authorization, or content related to new endorsement or authorization;

  or
- 2. Commission-approved school district program equivalent to III, B, 1, directly above;

  or

  Any commission-approved professional assessment.
- 3. In all cases, combination of post-baccalaureate program and additional hours

        required must be equivalent to master's degree, or to 45 quarter hours, or to 30 semester hours.

    C.   Renewal of Initial II teaching license requirements

        1.   Completion of all requirements in either III, B, 1, or III, B, 2, directly above, *and*

        2.   Professional development plan in accordance with current regulations.

IV.   Continuing Teaching License (CTL) (valid 5 years; option to renew)

    A.   Meet all requirements for Initial II Teaching License

    B.   Hold accredited master's degree or higher in arts and sciences, or advanced degree in the professions (all underlying degrees must also be from accredited institutions)

    C.   Have taught 5 years of at least one-half time on any non-provisional license appropriate for assignment (in any state)

    D.   Demonstrate minimum competencies, knowledge and skills by

        1.   Completion of TSPC-approved CTL program, or accredited doctorate degree in education

        2.   Certification by National Board of Professional Teaching Standards
or
Certificate of Clinical Competence awarded by Speech and Hearing Association for those holding communication discorders endorsement,
or
Completion of TSPC-approved school district program or any TSPC-approved professional assessment [not yet developed]

V.   Limited Teaching License (valid 3 years and renewable)

    A.   Valid at any level and designated for one or more highly specialized subjects of instruction for which Oregon does not issue a specific endorsement.

    B.   Valid for substitute teaching at any level but only in subjects listed on license.

    C.   Accredited associate's degree or its approved equivalent in objectively evaluated post-secondary education related to the intended subject of instruction is required.

    D.   Furnish fingerprints and provide satisfactory responses to character question contained in licensure application

VI.   Emergency Teaching License (valid for up to 1 year) when districts can demonstrate an emergency need

Teaching Authorizations

A first regular license, whether transitional or initial, is authorized for grade levels on basis of professional education, experience, previous licensure, and specialized academic course work. Oregon has following levels:

    I.   Early Childhood Authorization (grade 4 and below)

   II.   Elementary Authorization (grades 3 through 8)

  III.   Middle-Level Authorization (grades 5 through 9 of school designated as elementary school, middle school, or junior high school)

  IV.   High School Authorization (grades 9 through 12 of school designated as high school)

A. This level requires qualification for at least 1 specialty endorsement appropriate to secondary schools.

Subject Matter Endorsements

I. Educator must receive currently specified passing score on each of 1 or more tests of subject mastery for license endorsement.
   A. National Evaluation Series (NES): subject assessments in art, biology, general business, Chinese, chemistry, library media, family and consumer sciences, French, German, health, integrated science, language arts, basic and advanced mathematics, music, physical education, physics, social studies, Spanish, and ESOL
   B. Praxis II: subject assessments in agriculture, early intervention, hearing impaired, marketing, reading, speech, speech-language pathology, technology education, vision impaired
   C. Since there are no Praxis exams in drama, adapted physical education, Latin, Russian, and Japanese, transcript review is required for these endorsement areas. Contact TSPC (see Appendix 1)

Personnel Licenses

I. Transitional School Counselor License (valid 1 year; not renewable)
   Contact TSPC (see Appendix 1) for full details
II. Initial I School Counselor License (valid 3 years plus time to applicant's next birthday; renewable once)
   A. Valid as designated for regular counseling at specific grade levels; see TSPC (Appendix 1) for details
   B. Eligibility Requirements:
      1. Master's or higher degree in counseling, education, or related behavioral sciences from approved institution
      2. Completion of approved initial graduate program in school counseling
      3. Completion of approved practicum
      4. A passing score as currently specified on test of basic verbal and computational skills, unless
         a. Applicant held an Oregon educator license before 1985,
            or
         b. Applicant has regionally accredited doctoral degree.
      5. Passing score on test of knowledge of U.S. and Oregon civil rights laws at conclusion of approved course or workshop
      6. Furnish fingerprints and provide satisfactory responses to the character question contained in the licensure application
   C. Initial School Counselor License Renewal
      1. See Teaching Licenses, II, E, above
   D. Authorizations: contact TSPC (see Appendix 1) for details

III. Initial II School Counselor License (valid 3 years; renewable repeatedly under the following requirements below)
    A. Valid as designated for regular counseling at specific grade levels; see TSPC (Appendix 1) for details
    B. Eligibility Requirements:
        1. Six semester hours or 9 quarter hours of graduate-level academic credit must be completed after the Initial I School Counselor License has first been issued and be germane to the School Counselor License or directly germane to public school employment.
    C. Renewal of the Initial II School Counselor License requires a professional development plan.
    D. A school counselor may choose to become eligible for the Continuing School Counselor License in lieu of obtaining the Initial II School Counselor License.
    E. This rule applies to all Initial School Counselor Licenses issued after January 1999. See TSPC (Appendix 1) for certain specific time-frame requirements.

IV. Continuing School Counselor License (valid 5 years; renewable)
    A. Valid for counseling at all age or grade levels and for substitute teaching at any level in any specialty
    B. Eligibility Requirements
        1. Completed, beyond initial graduate program in school counseling, the following:
           a. Advanced program in counseling competencies consisting of at least 6 semester hours or 9 quarter hours of graduate credit or equivalent, *and*
           b. Practica in counseling early childhood or elementary students and middle-level or high school students
               i. If institution does not award credit directly, all advanced counseling competencies must be validated through approved assessments.
               ii. Such assessments may be waived when applicant holds regionally accredited doctoral degree in educational, vocational, or clinical counseling, or else in clinical or counseling psychology.
    C. Continuing School Counselor License Renewal
        1. Two requirements must be met during preceding 5-year period, as follows:
           a. Verification of Oregon public school employment, if available *and*
           b. Establishment, maintenance, and reporting of continuing professional development plan.

Administrative Licenses

I. Transitional Administrator (valid 18 months; not renewable)
    A. Master's or higher degree in arts and sciences or advanced degree in the professions from regionally accredited institution or approved foreign equivalent
    B. Depending upon applicant's experience as educator, or training and/or experience

as administrator, license may or may not be restricted to employing district. Contact TSPC (see Appendix 1) for additional details.

II.   Transitional Superintendent License (valid 3 years; nonrenewable)
    A.   Valid for superintendency when issued to person who has been a superintendent on regular assignment in any state; also valid for substitute teaching at any authorization level in any specialty
    B.   Eligibility Requirements
       1.   Applicant must have been employed as a superintendent for at least 5 years in any state and hold valid superintendent's license from that state
       2.   Furnish fingerprints and provide satisfactory responses to character question contained in licensure application
       3.   While holding license, applicants must
          a.   Complete Oregon school law and finance class,
            and
          b.   Complete the required civil rights exam.
    C.   Qualifying for Continuing Superintendent License
       1.   See II, B, 1–3, directly above
       2.   Complete 3 consecutive years of successful experience as superintendent at least half time or more in state of Oregon.

III.   Initial Administrative License (valid 3 years plus time to applicant's next birthday, renewable under the requirements below)
    A.   Master's or higher degree in arts and sciences or advanced degree in the professions from regionally accredited U.S. institution, or approved foreign equivalent of such degree, together with equally accredited bachelor's degree
    B.   Completion in Oregon or another U.S. jurisdiction, either as part of master's degree or separately, of initial graduate program in school administration at institution approved for administrator education by TSPC
    C.   Passing score on test of knowledge of U.S. and Oregon civil rights laws at conclusion of TSPC-approved course or workshop
    D.   Three academic years of experience as full-time licensed educator, on any license appropriate for assignment, in public or regionally accredited private school in any state, or other U.S. jurisdiction, or in approved Oregon schools
    E.   Through required course of study, assessments, and practica, candidate for Initial Administrator License must demonstrate knowledge, skills, and competencies as specified by Oregon's TSPC.
    F.   Renewal: Initial Administrator License may be renewed up to 2 times if applicant makes progress toward completion of Continuing Administrator License by completing at least 6 semester hours or 9 quarter hours of academic credit in approved Continuing Administrator License Program upon each renewal. A transcript of completed course work is required for renewal.

IV.   Continuing Administrator License (valid 5 years; renewable)
    A.   Completion, beyond both master's degree and the integrated or separate initial graduate program in school administration, of advanced program in administrative competencies consisting of at least 18 semester hours or 27 quarter hours of graduate credit or equivalent

B. Three years of successful experience on transitional or initial licenses administering at least half time in one or more of TSPC-approved schools in Oregon
C. Through required course of study, assessments, and administrative experience, candidate must demonstrate competencies specified by TSPC.
D. Passing score as currently specified by TSPC on test of professional knowledge for school administrators

Pennsylvania

Level I Certification

I. Instructional and Educational Specialist I (valid 6 years of service; nonrenewable)
   A. Hold a bachelor's degree and complete an approved education preparation program in the area requested with a cumulative grade-point average of 3.0 on a 4.0 scale.
   B. Receive the recommendation of the preparing college/university.
   C. Meet all Pennsylvania testing requirements.
      1. Applicant must register for the correct Pennsylvania required tests; consult the www.education.state.pa.us website for list of testing requirements by certificate type (see Appendix 1).
      2. All applicants must take the required tests for certification, except for those holding certification through the National Board for Professional Teaching Standards.
      3. All candidates for certification must meet the qualifying score for all applicable tests at the time their application for certification is received by the Bureau of School Leadership and Teacher Quality.
   D. Meet all citizenship and good moral character requirements.
II. Vocational Instructional I (valid 6 years of service; nonrenewable; valid 7 years of service if issued prior to October 1999.)
   A. Minimum of 2 years of wage-earning experience in addition to the learning period required to establish competency in the occupation to be taught.
   B. Successful completion of the occupational competency examination or evaluation of credentials for occupations where examinations do not exist.
   C. Eighteen credit hours in an approved program of vocational teacher education.
      1. For vocational I certificates issued on or after January 1, 2013, the 18 credit hours must include at least 3 credits, or 90 hours, or equivalent combination thereof, regarding accommodations and adaptations for diverse learners in an inclusive setting.
   D. Receive the recommendation of the preparing college/university.
   E. Meet all Pennyslvania testing requirements.
      1. All candidates for certification must meet the qualifying score for all applicable tests at the time their application for certification is received by the Bureau of School Leadership and Teacher Quality: consult website for list of testing requirements by certificate type (see Appendix 1).
   F. Meet all citizenship and good moral character requirements.
III. Administrative I: Principal K–12 (valid 5 years of service; nonrenewable) or Administrative: Vocational Director (valid 99 years)
   A. Three years of satisfactory instructional, educational specialist, supervisory, or administrative experience.

    B.   Complete an approved education preparation program including an internship in the area requested with a cumulative grade-point average of 3.0 on a 4.0 scale.

        1.   Principal programs must be graduate level.

    C.   Receive the recommendation of the preparing college/university.

    D.   Meet all Pennsylvania testing requirements.

        1.   See II, E, 1, above.

    E.   Meet all citizenship and good moral character requirements.

IV.   Administrative Provisional (valid 5 years of service; nonrenewable)

    A.   Bachelor's degree

    B.   Three years of professional experience in an educational setting related to the instructional process.

    C.   Verification of an employment offer as a principal, vice-principal, assistant principal, or vocational administrative director.

    D.   Meet all citizenship and good moral character requirements.

    E.   Must complete additional education and testing requirements within the first 2 years of employment.

V.   Supervisory (valid 99 years)

    A.   Five years of satisfactory service on an instructional or educational specialist certificate relevant to the area for which the supervisory certificate is sought.

    B.   Complete an approved graduate-level education preparation program including an internship in the area requested with a cumulative grade-point average of 3.0 on a 4.0 scale.

    C.   Receive the recommendation of the preparing college/university.

    D.   Meet all Pennsylvania testing requirements.

        1.   See II, E, 1, above.

    E.   Meet all citizenship and good moral character requirements.

VI.   Vocational Supervisor (valid 99 years)

    A.   Three years of satisfactory certified vocational teaching experience.

    B.   Complete an approved graduate-level education preparation program including an intership in the area requested with a cumulative grade-point average of 3.0 on a 4.0 scale.

    C.   Receive the recommendation of the preparing college/university.

    D.   Meet all Pennsylvania testing requirements.

        1.   See II, E, 1, above.

Level II Certification

I.   Instructional Certificates

    A.   Educators holding a Level I certificate who were awarded their initial baccalaureate degree after October 1, 1963, must provide evidence of 24 semester hour post-baccalaureate credits.

        1.   Effective September 1, 2011, educators who have been issued a Level I certificate after September 22, 2007, must have earned at least 6 post-baccalaureate credits of collegiate study in the area(s) of certification and/or designed to improve professional practice as part of the 24 semester hour post-

baccalaureate credits requirement. See CSPG No. 7 on website (see Appendix 1) for details.

B. Requires 3 years of satisfactory service on a Level I certificate

    1. Educator must possess at least 6 semiannual evaluations of satisfactory performance on the Level I certificate in the area for which the certificate was issued.

C. All instructional areas of certification will simultaneously convert to a Level II certificate provided all requirements have been met.

D. Requires completion of a Pennsylvania Department of Education approved induction program for educators initially certified June 1987 or after.

II. Education Specialist Certificates

A. Educators holding a Level I certificate who were awarded their initial baccalaureate degree after October 1, 1963, must provide evidence of 24 semester hour post-baccalaureate credits.

B. Requires 3 years of satisfactory service on the Level I certificate.

    1. Educator must possess at least 6 semiannual evaluations of satisfactory performance in Pennsylvania in each education specialist area for which a certificate has been issued for certificates issued on or after September 1, 2001.

C. Each educational specialist area of certification must be independently converted to a Level II certificate when all requirements are met.

D. Requires completion of a Pennsylvania Department of Education approved induction program for certificates issued on or after September 1, 2001.

III. Vocational Instructional Certificates

A. Educators who were issued a Vocational Instructional Level I certificate on or after January 1, 2013, may be recommended for Level II certification by their Pennsylvania-approved preparatory college/university after completing a total of 60 credit hours in addition to the 18 credits earned in Vocational I programs, including:

    1. At least 6 credits, or 180 hours, or an equivalent combination thereof, regarding accommodations and adaptations for students with disabilities in an inclusive setting; and

    2. At least 3 credits, or 90 hours, or an equivalent combination thereof, in teaching English language learners.

B. Requires a minimum of 3 years of satisfactory service in Pennsylvania in any occupational competency area(s) for which the certificate was issued.

C. Requires completion of a Pennsylvania Department of Education approved induction program.

D. Meet all Pennsylvania testing requirements; see Level I Certification, II, E, 1, above

E. All vocational areas of certification will simultaneously convert to a Level II certificate provided all requirements have been met.

IV. Administrative and Supervisory Certificates

A. Educational requirements

    1. The holders of administrative certificates issued in accordance with regulations established prior to September 1999 and who have served in the capacity of principal, assistant principal, or vice principal in a Pennsylvania public school

prior to January 1, 2008, have no additional educational requirements for Level II.

    a. Supervisory certificates have no additional educational requirements.

2. Educators granted administrative certificates prior to January 1, 2008, but who are employed for the first time in a position of principal, assistant principal, or vice principal in a Pennsylvania public school on or after January 1, 2008, must complete the Principal's Induction Program within 5 years of service to retain the certificate.

3. A principal certificate issued on or after January 1, 2008, requires the completion of an approved Principal's Induction Program, and shall be an Administrative I certificate.

    a. No individual may serve as principal, vice principal, or assistant principal on it for more than 5 service years in Pennsylvania.

B. Service requirements

1. Administrative I and Supervisory I certificates issued in accordance with regulations established prior to September 1, 1999, are made permanent by completion of 3 years of satisfactory service in Pennsylvania in each administrative/supervisory certificate area.

2. Administrative and Supervisory certificates issued in accordance with September 1, 1999, regulations are valid for 99 years.

3. Administrative I certificates issued in accordance with Act 45 of 2007 require 3 years of satisfactory Administrative I service in Pennsylvania.

4. Administrative Provisional I certificates issued in accordance with Act 24 of 2011 require 3 years of satisfactory administrative service in Pennsylvania.

V. Program Specialist Certificate

A. Most program specialist certificate holders possess a Pennsylvania Instructional certificate in order to be eligible for a program specialist certificate.

B. Service on a program specialist certificate is creditable toward meeting the experience requirements for Level II certification for the prerequisite Level I certificate and is charged against the period of validity of the prerequisite Level I certificate.

C. Once an educator has completed 3 years of combined satisfactory service on the instructional certificate and/or program specialist certificate and has satisfied all educational requirements for Level II certification, the educator may convert the prerequisite Instructional Level I certificate to a Level II certificate.

Types of Certificates

I. Instructional Certificates (default grade level is K–12 unless otherwise indicated)

A. Agriculture (7–12); art education; business, computer and information technology; Chinese; citizenship education (7–12); communication (7–12); cooperative education (7–12); English (7–12); environmental education; family and consumer science; French; German; health education; health and physical education; Hebrew; Italian; Japanese; Latin; library science; marketing (distributive) education;

mathematics (7–12); music education; Portuguese; reading specialist; Russian; safety/driver education (7–12); science—biology (7–12); science—chemistry (7–12); science—earth and space (7–12); science—general science (7–12); science—physics (7–12); social sciences (7–12); social studies (7–12); Spanish; special education—visually impaired (N–12); special education—hearing impaired (N–12); special education—speech/language impaired (N–I2); technology education.

B.   Early childhood (N–3), elementary education (K–6), middle level English (7–9), middle level mathematics (7–9), middle level social studies (7–9), middle level science (7–9) and special education (N–2) are no longer issued as of August 31, 2013.

C.   Grades PreK–4, Grades 4–8 with a concentration in English, mathematics, science and/or social studies, special education (PreK–8), and special education (7–12) are new certificates effective January 1, 2012.

II.   Educational Specialist Certificates (default grade level is K–12 unless otherwise indicated)

A.   Dental hygienist; elementary counselor (K–6); secondary counselor (7–12); home and school visitor; instructional technology; school nurse; school counselor (PreK–12).

III.   Supervisory Certificates (default grade level is K–12 unless otherwise indicated)

A.   Curriculum and instruction; pupil personnel services; special education; vocational education (7–12); single instructional area.

IV.   Administrative Certificate

A.   Principal (K–12); vocational administrative director (7–12).

V.   Letter of Eligibility

A.   Superintendent (K–12); Intermediate Unit Executive Director (K–12).

VI.   Vocational Certificate

Consult website for detailed information (see Appendix 1)

Rhode Island

Certification Overview

I. Three-Tier Certification System provides multi-year certificates that demonstrate the educator has met all Rhode Island requirements for certification; comparable to the National Association of State Directors of Teacher Education and Certification (NASDTEC) Stage 3 Licenses, which are recognized by other states for certificate reciprocity

    A. Initial Educator Certificate (valid 3 years; renewable) Held by all educators when they are certified for the first time in Rhode Island

    B. Professional Educator Certificate (valid 5 years; renewable) Awarded to holders of Initial Educator certificates once they demonstrate acceptable levels of performance while working under their certificate

    C. Advanced Educator Certificate (valid 7 years; renewable) Held by educators who consistently demonstrate highly effective practice

II. Preliminary Educator Certificate (valid 1 year) Allows educators who are not fully certified to serve as educators of record while pursuing certification

    A. Alternate Route Preliminary Certificate (valid 1 year; renewable) For prospective educators who:

        1. Are enrolled in a Rhode Island approved alternate route preparation program; and

        2. Have been offered a position in a district to serve as an educator of record while completing certification requirements

    B. Career and Technical Education / School Nurse Teacher Preliminary Certificate (valid 1 year; renewable) For prospective educators who:

        1. Have met specified requirements;
            and

        2. Have demonstrated that they have appropriate work experience in their respective fields.

        3. Holders can seek employment as teachers of record in employing agencies that are willing to employ them while the individuals pursue full certification.

    C. Emergency Preliminary Certificate (valid 1 year; renewable) For prospective educators at the request of employing agency when a fully certified and qualified educator who meets the criteria for the position cannot be secured

    D. Expert Residency Preliminary Certificate (valid 1 year; renewable; not available until January 1, 2015) For prospective educators who:

        I. Demonstrate sufficient preparation in subject matter, administrative expertise, or other certificate area specific requirements to be considered for positions as educators while pursuing certification

            a. Certified educators seeking to add new certification areas may also use this certificate as part of a route to certification in that area.

E.   Temporary Initial Educator Preliminary Certificate (valid 1 year; nonrenewable) For prospective educators who:
1.   Seek certification through reciprocity;
     and
2.   Meet all requirements for the Rhode Island Initial Educator certificate except for the Rhode Island certification testing requirements, including the English Language Competency Test, when applicable.
3.   This certificate allows the prospective educator time to meet the Rhode Island certification testing requirements while working in Rhode Island public schools.

F.   Visiting Lecturer Preliminary Certificate (valid 1 year; renewable; not available until January 1, 2015) For individuals who:
1.   Have distinctive qualifications and therefore a unique capacity to enhance educational programs in districts;
     and
2.   Have been offered employment in districts.
3.   This certificate is not a route to full certification.

G.   Permits
1.   Athletic Coach Permit (valid 5 years; renewable)
2.   Substitute Teacher Permit (valid 1 year; renewable)

III.   Certificates Available
A.   Teacher Certificates
1.   Early Childhood Certificates (PK–Grade 2 unless otherwise specified)
     a.   Early Childhood Education; Early Childhood Special Education (Birth–Grade 2); Early Childhood English as a Second Language Education; Early Childhood Bilingual and Dual Language Education
2.   Elementary Certificates (Grades 1–6)
     a.   Elementary Education; Elementary and Middle Level Special Education—Mild Moderate; Elementary English as a Second Language Education; Elementary Bilingual and Dual Language Education
3.   Middle Grades Teacher Certificates (Grades 5–8)
     a.   English; English as a Second Language; Mathematics; Science; Social Studies; World Languages
4.   Secondary Grades Teacher Certificates (Grades 7–12)
     a.   Agriculture; Bilingual and Dual Language; Biology; Business Education; Career and Technical Education; Chemistry; English; English as a Second Language; General Science; Mathematics; Physics; Social Studies; World Languages
5.   All Grades Teacher Certificates (Grades PK–12)
     a.   Adapted Physical Education; Art; Bilingual and Dual Language; Dance; English as a Second Language Specialist; English as a Second Language Teacher; Family and Consumer Science; Health; Library Media; Music; Physical Education; School Nurse Teacher; Technology Education; Theatre
6.   Special Education Teacher Certificates
     a.   Elementary/Middle Special Education (Grades K–8); Middle/Secondary Special Education Teacher (Grades 7–12); All Grades Special Education—

Blind and/or Visually Impaired (Grades PK–12); All Grades Special Education—Deaf and Hard of Hearing Teacher (Grades PK–12); All Grades Special Education—Severe Intellectual Disability Teacher (Grades PK–12)

B.   Administrator Certificates
1.   Building Level Administrator; District Level Administrator—Curriculum and Instruction; and Administrator of Curriculum and Instruction; District Level Administrator—Special Education and Administrator of Special Education; School Business Administrator; Superintendent of Schools

C.   Support Professionals
1.   Reading Specialist / Consultant; School Counselor; School Psychologist; School Social Worker, Speech and Language Pathologist

D.   Permits
1.   Substitute Teacher; Athletic Coach

Requirements for Teaching Certificates

I.   Early Childhood (PK to Grade 2) and Elementary (Grades 1–6)
A.   Initial Educator Certificate (valid 3 years)
1.   Bachelor's degree from a regionally accredited institution;
2.   Completion of Rhode Island–approved program in appropriate field at specific Rhode Island institutions of higher education; reciprocity; or transcript analysis—see I, B, directly below;
3.   Completion of a minimum of 12 weeks of student teaching in this area and a minimum of 60 hours field experience prior to student teaching
4.   Demonstration of meeting the professional competencies of the Rhode Island Professional Teaching Standards (RIPTS);
5.   Demonstration of meeting specified content competencies;
a.   These may include those prescribed by National Association for the Education of Young Children (NAEYC) or by the Association for Childhood Education International and Content Specific Standards (ACEI)
b.   For Special Education, these may include those prescribed by the Council for Exceptional Children (CEC)
c.   For language certifications, these may include those prescribed by Teachers of English to Speakers of Other Languages (TESOL)
6.   Assessment Requirements
a.   Applicants must achieve a passing score of 174 on the Praxis II Education of Young Children (0021/5021) and a passing score of 170 on the Praxis II Early Childhood: Content Knowledge (0022/5022);
     or
     Applicants must achieve a passing score of 160 on the Principles of Learning and Teaching Test K–6 (0622/5622) and passing scores on the Praxis II Elementary Multiple Subjects (5031).
b.   Applicants prepared in a program where the language of instruction was not English must achieve a passing score of 64 on the Versant Pro Speaking and Writing English assessments.

7. Other requirements as specified.
B. Current Routes to Certification
  1. Completion of Rhode Island–approved program in appropriate field at specific Rhode Island institutions of higher education
  2. Reciprocity
     a. Applicants seeking certification through reciprocity (recognition of preparation or certification in another state) must demonstrate that they meet all Rhode Island certification assessment requirements, hold the additional required certificate, and meet all experience requirements when applicable.
     b. Applicants can attain certification by completing a state-approved program for Educator Certification in a state other than Rhode Island within the last 5 years,
        or
        By demonstrating that they hold a currently valid full certificate in another state.
  3. Transcript Analysis
     a. Applicants who have not completed an approved program or do not meet reciprocity requirements can be certified by transcript analysis until December 31, 2014. Beginning January 1, 2015, a credential review process will replace transcript analysis in areas for which there are no Rhode Island–approved preparation programs. For details consult www.ride.ri.gov/TeachersAdministrators/EducatorCertification.aspx
II. Middle Grades Certificates (Grades 5 – 8)
A. Three options are available to attain middle grades certification. For certificate-specific details, consult http://www.ride.ri.gov/TeachersAdministrators/Educator Certification/CertificationRequirements.aspx
  1. Common Requirements for 3 Options
     a. Bachelor's degree from a regionally accredited institution;
     b. Completion of an approved program in this area;
     c. Specified hours of student teaching, field experience, and/or practicum;
     d. Demonstration of meeting the professional, content, and pedagogical competencies as specified;
     e. Meet specific Rhode Island assessment requirements; for details, consult http://www.ride.ri.gov/TeachersAdministrators/EducatorCertification/ CertificationRequirements.aspx
        and
     f. Other requirements as specified.
  2. Option 1: Stand Alone
     a. Includes completion of an approved program for the preparation of middle grades teachers and other requirements specific to middle grades, including demonstration of the pedagogical competencies of the Association for Middle Level Education (AMLE)
  3. Option 2: Extend an Elementary Education Certificate
     a. For holders of elementary education certificates

        4.   Option 3: Extend a Secondary Grades Certificate

          a.   For holders of secondary education certificates

III.   Secondary (Grades 7–12)

    A.   Initial Educator Certificate (valid for 3 years)

        1.   Bachelor's degree from a regionally accredited institution;

        2.   Completion of Rhode Island–approved program in appropriate field at Rhode Island institution of higher education; reciprocity; or transcript analysis—see 5, b, directly below

        3.   Demonstration of meeting the professional competencies of the Rhode Island Professional Teaching Standards (RIPTS);

        4.   Demonstration of meeting specified professional, pedagogical, and content competencies;

          a.   For specifics, consult http://www.ride.ri.gov/TeachersAdministrators/ EducatorCertification/CertificationRequirements.aspx

        5.   Assessment requirements

          a.   Achieve a passing score of 157 on the Praxis II Principles of Learning & Teaching—Grades 7–12 (0624/5624) with a score of 157 or higher and passing score on specified content area assessment(s).

          b.   Applicants prepared in a program where the language of instruction was not English must achieve a passing score of 64 on the Versant Pro Speaking and Writing assessments; and

        6.   Other requirements as specified.

Administrators and Support Professionals

For detailed certification information, consult http://www.ride.ri.gov/TeachersAdministrators/ EducatorCertification/CertificationRequirements.aspx

South Carolina

Note on "Highly Qualified" Requirement

1. Teachers of core academic subjects must not only be properly certified, but must also meet the "highly qualified" teacher requirements of the federal No Child Left Behind Act of 2001 (Pub. L. No. 107-110), which requires public school elementary and secondary teachers to meet their state's definition of highly qualified teacher for each core academic subject they teach.
2. According to No Child Left Behind, these subjects are English, reading or language arts, math, science, history, civics and government, geography, economics, the arts and foreign language.
3. Special education teachers and teachers of English language learners must be highly qualified if they teach core academic subjects to their students.
4. Out-of-field permits may be issued for administrators, eligible teachers, library media specialists, and guidance counselors. Contact the South Carolina Office of Educator Services (see Appendix 1) to determine what subject area teachers are eligible for out-of-field permits.
5. For more information about Highly Qualified requirements, call the Office of Federal and State Accountability at 803-734-3454.

Steps to Certification

To access step-by-step instructions for required materials, specific forms and how to submit them for each of the categories below, consult http://ed.sc.gov/agency/se/Educator-Services

I. Uncertified Applicants. For those who have completed an approved teacher-education program but have not yet been certified
   A. Submit an official, sealed transcript from each college or university attended, as well as a college recommendation form signed by designated college official.
   B. Submit passing scores for the required Praxis II specialty area exams; and submit a passing score on the Principles of Learning and Teaching (PLT) in the specific grade level.
II. Reciprocal Applicants
   A. Applicants with a valid standard certificate issued by another state, a United States territory, or the Department of Defense Dependents Schools (DODDS), may be eligible for certification through South Carolina's reciprocity agreement.
      1. Interstate reciprocity does not apply to Career and Technology Education Work-Based licensure.
   B. To evaluate status of existing credentials, review South Carolina's current reciprocity agreement with the states, territories, and countries on website, see Appendix 1

C. Individuals with certification from the National Board for Professional Teaching Standards (NBPTS), upon application and a valid standard out-of-state certificate, will receive a professional license in their field.

D. Reciprocal Certificate Types
1. Reciprocal Initial Certificate (valid for 3 academic school years)
   a. For those with less than 3 years of teaching experience, or for those who do not have 27 months of full or part-time PreK–12 school teaching experience in the last 7 years on that valid standard license
   b. Requirements
      i. Must present valid standard out-of-state license
      ii. Subject/s shown on the license must be considered comparable to a subject/s issued in South Carolina.
      iii. All licensure areas issued in that state will also be issued on the South Carolina license provided the areas are initially requested on the application. Areas not requested initially would have to meet South Carolina's add-on requirements at the date of the request.
      iv. Content exams will not be required for licensure purposes, however, may be required for Highly Qualified status.
      v. The appropriate level of Principles of Teaching and Learning (PLT) and South Carolina's system for assisting, developing, and evaluating professional teaching (ADEPT) must be presented during the life of the Initial license and before the Professional license is issued.
2. Reciprocal Professional License (will be valid for 5 academic school years)
   a. Must present verification of 27 months of full- or part-time PreK–12 school teaching experience in the last 7 years on that valid standard license.
   b. See Reciprocal Initial License, 1, b, directly above
3. Reciprocal Professional License (National Board Certification: Will be valid for the remainder of the National Board certification)
   a. Requires valid National Board Certification and valid standard out-of-state certificate
   b. Subject/s shown on the NBC certificate must be considered comparable to the subject/s issued in South Carolina.
   c. Applicant will be given professional license in the NBC area only; or, if the reciprocal professional requirement applies, a license can be issued in those areas for the remainder of the NBC period.

Required Credentials

For complete requirements for each position, consult website; see Appendix 1

I. District professional staff, including district administrators and district consultants, curriculum specialists, and coordinators
   A. Master's degree and certification in the area of primary responsibility
II. School administrators and professional support staff
   A. Master's degree and certification in the area of primary responsibility

III.   Teachers of special education
    A.   Acceptable certification, determined by the area of disability in which all or the majority of the teacher's students are classified.
        1.   Acceptable certification for a resource or itinerant special education teacher is determined by the area of disability in which the majority of the teacher's students (i.e., caseload) are classified.
    B.   Teachers of core academic subjects must also meet No Child Left Behind requirements.

IV.   Teachers of PreKindergarten–Grade 6; Grades 7–8; Grades 9–12
    A.   Acceptable certification and all mandatory attendant training
    B.   Teachers of core academic subjects must also meet No Child Left Behind requirements.
    C.   Teachers of credit-bearing courses in grades 7 and 8 must either hold middle-level certification in the content area, secondary certification in the content area, or hold middle school certification.
        1.   Additionally, these teachers must have passed either the middle-level or secondary Praxis II exam in the content area or the National Teacher's Examination in the content area.
    D.   Teachers of Career and Technology Education must have acceptable certification and all mandatory attendant training but are not required to meet "Highly Qualified" standards.

South Dakota

Teacher Certification

Please note that South Dakota has aligned all teacher education programs to national standards where applicable. A complete record of standards can be obtained at http://doe.sd.gov/oatq/teacheredprograms.aspx

I. General Requirements for All Certification Levels:
    A. Verification from accredited institution that applicant has met the standards of an approved program and can be recommended for certification
    B. Notarized citizenship statement and verification that applicant has not been convicted of any crime involving moral turpitude, including traffic in narcotics
    C. Completion of human relations (HR) and South Dakota Indian studies (SDIS) courses
    D. If an applicant meets all the stated requirements for certification with the exception of SDIS and HR, a 5-year certificate can be issued with the understanding that both SDIS and HR must be completed as course work to renew the initial certificate.

II. Initial Certification Requirements (valid 5 years):
    A. A completed online initial application form (online form is at http./doe.sd.gov/oatq/teachercert.aspx)
    B. Official transcripts from each accredited postsecondary institution attended
    C. Official copy of all passing test scores including any subtest scores provided on the state certification exams
    D. Teachers new to the profession or to the state are required to pass Praxis II tests specific to the content areas they will be teaching.
        1. The department may issue a 1-year certificate allowing an applicant to complete required Praxis.
        2. Testing information is at http://doe.sd.gov/oatq/praxis.aspx
    E. Teachers new to the profession also must take the Principles of Learning and Teaching test that most accurately matches their level of preparation.
    F. Teachers who have had any contracted teaching experience on a valid certificate outside of their basic teaching program requirements, including student teaching, practicum, or internship, can either show verification of teaching experience at http://doe.sd.gov/oatq/teachercert.aspx or submit a copy of Praxis II PLT test scores.
    G. Institutional statement completed and submitted by the certifying office of the college/university where preparation was made
    H. Applicants whose programs are more than 5 years old must provide documentation of 6 educational credits from an accredited institution in the 5 years immediately preceding the date of application.
        1. The department may issue a 1-year certificate allowing an applicant to complete required college credits.

III. K–8 Elementary Education Program Requirements:
    A. General and Initial Certification requirements (see I and II, directly above)

    B. Course work sufficient to constitute an elementary education major

    C. Demonstrated competencies in all of the following areas:

        1. Knowledge of the developmental characteristics of the elementary-level learner and of the student with disabilities

        2. Knowledge of curriculum development that uses South Dakota and other established K–12 academic standards to design a successful instructional program that facilitates student achievement

        3. Integration of technology into teaching and learning

        4. Verification that the applicant has completed studies and field experiences in all of the following:

            a. Design of curriculum and instructional strategies for middle-level learners

            b. Developmental characteristics of the middle-level learner

            c. Concepts of middle-level education or the middle-level learner

IV. 7–12 Secondary Education Program Requirements

    A. General and Initial Certification requirements (see I and II, directly above)

    B. Course work sufficient to constitute an academic major

    C. Demonstrated competencies in all of the following areas:

        1. Competency in the teaching of content area literacy and instructional methods in the content area specific to the discipline

        2. Knowledge of the developmental characteristics of the secondary-level learner and of the student with disabilities

        3. Knowledge of curriculum development that uses South Dakota and other established K–12 academic standards to design an instructional program that facilitates student achievement

        4. Integrating technology into teaching and learning

        5. Concepts of middle-level education or the middle-level learner

        6. Verification that the candidate has completed studies and field experiences in the following:

            a. Design of curriculum and instructional strategies for middle-level learners

            b. Developmental characteristics of the middle-level learner

V. 5–8 Middle-Level Education Program Requirements

    A. General and Initial Certification requirements (see I and II, directly above)

    B. Course work sufficient to constitute a middle school education major

    C. Demonstrated competencies in all of the following areas:

        1. Teaching middle-level reading

        2. Integrating technology into teaching and learning

        3. Knowledge of the developmental characteristics of the middle-level learner and of the student with disabilities

        4. Knowledge of curriculum development that uses South Dakota and other established K–12 academic standards to design an instructional program that facilitates student achievement

        5. Integrating technology into teaching and learning

VI. Alternative Certification

    A. Limited to 7–12 or K–12 age/grade span authorizations issued at the approved education program level

B. To be eligible for the program, an applicant must have the following:
1. A bachelor's degree or higher, with the bachelor's degree obtained at least 2 years prior to admittance into the alternative certification program
2. An overall grade-point average of 2.5 or higher on an undergraduate transcript
3. A college major in the subject area to be taught or has 5 years of experience in a related field
4. An offer of employment from a South Dakota accredited school system that operates a mentoring program approved by the department
5. A criminal background investigation done by the school district
6   Adherence to the Code of Professional Ethics, as adopted by the Professional Teachers Practices and Standards Commission
7. A screening interview with school personnel and the department's program coordinator,
    and
8. An official copy of all test scores, including any subtest scores provided by the testing company on the state certification exams for each subject or area authorization, and for the pedagogy exam for each age or grade span in which the alternative certification applicant will be certified.

Reading Specialist

I. K–12 reading specialist program shall require all of the following:
A. A master's degree with an emphasis in reading
B. Three years of teaching experience in a K–12 setting
C. The required courses and experiences of a K–12 reading specialist program shall meet the International Reading Association (IRA) standards, 2003 edition.
D. The program shall require candidates to demonstrate the content, pedagogical, and professional knowledge and skills identified in the IRA standards.

Certification Changes for Endorsement Programs

I. For the most part, South Dakota cannot award an endorsement without a valid South Dakota teaching certificate.
II. An additional authorization can be issued on a certificate, or a transcript analysis may be requested by completing the South Dakota Department of Education's Additional Authorizations application.
III. An additional authorization may be issued on a certificate with:
A. Verification of completion of an approved education program by a certifying officer or verification of completion of education endorsement program requirements by a certifying officer or by the department. Course work for education endorsement programs must be completed with a grade of "C" or higher at an accredited postsecondary institution. Course work earned at accredited community colleges and postsecondary vocational schools must be approved by the department or the certifying officer prior to enrollment in the course,

or

B. An official copy of all Praxis II test scores including any subtest scores provided by the testing company on the state certification exam for each subject or area authorization for endorsement programs for which the applicant is applying.

C. Submission of official transcript

Administration

I. Elementary and Secondary Principal Certificate Authorization

   A. Preschool–grade 12, preschool–grade 8, or grade 7–grade 12 principal programs shall require all of the following:

      1. Master's degree in education

      2. Three years of verified experience on a valid certificate in an accredited K–12 school, 1 year of which includes classroom teaching experience or direct services to students

         a. The 3 years of verified experience may be waived if candidate receives passing score on Educational Leadership Praxis II test.

      3. Demonstrated competence related to the age/grade span for which authorization is sought

      4. Internship to include all job responsibilities at the age/grade span for which authorization is sought

         a. For a preschool–grade 12 principal program, the internship must include time spent in at least 2 of the levels of elementary school, junior high/middle school, or secondary school.

   B. The required courses and experiences of a preschool–grade 8 or grade 7–grade 12 principal program shall meet the Educational Leadership Constituent Council (ELCC) standards, 2001 edition.

   C. The program shall require candidates to demonstrate the applicable content, pedagogical, and professional knowledge and skills identified in the ELCC.

   D. The principal programs may be developed with multiple options to earn eligibility for a preschool–grade 12 principal program within the same master's degree or as an additional certification-only principal program.

II. Superintendent Certificate Authorization

   A. Preschool–grade 12 career school superintendent program shall require:

      1. Completion of an education specialist or doctoral degree

      2. Three years of verified experience on a valid certificate in an accredited K–12 school

         a. One year to include classroom teaching experience or direct services to students

         b. Experience to allow for participation of the cooperating superintendent

      3. Internship in all job responsibilities

   B. Required courses and experiences of a preschool–grade 12 career school superintendent program shall meet ELCC standards, 2001.

   C. The program shall require candidates to demonstrate the applicable standards identified in the ELCC.

III.   Administrative Endorsement Requirements
    A.   Principal endorsement, preschool–grade 8, grade 7–grade 12, or preschool–grade 12
        1.   Bachelor's degree in education
        2.   Minimum of 15 graduate semester hours of course work, plus practicum or internship experiences, or a combination thereof, which address the specific competencies mandated by law
        3.   Three years of verified experience in an accredited K–12 school, 1 year of which includes classroom teaching experience or direct service to students
            a.   The 3 years of verified experience may be waived if candidate receives passing score on Educational Leadership Praxis II test.
        4.   Valid for 5 years only, unless the holder has also previously completed a master's degree in education
    B.   School superintendent endorsement, preschool–grade 12
        1.   Master's degree, plus 15 graduate semester hours which address the specific competencies mandated by law
        2.   Three years of verified experience on a valid certificate in an accredited K–12 school, 1 year of which includes classroom teaching experience or direct services to students
        3.   Valid for 10 years only; and within the first 5 years of validity, holder must complete 6 additional graduate semester hours addressing specific competencies mandated by law; and by end of validity, all legal requirements must be satisfied.
    C.   Principal endorsement program, preschool–grade 12
        1.   Master's degree with a preschool–grade 8 or 7–12 principalship
        2.   Completion of course work specific to the preschool–grade 8 or 7–12 principal endorsement sought
        3.   Three years of verified experience in an accredited K–12 school, 1 year of which includes classroom teaching experience or direct services to students
            a.   The 3 years of verified experience may be waived if candidate receives passing score on Educational Leadership Praxis II test.

School Counselor Certificate Authorization

I.   A preschool through grade 12 school counselor education program shall require a master's degree in school guidance or counseling.
    A.   The required courses and experiences of a preschool–grade 12 school counselor education program shall meet the Council on Accreditation of Counseling and Related Education Programs (CACREP) standards, 2001 edition.
    B.   The program shall require candidates to demonstrate the applicable content, pedagogical, and professional knowledge and skills identified in the CACREP standards.

Certificate Renewal

I.   Individuals who wish to renew a current South Dakota teaching certificate or update a lapsed certificate need specific items to complete an online application; for details, contact the Department of Education (see Appendix 1)

II. Certified staff with advanced certification or degrees, including National Board certification, master's degrees, specialist degrees, and doctoral degrees, must document 6 credits, which can be a combination of continuing education contact hours and university credits.

III. Certified staff with only a bachelor degree must document six credits.
   A. Three of these six credits—or five of nine quarter credits—must be earned at the university level; and those hours must be recognized on an official college transcript.

IV. Applicants renewing an initial 5-year certificate
   A. Must verify completion of 2 departmentally approved 3 credit courses, 1 in human relations and another in South Dakota Indian studies.

V. Applicants renewing an initial 1-year certificate must verify completion of any deficiencies such as Praxis II tests or recent credits on a college transcript.

VI. Applicants updating a lapsed certificate must verify completion of any deficiencies in excess of 6 semester hours that were identified at the reissuance of the lapsed certificate.

Reciprocity

I. South Dakota has reciprocity with any accredited out-of-state teacher preparation program that is also offered in South Dakota.

II. Reciprocity applicants must provide a sign-off from the university from which they obtained their degree along with supporting transcript documentation.

III. Successful applicants will be granted a 1-year certificate, during the course of which they must complete and pass both the Praxis II pedagogy and content tests for each area of certification.

Tennessee

Types of Teacher Licenses

I. Apprentice License (valid 5 years; renewable)
   A. Initial license issued to applicant who completes approved teacher preparation program or who meets reciprocal requirements with less than 1 year of teaching experience
   B. Five-year validity to allow 3 years of teaching in Tennessee public or state-accredited private school; validity expires after 3 years of teaching in approved Tennessee school
II. Out-of-State Teacher's License (valid 5 years; renewable)
   A. Initial license issued to out-of-state applicant who meets Tennessee licensure requirements; equivalent to Apprentice License
   B. Requires at least 1 year of acceptable teaching experience in another state
III. Professional License (valid 10 years; renewable)
   A. Accrue minimum of 3 years of acceptable experience in an approved school and receive positive local evaluation in Tennessee public or state-accredited private school
      1. Three years of experience may combine in-state with out-of-state experience, but last year must be in Tennessee public school to participate in local evaluation process
IV. Transitional License (1 year; renewable no more than 2 times)
   A. Applies only to candidates holding at least a bachelor's degree who may or may not have yet completed all required licensure exams.
   B. Requirements:
      1. Bachelor's degree from a regionally accredited institution of higher education and content in one of the following 3 ways:
         a. Acceptable major in the endorsement area,
            or
         b. Verification of at least 24 semester hours in the teaching content area,
            or
         c. Pass the required PRAXIS II content exam(s) for the endorsement area sought.
      2. Statement signed by a Tennessee director of schools stating intent to employ the candidate as directed by the Transitional License application
      3. Verification by the institution of higher education or approved education organization of enrollment in and/or admission to the Transitional License program
V. Apprentice Occupational Education License (valid 3 years; renewable)
   A. Issued in two areas:
      1. Health Science and Technology
      2. Trade and Industry

    B.   Contact Office of Teacher Licensing (see Appendix 1) for complete list of endorsement areas and related requirements for each

  VI. Professional Occupational Education License (valid 10 years; renewable)

    A.   Hold Apprentice Occupational Education License

    B.   Evaluation by approved university of candidate's knowledge and skills to determine specific course work required

  VII. Apprentice Special Group Licenses (valid 5 years)

    A.   Initial license issued for the following areas (Grades PreK–12): school counselor, school psychologist, school social worker, speech language pathologist, and school audiologist

  VIII. Professional School Service Personnel License (valid 10 years)

    A.   Serve in endorsement area (see VII, A, directly above) for a minimum of 3 years

       1.   Last year of 3 years of service in Tennessee public or state-accredited private school with receipt of positive local evaluation

Teacher License Requirements

    I. Tennessee College/University Program Route to Licensure

    A.   Hold a bachelor's and/or master's degree from a teacher preparation program at a regionally accredited college/university

       1.   Program to include all required professional courses, student teaching, and/or internship

    B.   Pass all appropriate portions of the Praxis Series Exam

    C.   Receive recommendation from college/university to Tennessee Office of Teacher Licensing

    II. Out-of-State Route to Licensure

    A.   Complete a teacher preparation program or meet reciprocity requirements

    B.   Hold a bachelor's and/or master's degree from a regionally accredited college/university

    C.   Pass all appropriate portions of the Praxis Series Exam, unless:

       1.   Fully certified/licensed in another state before July 1, 1984,
or

       2.   Hold full, valid license in an endorsement area available in Tennessee from a state having a reciprocal agreement with Tennessee and meet all guidelines defined in reciprocal agreement; submit documentation to Office of Teaching Licensing (see Appendix 1) for determination of possible eligibility without testing.

    III. Endorsements

Administrator (Aspiring PreK–12; Beginning PreK–12; Professional PreK–12; Exemplary preK–12); Bible 7–12; Biology 7–12; Business Education 7–12; Business Technology 7–12; Early Child Care Services 9–12; Chemistry 7–12; Coop Coordinator; Dance K–12, Driver Education 7–12; Early Childhood Education PreK–3; Early Development/Learning PreK–K; Earth Science 7–12; Economics 7–12; Elementary K–6; English 7–12; English as Second Language PreK–12; Family & Consumer Sciences 5–12; Food Production & Management Services 9–12; Food Service Supervisor;

Foreign Language Other (7–12; PreK–12); French (7–12; PreK–12); Geography 7–12; German (7–12; PreK–12); Gifted Education PreK–12; Government 7–12; Health & Wellness K–12; History 7–12; JROTC; Latin (7–12; PreK–12); Library Information Specialist PreK–12; Marketing 7–12; Mathematics 7–12; Middle Grades (4–8); Music (Instrumental/General K–12; Vocal/General K–12); Physical Education K–12; Physics 7–12; Psychology 9–12; Reading Specialist PreK–12; Russian (PreK–12; 7–12); School Counselor PreK–12; School Psychologist PreK–12; School Audiologist PreK–12; Speech Language Pathologist PreK–12; School Social Worker PreK–12; Sociology 9–12; Spanish (7–12; PreK–12); Special Education (Comprehensive K–12; Early Childhood Education PreK–3; Hearing PreK–12; Modified K–12; Speech/Language Teacher PreK–12; Vision PreK–12); Speech Communications 7–12; Superintendent; Supervisor of Attendance; Supervisor of Materials; Technology/Engineering Education 5–12; Theatre K–12; Visual Arts K–12; Agriculture Education 7–12

Administrator (PreK–12)

I. Beginning Administrator License or Instructional Leadership License— Beginning (valid 5 years)
   A. Complete approved graduate program in school administration and supervision at accredited institution of higher education (IHE)
   B. Passing grades on state-required test/assessment
   C. Receive recommendation for license by an approved leadership preparation program
II. Professional Administrator License (valid 10 years; renewable)
   or
   Instructional Leadership License—Professional (valid 5 years; renewable)
   A. Hold Beginning Administrator License or Instructional Leadership License—Beginning
   B. Obtain employment as assistant principal, principal, or supervisor of instruction in Tennessee public or state-accredited private school
   C. Complete customized professional development program jointly developed by administrator, superintendent, Tennessee IHE, and mentor
   or
   Complete state beginning administrator academy program based upon Tennessee Instructional Leadership Standards (TILS)
   D. Receive successful local evaluation by superintendent or designee based upon TILS
   E. Serve successfully in administrator position at least 2 years.

Librarian

I. Licensing requirements
   A. Complete graduate-level program leading to a master's degree with major in library information; or have master's degree and complete graduate-level library licensing program
   B. Receive recommendation for licensure from college/university attended
   C. Receive passing scores on appropriate parts of Praxis series examination

Texas

The rules adopted by the State Board for Educator Certification (SBEC) are part of a larger body of state agency rules that are collected and published as the Texas Administrative Code. The SBEC may adopt new rules or amendments to or repeals of existing rules at any time. Go to Texas Education Agency website at http://www.tea.state.tx.us for most recent rule changes.

Certification Overview

I. General Certification Requirements
    A. Hold bachelor's degree from institution of higher education that at the time was accredited or otherwise approved by an accrediting organization recognized by the Texas Higher Education Coordinating Board
        1. Texas institutions do not offer a degree in education, so every teacher must have an academic major as well as teacher-training courses.
            a. Only exemption is for individuals seeking Career and Technical Education certification to teach certain courses, such as welding or computer-aided drafting
    B. Complete teacher training through an approved program, offered through colleges and universities, school districts, regional service centers, community colleges, and other entities
    C. Successfully complete appropriate teacher certification tests for subject and grade level. Specific Texas Examinations of Educator Standards (TExES) and Examination for the Certification of Educators in Texas (ExCET) and other tests are required, depending on applicant's background and certification sought; contact TEA at http://www.tea.state.tx.us for list of certification tests and information on which tests are required.
        1. Teachers certified in another state must submit an application for a review of credentials.
II. Routes to Educator Certification
    A. University-based Programs
        1. Undergraduate certificate earned as part of baccalaureate degree program
        2. Post-baccalaureate programs designed to prepare baccalaureate degree holders seeking educator certification.
    B. Alternative Programs for Educator Preparation
        1. TEA-approved programs available at some institutions of higher education. These may involve university course work or other professional development experiences as well as intense mentoring and supervision during candidate's first year in role of educator.
        2. Some regional education service centers, large school districts, and private entities offer alternative programs of preparation.

C. Additional Certification Based on Examination: for teachers holding a classroom teaching certificate and bachelor's degree
    1. Such teachers may add classroom certification areas by successfully completing appropriate certification examination(s) for area(s) sought.
    2. Certification by examination not available for:
        a. Initial certification
        b. Career and Technical Education, except for marketing; certification based on skill and work experience
        c. Certification other than classroom teacher (e.g., counselor, principal, superintendent, school librarian, educational diagnostician)
        d. Certificate for which no certification examination has been developed

D. Certification Based on Credentials from Another Jurisdiction
    1. Applicants holding an acceptable certificate or credential from another state, U.S. territory, or country may apply for a Texas certificate. Credential must be equivalent to a certificate issued by TEA and must not have been revoked, suspended, or pending such action.
    2. One-Year Certificate in one or more subject areas may be issued to applicant who holds a standard credential issued by jurisdiction outside Texas and who meets specified requirements as determined by TEA credentials review. Applicant may also request exemption from Texas test based on comparable test in another jurisdiction.

E. Temporary Teacher Certificate: Applicant holding bachelor's degree or higher from accredited institution of higher education with academic major related to at least 1 area of Texas public school curriculum and to 8–12 certificate structure that currently has TExES exam may apply for transcript review by TEA. Training may be provided by an approved school district. Currently, no school districts participating.

Certificate Types, Classes, and Renewal

I. Types of Certificates: Designates period of validity, personnel, and requirements for each certificate (CPE stands for continuing professional education)
  A. Standard (valid 5 years, renewable with 150 CPE hours)
    1. Replaced lifetime provisional and professional certificates, and educators holding lifetime certificates have been exempted from renewal process.
        a. Note: Since educators adding certificates after September 1, 1999, will be issued a Standard Certificate that must be renewed, it is likely that many current educators will hold both lifetime and Standard Certificates.
    2. Standard teacher certificate requirements
        a. See Certification Overview, I and II, above
  B. One-year (nonrenewable)
    1. Issued for out-of-state or out-of-country candidates
  C. Probationary (valid 1 year; renewable for up to 2 more years)
    1. Issued to individual enrolled in educator preparation program and serving in supervised internship to satisfy field experience requirements of the certificate.

          a.   Holder must be employed by accredited Texas public or private school in position appropriate for certificate sought.

    2.   Probationary principal certificate eligibility requirements

          a.   Hold at least a bachelor's degree,

          b.   Meet admission requirements of educator preparation program, *and*

          c.   Qualify for internship as defined by the program.

    3.   Probationary superintendent eligibility requirements

          a.   Hold a Texas standard principal certificate or its equivalent from another state or country, provided applicant passed TEA-approved principal certificate examination, *and*

          b.   Hold at least a master's degree.

    4.   Renewal contingent on enrollment of applicant in educator preparation program and employment in appropriate position, with mentoring and supervision throughout validity period.

D.   Temporary Teacher (valid for 2 years, nonrenewable). Currently, no school districts participating.

    1.   Applicant must obtain a teaching position and be trained by an approved school district.

    2.   Successfully complete TEA transcript review

    3.   Applicant must pass national fingerprint-based criminal history background check.

    4.   May be issued for grades 8–12 in curriculum areas that currently have TexES exam

    5.   Requires passing scores on 8–12 Pedagogy and Professional Responsibilities (PPR) TExES exam and on appropriate 8–12 TExES content exam

E.   Emergency Permit (valid for 1 school year, renewable for no more than 2 additional school years)

    1.   Issued to degreed individual who does not have any appropriate certificate required for assignment

F.   Non-Renewable Permit (valid for 1 year, nonrenewable)

    1.   Issued to degreed individual who has completed educator preparation program but has not yet passed TExES test(s)

II.   Classes of Certificates

A.   Superintendent (valid 5 years; renewable with 200 CPE hours)

B.   Principal (valid 5 years; renewable with 200 CPE hours)

C.   Classroom teacher (valid 5 years; renewable with 150 CPE hours)

D.   Student Services, for instructional educator other than classroom teacher, including reading specialist (valid 5 years; renewable with 200 CPE hours)

E.   Master teacher, including master reading, math, science, and technology teacher (valid 5 years; renewable with 200 CPE hours)

F.   School librarian (valid 5 years; renewable with 200 CPE hours)

G.   School counselor (valid 5 years; renewable with 200 CPE hours)

H.   Educational diagnostician (valid 5 years; renewable with 200 CPE hours)
I.   Educational aide I, II, and III (valid 5 years; no renewal CPE requirements)

III.   Certificate Renewal
   A.   Standard Requirements
      1.   Hold a valid Standard Certificate that has not been, nor is in the process of being, sanctioned by TEA,
      2.   Successfully complete a criminal history review,
      3.   Not be in default on a student loan or in arrears of child support,
      4.   Complete the required number of clock hours of continuing professional education (CPE),
         and
      5.   Submit online application to TEA with appropriate renewal fee.

Administrator Certification

I.   Principal Certificate (valid 5 years; renewable with 200 CPE hours)
   A.   Requirements for certificate
      1.   Successfully complete a TEA-approved principal preparation program and be recommended for certification by that program
      2.   Successfully pass TExES Principal certification exam
      3.   Hold master's degree from institution of higher education that at the time was accredited or otherwise approved by an accrediting organization recognized by the Texas Higher Education Coordinating Board
      4.   Hold a valid classroom teaching certificate
      5.   Have 2 years of creditable teaching experience as classroom teacher

II.   Superintendent Certificate (valid 5 years; renewable with 200 CPE hours)
   A.   Requirements for certificate
      1.   Satisfactorily pass TExES superintendent certification exam
      2.   Successfully complete a TEA-approved superintendent preparation program and be recommended for certification by that program
      3.   Hold master's degree from an accredited institution of higher education that at the time was accredited or otherwise approved by an accrediting organization recognized by the Texas Higher Education Coordinating Board
      4.   Hold a principal certificate or the equivalent issued under this title or by another state or country
   B.   Induction for New Superintendents
      1.   One-year mentorship for first-time superintendents (including those new to state)
         a.   Include at least 36 clock hours of professional development directly related to identified standards
      2.   Mentorship program must be completed within the first 18 months of employment as superintendent

Utah

Educator Licenses

I. Letter of Authorization (valid for up to I year; renewable annually, not to exceed 3 years)—Temporary license issued to meet special needs at the request of local school authorities
   A. Educators involved in an alternative route to licensure (ARL) hold a temporary license until they complete the first year of an approved alternative preparation program.
      1. ARL candidates who submit documentation of progress and a successful end-of-year evaluation are moved from "temporary" to "ARL" license status for years 2 and 3 of the prelicensure program.
   B. Local boards may request from the state board a letter of authorization for educators employed by the local board who have not completed requirements for areas of concentration or endorsements.
   C. An authorization is approved for 1 school year and may be renewed for a total of 3 school years.
II. Level 1 Licensure (valid for 3 years; renewal dependent on experience)
   A. Requires one of the following:
      1. Completion of an approved Utah educator preparation program, *or*
      2. Completion of an approved Utah alternative preparation program, *or*
      3. Eligibility under the Compact for Interstate Qualification of Educational Personnel.
         a. A Level 1 license is issued to a graduate of an educator preparation program from an accredited institution of higher education in another state who meets Utah's requirements. Effective December 1, 2012, individual must hold the license in the other jurisdiction before a Utah license is issued.
         b. If the applicant has 3 or more continuous years of previous educator experience in a public or accredited private school, a Level 2 license may be issued upon the recommendation of the employing Utah Local Education Agency (LEA) after at least 1 year of teaching in Utah.
   B. All applicants for a Level 1 license or an endorsement in a No Child Left Behind (NCLB) core academic subject area must take and pass a state-approved content examination.
   C. License is valid for 3 years
      a. License holders with 3 years of teaching experience in Utah may not renew the license, but rather must meet the requirements for upgrade to a Level 2 license (See III, A, below)

    b.   A 1-year extension may be requested by the employing district/charter school if the individual has not yet met the requirements for upgrade.

  D. Renewal for those without 3 years of teaching in Utah requires 100 license renewal points every 3 years and a fingerprint background check within a year.

  E. All educators must have a Professional Learning Plan signed by their administrator for renewal; consult: http://schools.utah.gov/cert/License-Renewals/Professional-Learning-Plan.aspx

  F. "Active" educators (http://schools.utah.gov/cert/License-Renewals/Definitions.aspx) must also have at least 2 hours of professional development on Youth Suicide Prevention in order to renew their license.

  G. Complete the Utah Educator Ethics Review online at www.utah.gov/teachers

III. Level 2 License (valid 5 years; renewable)

  A. Prior to upgrade from Level 1 to Level 2, holders of Level 1 Utah Educator Licenses issued after January 1, 2003, must complete all requirements of the Entry Years Enhancement (EYE) program, a structured support program providing novice teachers with 3 years of school, district, and state support.

    1. All new educators are required to participate in EYE, and all requirements must be completed within the first 3 years of service in Utah.

    2. Requirements for EYE include:

      a. Hold a Level 1 Utah Educator License,

      b. Complete a professional portfolio,

      c. Receive 2 successful professional evaluations per year for 3 years in a Utah public or accredited private school,

      d. Achieve a score of 160 or better on the Praxis II Principles of Learning and Teaching at the appropriate level of educational preparation,

      e. Work with a trained mentor for 3 years,

      f. Complete any additional district/school requirements,

      g. Receive a district/school recommendation for upgrade to Level 2, *and*

    3. Because this program continues to change and develop, refer to the most recent version of its requirements at http://www.schools.utah.gov/cert

    4. Complete the Utah Educator Ethics Review online at www.utah.gov/teachers

  B. Renewal requires completion of:

    1. 200 license renewal points every 5 years, which may include 35 points per year for 3 out of the last 5 years, for teaching experience at a public or accredited private school;

    2. A fingerprint background check within a year;

    3. All educators must have a Professional Learning Plan signed by their administrator for renewal; consult: http://schools.utah.gov/cert/License-Renewals/Professional-Learning-Plan.aspx

    4. "Active" educators (http://schools.utah.gov/cert/License-Renewals/Definitions.aspx) must also have at least 2 hours of professional development on Youth Suicide Prevention in order to renew their license.

    5. Complete the Utah Educator Ethics Review online at www.utah.gov/teachers

IV. Level 3 License (valid for 7 years; renewable)
   A. Requires eligibility to hold a Level 2 License and one of the following in the educator's field of practice:
      1. Doctoral degree,
         or
      2. National Board for Professional Teaching Standards (NBPTS) Certificate,
         or
      3. American Speech-Language-Hearing Association (ASHA) Certificate of Clinical Competence.
      4. Complete the Utah Educator Ethics Review online at www.utah.gov/teachers
   B. Renewal same as Level 2; see III, B, above; and in addition:
      1. For NBPTS holders, renewal of that certificate is required.
      2. For speech-language pathologists, verification of continued membership in ASHA is required.
 V. District/Charter School-Specific Competency-Based License (nonrenewable). Rather than being a permanent license, these licenses are now parallel to the other licenses, with the same duration and renewal requirements.
   A. Only district school board chair or charter school board chair may submit application on behalf of educator, demonstrating that other licensing routes for the applicant are untenable or unreasonable.
   B. Request must be made within 60 days after the date of individual's first day of employment:
   C. Teachers of one or more core academic subjects shall provide specific documentation of eligibility.
      1. Core academic subjects include English, reading or language arts, mathematics, science, foreign languages, civics and government, economics, arts, history, and geography.
      2. Specific documentation of eligibility includes possession of a bachelor's degree and either:
         a. For Grades K–6 satisfactory results of approved test including subject knowledge and teaching skills in the required core academic subjects,
            or
         b. For Grades 7–12 competency in each core academic subject to be taught, as demonstrated by completion of an academic major, a graduate degree, course work equivalent to an undergraduate academic major, advanced certification or credentialing, or results/scores of a rigorous state core academic subject test in each core academic subject in which the teacher teaches.
   D. Teacher of non-core subjects shall provide documentation of both:
      1. A bachelor's degree, associate degree, or skill certification; and
      2. Skills, talents, or abilities specific to teaching assignment.
   E. The district/charter school specific competency-based license is only valid in the district/charter school requesting the license.
   F. Complete the Utah Educator Ethics Review online at www.utah.gov/teachers

Concentrations and Endorsements

I. Each educator license must have at least one area of concentration from the following list: Early childhood K–3, elementary K–6, elementary 1–8, secondary 6–12, administrative/ supervisory, school counselor, school psychologist, school social worker, special education K–12, preschool special education (Birth–Age 5), communication disorders/ audiology, or speech language pathology

II. Licenses may also bear appropriate endorsements relating to subject or specific assignments (e.g., biology, English as a second language, hearing or visually impaired, mild/ moderate disabilities, severe disabilities, Spanish, library media, etc.)

Vermont

Eligibility for Initial Licensure

I. Eligibility requirements
   A. Graduation from a Vermont-approved educator preparation program with a recommendation for licensure from the institution;
      or
   B. Graduation from an approved teacher preparation program from a state with which Vermont has signed a NASDTEC interstate reciprocity contract. The qualifications of persons certified in a state with which Vermont does not have reciprocity, as well as all educators seeking vocational and support services licensure, will be evaluated on an individual basis;
      or
   C. An out-of-state applicant shall be issued a comparable license and endorsement(s) if he or she:
      1. Is licensed through an alternative route in a state with which Vermont has signed a NASDTEC interstate reciprocity contract,
         and
      2. Either has a recommendation from a state-approved alternate route program
         or
         has provided satisfactory service under a non-conditional license as an educator in a school in an assignment covered by the endorsement sought on at least a half time basis for not fewer than 3 years during the 7 years immediately preceding the application for a Vermont license,
         and
      3. Meets the contract and ancillary requirements as defined in the contract.
   D. Alternative Routes to Licensure
      1. An individual who holds at least a bachelor's degree from a regionally accredited or state-approved institution and who has successfully completed a major, or its equivalent, in the liberal arts and sciences, or in the content area of the endorsement sought, may be licensed by completing an alternate preparation process approved by the Standards Board.
         a. For endorsement areas requiring an advanced degree, the individual must hold the specified advanced degree in order to be deemed eligible to proceed with any other alternate preparation process approved by the Standards Board.
      2. Academic Review for Individual Seeking Licensure as an Administrator.
         a. An applicant for a Vermont administrator license who has not completed an approved preparation program (including Peer Review) may be evaluated by the Standards Board, or its designee, on an individual basis by academic review of course work appearing on an official transcript

for which the applicant received graduate credit to establish whether the applicant meets the competency requirements of these rules.

    b.   Administrator candidates must also meet the internship, the examination, and requirements for updated knowledge and skills as established by the Standards Board.

E.   Transcript Review. The VSBPE shall evaluate on an individual basis by transcript review any applicant for Vermont licensure whose category of licensure is not covered by the reciprocity contract or in an endorsement area for which Vermont has no educator preparation program.

F.   An applicant for Vermont licensure who holds an out-of-state license and is certified by the National Board for Professional Teaching Standards (NBPTS) shall be issued a license in the applicable endorsement area.

II.   General requirements for all licensure candidates

   A.   The applicant must hold a baccalaureate degree from a regionally accredited or Vermont-approved institution and must have successfully completed a major, or its equivalent, in the liberal arts and sciences or in the content area of the endorsement sought.

      1.   Exceptions include an applicant for a Career and Technical Education endorsement, or an educator who holds a Career and Technical Education endorsement; however, an applicant for a Career and Technical Education endorsement shall hold at least an associate's degree or the equivalent in order to qualify for Level I Licensure.

      2.   Applicants for the Junior ROTC Instructor endorsement need not hold a bachelor's degree.

      3.   Candidates for a school nurse endorsement must hold a baccalaureate degree from a nationally accredited 4-year nursing program.

         a.   Candidates for an associate school nurse endorsement must hold an associate degree.

   B.   Demonstrated ability to communicate effectively in speaking, writing, and other forms of creative expression, and ability to apply basic mathematical skills, critical thinking skills, and creative thinking skills

   C.   Documentation of the specified content knowledge, performance standards, and additional requirements, if any, for the endorsement(s) being sought

   D.   Documentation of required student teaching or administrative internship experience

      1.   Student Teaching: Evidence of at least 12 consecutive weeks of student teaching, or an equivalent learning experience as determined by Standards Board policy or by the requirements of the endorsement

      2.   Administrative Internship: Evidence of at least 300 hours of an administrative internship for those seeking an initial administrator endorsement

   E.   The educator has knowledge and skills in the content of his or her endorsement(s) at a level that enables students to meet or exceed the standards represented in both the fields of knowledge and the vital results of *Vermont's Framework of Standards and Learning Opportunities, Common Core, and/or Next Generation Science Standards.*

   F.   The educator fulfills general competencies in teaching; for details, consult http://education.vermont.gov/new/html/maincert.html

G. Testing requirements
   1. Praxis Core Academic Skills Test for Educators for initial licenses, including school psychologist, guidance counselor, school nurse, and all other support services personnel
      a. Meet scores on 3 individual core tests (reading—156, writing—162, and mathematics—150)
   2. Praxis II for applicants seeking initial license or additional endorsement in any of the following areas:
      a. Mathematics, social studies, English, science, elementary education, art, music, physical education, modern or classical languages, reading, ESL, Speech/Language Pathologists (S/LPs), audiologists, school psychologists, and American sign language (ASL)
      b. For middle grades: English, mathematics, science, or history/social science
   3. Exemptions from Praxis testing requirements only if:
      a. Applicant qualifies for licensure under interstate reciprocity,
         and
         Has at least 3 years of employment experience under a non-conditional license within the past 7 years as licensed educator in endorsement area being sought,
         or
      b. Applicant qualifies for licensure in the endorsement under the NASDTEC interstate reciprocity agreement,
         and
         Has achieved National Board certification in the applicable endorsement area.

Licensure Levels and Types with Renewal Requirements

I. Level I: Professional Educator License (valid 3 years; renewable)
   A. Issued to an applicant who has satisfactorily met all requirements for licensure
      1. See general requirements for all licensure candidates, II, A–G, above.
II. Level II: Professional Educator License (valid 7 years; renewable)
   A. Issued, upon recommendation of a local or regional standards board, to educator who has:
      1. Successfully practiced in endorsement area for 3 years under Level I license,
         and
      2. Submitted an approved Individual Professional Learning Plan (IPLP) developed through analysis of professional practice and student learning data that articulates the educator's professional development goals for the ensuing licensure period,
         and
      3. Provided verification from a supervising administrator that the educator has demonstrated the competencies required by the endorsement at a professional level.

    B.   Applicants for licensure through interstate reciprocity may be eligible for an endorsement on a Level II license upon presentation of satisfactory evidence of 3 successful years of practice in the endorsement area under a nonconditional license within the last 7 years.

III.   Apprenticeship License. For individuals seeking Career and Technical Education Endorsements (valid 3 years, not renewable)

IV.   Provisional License or Endorsement (valid 2 years, not renewable)

    A.   A superintendent may apply to the VSBPE for a provisional license or endorsement when the local district is unable to find an appropriately licensed and/or endorsed applicant after making all reasonable efforts to do so.

    B.   The application for a provisional license or endorsement shall include a plan for obtaining a Level I license or endorsement and an explanation of how the applicant will be mentored and supervised during the 2-year period of the provisional license.

    C.   Qualifications

        1.   Possess a baccalaureate degree (except for associate school nurse, an associate's degree) and meet at least 1 of the following criteria:

            a.   Possess any valid educator license from Vermont or another state,
               or

               Possess any expired Vermont educator license or any expired license from another state, provided the license expired no longer than 10 years ago,
               or

               Have a major in the content area of the provisional endorsement sought,
               or

               Have successfully completed the Praxis II for the provisional endorsement sought.

    D.   A provisional license or endorsement shall not be renewed. With extenuating circumstances that prevented the individual from completing the approved plan for Level I licensure, an extension of 1 year may be granted.

V.   Emergency Licenses and Endorsements (valid for school year issued; not renewable)

    A.   See IV, A, directly above, except for emergency license or endorsement

    B.   Emergency licenses and endorsements shall be issued only to individuals who hold a baccalaureate degree or its equivalent (except career and technical education) but do not meet the qualifications for a provisional license (see IV, C, directly above).

    C.   The application for an emergency license shall include an explanation of how the applicant will be mentored and supervised.

    D.   No emergency endorsements will be issued for Special Educator, Consulting Teacher, Early Childhood Special Educator, Intensive Special Education Teacher, Teacher of the Blind and Visually Impaired, Teacher of the Deaf and Hard of Hearing, Career and Technical Education Special Needs Coordinator, School Nurse, Associate School Nurse, School Psychologist, Educational Speech Language Pathologist, School Counselor, Career and Technical Education School Counseling Coordinator, School Social Worker, Junior ROTC Instructor, or Driver and Traffic Safety Education, school nursing, school psychologist, educational speech-language pathologist, school counseling, school social worker, junior ROTC instructor, or driver's education instructor.

VI. Renewal Requirements

A. Level I Renewal

1. To receive a 3-year renewal, the educator shall show professional growth through completion of a minimum of 3 credits or 45 hours of professional learning in the endorsement area.

2. Level I endorsement holders who have practiced in Vermont in the endorsement area after 3 years shall seek a recommendation from their local or regional standards board for a Level II endorsement.

   a. An educator who does not receive a recommendation for a Level II endorsement upon initial application shall renew the Level I endorsement after 3 years of professional practice and reapply for a Level II license prior to the expiration of the renewal.

   b. Level I endorsement of an educator who does not receive a recommendation for a Level II endorsement after another 3 years of professional practice shall become lapsed.

   c. Level I license holders employed as educators in Vermont but who have not practiced in a particular endorsement area for 3 years shall seek a recommendation for renewal of that Level I endorsement through their local or regional standards board.

   d. Educators may renew Level 1 endorsements under which they are not currently teaching by completing 3 credits or 45 hours of professional learning for each renewal. There is no limit to the number of times these endorsements may be renewed.

   e. An educator shall present evidence of any required additional licenses or credentials specific to a particular endorsement.

B. Level II Renewal

1. Level II license holders shall seek a recommendation for renewal of their Level II license and endorsement(s) from their local or regional standards board.

2. The local or regional standards board shall recommend renewal of a Level II endorsement if the applicant presents a professional portfolio that includes:

   a. Current Individual Professional Learning Plan (IPLP)

   b. Documentation of professional growth pursuant to the IPLP goals, including documentation of a minimum of 9 credits or 135 hours of professional learning, at least 3 credits or 45 hours of which must address the specific content knowledge and performance standards of each endorsement recommended for renewal

   c. Evidence of any required additional licenses or credentials specific to a particular endorsement

   d. Approved IPLP developed through analysis of professional practice and student learning data that articulates the educator's professional learning goals for the ensuing licensure period

   e. A portfolio submitted by an educator for National Board Certification shall be considered sufficient professional development for renewing the comparable endorsement.

Endorsements

I.   In order to be valid, each professional educator's license shall have 1 or more endorsements.

II. Endorsements limited in time, grade level, or scope may be issued by the VSBPE based on the applicant's background and experience, permitting practice in a specialized area within a broader endorsement field.

III. The holder of any license who wishes to qualify for an additional endorsement via transcript review shall present evidence of meeting the content knowledge and performance standards and additional requirements, if any, of the endorsement.

   A. A minimum of 18 credit hours in the endorsement field is required.

IV. Endorsements may be obtained in the following areas:

   A. Administrator Endorsements

      1. Assistant Director for Adult Education

      2. Career and Technical Center Director

      3. Director of Special Education

      4. Principal

      5. Superintendent

      6. Supervisor

   B. Art (Grades PreK–6, 7–12, or PreK–12); Associate School Nurse (Grades PreK–12); Business Education (Grades 5–12); Career & Technical Education School Counseling Coordinator (Grades 9–12); Computer Science (Grades 7–12); Cooperative Career and Technical Education Coordinator (Grades 9–12); Dance (Grades PreK–12); Design and Technology Education (Grades 5–12); Driver & Traffic Safety Education (Grades 9–12); Early Childhood Education (Grades Birth to Grade 3, K–3, Birth to Age 6); Educational Technology Specialist (Grades PreK–12); Elementary Education (Grades K–6); English (Grades 7–12); English as a Second Language (ESL) (Grades PreK–6, 7–12, or PreK–12); Family and Consumer Sciences (Grades 5–12); Health Education (Grades PreK–6, 7–12, or PreK–12); Junior Reserve Officer Training Corps (ROTC) Instructor (Grades 9–12); Library Media Specialist (Grades PreK–12); Mathematics (Grades 7–12); Middle Grades (with 1 or more of the required content areas of Mathematics, English/ Language Arts, Science, and Social Studies) (Grades 5–9); Modern and Classical Languages (Grades PreK–6, 7–12, or PreK–12); Music (Grades PreK–6, 7–12 or PreK–12); Physical Education (Grades PreK–6, 7–12, or PreK–12); Reading/ English Language Arts Coordinator (for holder of endorsement in either Early Childhood, Elementary Ed, Middle Grades, Secondary Education, or Special Education) (Grades PreK–12); Reading/English Language Arts Specialist (for holder of endorsement in either Early Childhood, Elementary Ed, Middle Grades, Secondary Education, or Special Education) (Grades PreK–12); School Counselor (Grades PreK–12); School Nurse (Grades PreK–12); School Psychologist (Grades

PreK–12); School Social Worker (Grades PreK–12); Science (Grades 7–12); Social Studies (Grades 7–12); Theater Arts (Grades PreK–12); Career and Technical Special Needs Coordinator (Grade 8 to Adulthood); Consulting Teacher (Grades K–8, Grades 7–Age 21, or K through Age 21); Early Childhood Special Educator (Birth to Age 6); Intensive Special Education Teacher (Age 3 through Age 21); Special Educator (Grades K–8, Grades 7–Age 21, or K through Age 21); Educational Speech Language Pathologist (Age 3 through Age 21); Teacher of the Blind and Visually Impaired (Age 3 through Age 21); Teacher of the Deaf and Hard of Hearing (Age 3 through Age 21); Online Teaching Specialist

Virginia

General Requirements for Licensure

I.   Applicants for licensure must:
   A. Be at least 18 years of age,
   B. Pay appropriate fees and complete application process,
   C. Have earned a baccalaureate degree (with the exception of the Technical Professional License) from a regionally accredited institution of higher education (IHE) and meet requirements for the license sought. Persons seeking initial licensure who graduate from Virginia IHEs shall only be licensed as instructional personnel by the Board of Education if the endorsement areas offered at such institutions have been assessed by a national accrediting agency or by a state approval process with final approval by the Board of Education;
   and
   D. Possess good moral character.
II. All candidates seeking an initial Virginia teaching license who hold at least a baccalaureate degree from a regionally accredited college or university must obtain passing scores on professional teacher assessments within the 3-year validity of the initial provisional license except:
   A. Candidates for the the Career Switcher Program that requires assessments as prerequisites
   B. Candidates seeking a Technical Professional License, the International License, School Manager License, or the Pupil Personnel Services License
   C. Individuals who hold valid out-of-state licenses (full credential with no deficiencies) and who have completed a minimum of 3 years of full time, successful teaching experience in a public or accredited nonpublic school (K–12) in another state
III. Those seeking an initial endorsement in early/primary education preK–3, elementary education preK–6, special education—general curriculum, special education—hearing impairments, special education—visual impairments, and individuals seeking an endorsement as a reading specialist must obtain passing scores prescribed by the Board on reading instructional assessment.
IV. For all individuals seeking an initial endorsement authorizing them to serve as principals and assistant principals in the public schools, a school leaders assessment prescribed by the Board of Education must be met:
   A. Individuals seeking an initial administration and supervision endorsement who are interested in serving as central office instructional personnel are not required to take and pass the school leaders assessment prescribed by the Board of Education.
V.   Individuals seeking initial licensure must:
   A. Demonstrate proficiency in the use of educational technology for instruction
   B. Complete study in child abuse recognition and intervention in accordance with

curriculum guidelines developed by the Board of Education in consultation with the Department of Social Services

   C. Provide evidence of completion of certification or training in emergency first aid, cardiopulmonary resuscitation (CPR), and the use of automated external defibrillators (AED)

   D. Receive professional development in instructional methods tailored to promote student academic progress and effective preparation for the Standards of Learning end-of-course and end-of-grade assessments.

Types of Licenses

Unless otherwise indicated, licenses are valid for 5 years and renewable. For full information on the licenses listed below, refer to pages 8–11 of the Virginia Licensure Regulations for School Personnel at http://www.doe.virginia.gov/teaching/licensure/licensure_regs.pdf

    I. Provisional License (valid 3 years; nonrenewable)
   II. Collegiate Professional License
  III. Postgraduate Professional License
  IV. Technical Professional License
   V. School Manager License
  VI. Pupil Personnel Services License
 VII. Division Superintendent License
VIII. International Educator License (valid up to 3 consecutive years; nonrenewable)
  IX. Teach for America License (valid 2 years; nonrenewable)

Alternate Routes to Licensure

    I. Career Switcher alternate route to licensure for career professions:
     A. Available to career switchers who seek teaching endorsements preK through grade 12 with the exception of special education.
     B. An individual seeking a Provisional License through the career switcher program must meet the following prerequisite requirements:
       1. Completed application
       2. Baccalaureate degree from a regionally accredited college or university
       3. Completion of requirements for an endorsement in a teaching area or the equivalent through verifiable experience or academic study
       4. A minimum of 5 years of full-time work experience or its equivalent
       5. Virginia qualifying scores on the professional teacher assessments as prescribed by the Board of Education
     C. The Provisional Career Switcher License is awarded at the end of Level I preparation and is valid for 1 year. The candidate must complete all components of the career switcher alternate route for career professions.
     D. Level I requirements must be completed during the course of a single year and

may be offered through a variety of delivery systems, including distance learning programs. Career Switcher programs must be certified by the Virginia Department of Education. If an employing agency recommends extending the Provisional License for a second year, the candidate will enter Level III of the program.

1. Level I preparation includes:
    a. Minimum of 180 clock hours of instruction, including field experience
2. Level II preparation during first year of employment includes:
    a. Seeking employment in Virginia with the 1-year Provisional Career Switcher License
    b. Continued Level II preparation during the first year of employment with a minimum of 5 seminars that will include a minimum of 20 cumulative instructional hours
    c. One year of successful, full-time teaching experience in a Virginia public or accredited nonpublic school under a 1-year Provisional License, under the direction of a trained mentor
    d. Upon completion of Levels I and II of the Career Switcher alternate route to licensure program and submission of a recommendation from the Virginia educational employing agency, the candidate will be eligible to apply for a 5-year renewable license.
3. Level III preparation, if required, includes:
    a. Postpreparation, if required, to be conducted by the Virginia employing educational agency to address the areas where improvement is needed as identified in the candidate's professional improvement plan
    b. Upon completion of Levels I, II, and III of the Career Switcher alternate route to licensure program and submission of a recommendation from the Virginia educational employing agency, the candidate will be eligible to receive a 5-year renewable license.

E. Verification of program completion will be documented by the certified program provider and the division superintendent or designee.
F. Certified providers implementing a Career Switcher program may charge a fee for participation in the program.

II. Other Alternate Routes to Licensure are available for individuals employed by a Virginia educational agency, individuals seeking licensure via an alternative program offered through institutions of higher education, or via experiential learning. For more information, contact the Virginia Department of Education (see Appendix 1).

Requirements

I. General requirements:
    A. Completion of an approved program, including:
        1. A degree from a regionally accredited college or university in the liberal arts and sciences (or equivalent)
        2. Professional teacher assessments requirement prescribed by the Board of Education

3. Specific endorsement requirements
4. Professional studies requirements,
   or

B. If employed by a Virginia public or nonpublic school, completion of the Alternate Route to Licensure.

II. Professional studies requirements—which may be met through integrated course work or modules—total 15 semester hours for adult education, preK–12 endorsements, and secondary grades 6–12 endorsements; for early/primary preK–3, elementary education preK–6, and special education, the total is 18 semester hours.

A. Human growth and development (birth through adolescence): 3 semester hours

B. Curriculum and instructional procedures: 3 semester hours

C. Classroom and behavior management: 3 semester hours

D. Foundations of education: 3 semester hours

E. Reading:
   1. Early/primary preK–3 and elementary education preK–6 language acquisition and reading: 6 semester hours
   2. Middle education—language acquisition and reading in the content areas: 6 semester hours
   3. Special education—language acquisition and reading: 6 semester hours
   4. Secondary education—reading in the content area: 3 semester hours

F. Supervised classroom experience:
   1. Full-time classroom experience for a minimum of 300 clock hours (including pre- and postclinical experiences) with at least 150 clock hours spent supervised in direct teaching activities
   2. One year of successful full-time teaching experience in the endorsement area in a public or accredited nonpublic school may be accepted in lieu of the supervised teaching experience.

Endorsements for Early/Primary Education, Elementary Education, and Middle Education

Note: The Alternate Route requirements apply to individuals seeking licensure outside of state-approved programs and through the Alternative Route to Licensure. IHEs with approved programs in Virginia are not subject to specific semester-hour requirements since they incorporate state competencies into their programs.

I. Early/primary education preK–3 endorsement requirements:
   A. Graduation from an approved teacher preparation program in early/primary education preK–3,
      or
   B. A degree from a regionally accredited college or university in the liberal arts and sciences (or equivalent) and completed course work that covers the early/primary education preK–3 competencies and fulfills the following 48 semester-hour requirements: English (12 semester hours), mathematics (9 semester hours), science

(9 semester hours in at least 2 science disciplines), history (6 semester hours), social science (6 semester hours), arts and humanities (6 semester hours).

II.   Elementary education preK–6 endorsement requirements:
   A.   Graduation from an approved teacher preparation program in elementary education preK–6,
        or
   B.   The candidate for the elementary education preK–6 endorsement must have a bachelor's degree or higher from a regionally accredited college or university majoring in the liberal arts and sciences (or equivalent) and fulfill the following 57 semester-hour requirements: English (12 semester hours), mathematics (12 semester hours), science (12 semester hours in at least 2 science disciplines), history (9 semester hours), social science (6 semester hours), arts and humanities (6 semester hours).

III.   Middle education 6–8 endorsement requirements:
   A.   Graduation from an approved teacher preparation discipline-specific program in middle education 6–8 with at least 1 area of academic preparation from the areas of English, mathematics, science, and history and social sciences,
        or
   B.   A degree from a regionally accredited college or university in the liberal arts and sciences (or equivalent); and completed a minimum of 21 semester hours in at least 1 area of academic preparation (concentration) that will be listed on the license; and completed minimum requirements for those areas in which the individual is not seeking an area of academic preparation. Areas: English (21 semester hours), mathematics (21 semester hours), science (21 semester hours), history and social sciences (21 semester hours).

Endorsements for PreK–12 and Secondary Grades 6–12, Special Education, and Adult Education

Note: The Alternate Route requirements apply to individuals seeking licensure outside of state-approved programs and through the Alternative Route to Licensure. IHEs with approved programs in Virginia are not subject to specific semester-hour requirements since they incorporate state competencies into their programs.

I.   Individuals seeking licensure with preK–12 endorsements, special education, secondary grades 6–12 endorsements, and adult education may meet requirements through the completion of an approved program or, if employed by a Virginia public or nonpublic school, through the Alternative Route to Licensure. Components of the licensure program include a degree in the liberal arts and sciences (or equivalent), professional teacher assessment requirements prescribed by the Board of Education, specific endorsement requirements, and professional studies requirements. For further details on course distributions in each subject field, as well as for additional teaching endorsement areas, contact the Virginia Department of Education (see Appendix 1).
   A.   Visual Arts, preK–12, semester hours 36
   B.   Biology, semester hours.. 32
   C.   Chemistry, semester hours.. 32

D. Earth science, semester hours... 32

E. English, semester hours... 36

F. English as a second language preK–12, semester hours...................... 24

G. Foreign language (preK–12), semester hours 30

H. Health and physical education (preK–12), semester hours.................. 45

I. History and social sciences, semester hours....................................... 51

J. Library media (preK–12), semester hours 24

K. Mathematics, semester hours 36

L. Music (vocal/choral/instrumental) prek–12, semester hours............. 42

M. Physics, semester hours.. 32

II. Professional studies requirements: 15 semester hours
   A. See Requirements II, A–F, above, with an emphasis on preK–12, Secondary Grades 6–12, Special Education, and Adult Education

Support Personnel Licensure Requirements

I. Administration and Supervision, preK–12
   A. Level I endorsement
      1. Master's degree from a regionally accredited college or university
      2. Three years of successful, full-time experience in a public school or accredited nonpublic school in an instructional personnel position that requires licensure in Virginia
      3. Completed an approved program in administration and supervision from a regionally accredited college or university
      4. Completed a minimum of 320 clock hours of a supervised internship that provided exposure to multiple sites (elementary, middle, high, central office, agency) with diverse student populations
      5. Satisfied the requirements for the school leaders licensure assessment prescribed by the Board of Education
         a. Individuals seeking an initial administration and supervision endorsement who are interested in serving as central office instructional personnel are not required to take and pass the school leaders assessment prescribed by the Board of Education.
   B. Out-of-state administration and supervision endorsement
      1. Master's degree from a regionally accredited college or university
      2. Current, valid out-of-state license (full credential) with an endorsement in administration and supervision
   C. Level II endorsement
      1. Successful service as a building-level administrator for at least 5 years in a public school or accredited nonpublic school
      2. Successful completion of a formal induction program as a principal or assistant principal
      3. Recommendation from a Virginia school division superintendent
      4. Two or more of the following Board of Education criteria: improved student achievement; effective instructional leadership; positive effect on school climate

or culture; earned doctorate in educational leadership or evidence of formal professional development in the areas of school law, school finance, supervision, human resource management, and instructional leadership; completion of a high-quality professional development project designed by the division superintendent

II. Division Superintendent
   A. Option 1
      1. An earned doctorate degree in educational administration or educational leadership from a regionally accredited college or university
      2. Five years of educational experience in a public or accredited nonpublic school, of which 2 must be teaching experience at the preK–12 level and 2 must be in administration/supervision at the preK–12 level,
         or
   B. Option 2
      1. An earned master's degree from a regionally accredited college or university plus 30 completed hours beyond the master's degree
      2. Completed requirements for administration and supervision preK–12 endorsement that includes demonstration of competency. For more information, contact the Virginia Board of Education (see Appendix 1),
         or
      3. Have completed 5 years of educational experience in a public or accredited nonpublic school, 2 of which must be teaching experience at the preK–12 level and 2 of which must be in administration/supervision at the pre K–12 level.
   C. Option 3
      1. An earned master's degree from a regionally accredited college or university
      2. A current, valid out-of-state license with an endorsement as a division/district superintendent
      3. Five years of educational experience in a public or accredited nonpublic school, of which 2 must be teaching experience at the preK–12 level and 2 must be in administration/supervision,
         or
   D. Option 4
      1. Master's degree, or its equivalent, from a regionally accredited college or university
      2. Have held a senior leadership position such as chief executive officer or senior military officer
      3. Be recommended by a school board interested in employing the individual as superintendent.

III. School Counselor PreK–12. Endorsement requirements:
   A. An earned master's degree from an approved counselor education program, with at least 100 clock hours of clinical experiences in the preK–6 setting and 100 clock hours of clinical experiences in the grades 7–12 setting,
      and
      Two years of successful full-time teaching experience or 2 years of successful experience in guidance and counseling in a public or accredited nonpublic school.

Two years of successful full-time experience in guidance and counseling under a Provisional License may be accepted to meet this requirement.

IV.   Additional Support Personnel. Each license and endorsement listed below has specific requirements. For details, contact the Virginia Department of Education (see Appendix 1)

A.   Mathematics Specialist for Elementary and Middle Education
B.   Reading Specialist
C.   School Manager License
D.   School Psychologist
E.   School Social Worker
F.   Special Education—Speech-Language Pathologist, preK–12
G.   Vocational Evaluator

Washington

The Professional Educator Standards Board has adopted changes to the Washington Administrative Code that change the validity and renewal of a residency teacher certificate on September 1, 2011. All candidates who have not had a residency teacher certificate reissued with a defined expiration date under the current calculation will move to one validity date system effective September 1, 2011.

General Certificate Information

I. The teacher certificate authorizes service in the primary role of teacher.

II. The administrator certificate authorizes service in the primary role of building-level administration (principal), program administration (program administrator), and district-wide general administration (superintendent).

III. The educational staff associate (ESA) certificate authorizes service as school psychologist, counselor, social worker, school nurse, physical therapist, occupational therapist, or speech-language pathologist or audiologist.

IV. Levels of Certificates available to first-time applicants:

   A. Teaching Certificates
      1. Residency Teaching Certificate
      2. Professional Teaching Certificate

   B. Administrator Certificates
      1. Residency Administrator Certificate—Principal and Program Administrator
      2. Professional Administrator Certificate—Principal and Program Administrator
      3. Initial Administrator Certificate—Superintendent Only
      4. Continuing Administrator Certificate—Superintendent Only

   C. Educational Staff Associate Certificates
      1. Residency ESA Certificate—School Counselor, Psychologist
      2. Professional ESA Certificate—School Counselor, Psychologist
      3. Initial ESA Certificate—School Nurse, Occupational Therapy, Physical Therapy, School Speech Language Pathologist/Audiologist, Social Worker
      4. Continuing ESA Certificate—School Nurse, Occupational Therapy, Physical Therapy, School Speech Language Pathologist/Audiologist, Social Worker

V. Candidates for all certificates must complete course work in issues of abuse, which must include information related to:

   A. Identification of physical, emotional, sexual, and substance abuse;
   B. The impact on learning and behavior;
   C. The responsibilities of a teacher, administrator, or ESA to report abuse or to provide assistance to victimized children;
      and
   D. Methods of teaching about abuse and its prevention.

Teaching Certificates

I.   Residency Teaching Certificate (valid minimum of 4 years)
   A.   Baccalaureate degree from regionally accredited institution and completion of state-approved teacher education program
   B.   Completion of 1 endorsement
   C.   Passed a WEST-B (Washington Educator Skills Test-Basic skills reading, writing, and math) and a WEST-E (Washington Educator Skills Test-Endorsements) content test in each endorsement area
   D.   Residency teacher certificate is issued without a defined expiration date. Once certificate holders are employed and reported as teachers by a Washington school district on the Washington State personnel report (S-275) with 1.5 FTE experience, their certificate will expire immediately following June 30. Those teachers will need to submit a residency reissuance application to have a new certificate issued with a 3-year expiration date. Until this takes place, the certificate is valid without a defined expiration date.
   E.   Certificate Endorsements
      1.   Endorsements indicate the content area(s) and/or specializations for which the teacher is prepared.
      2.   Teachers may obtain endorsements on their Washington certificate in several ways:
         a.   Program. By completing a college/university program approved to offer the endorsement. This can be in-state or out-of-state.
         b.   National Board for Professional Teaching Standards. By earning National Board certification in a Washington endorsement area
         c.   Testing. Through WEST-E testing in an area compatible with an endorsement for which they already qualify and are experienced

II. Professional Teacher Certificate (valid for 5 years; renewed upon completion of 150 clock hours every 5 years)
   A.   Specific Washington state–approved second-level professional certificate program that all teachers are expected to earn within the 5-year reissuing of the Residency Teaching Certificate (see I, D, directly above),
   B.   As of September 1, 2011, to earn a professional certificate, teachers must:
      1.   Have 2 years of teaching experience,
         and
      2.   Pass the new professional certificate assessment (portfolio of evidence). Teachers can register to take the assessment any time prior to the expiration of their residency certificate, but typically do so during their third or fourth year of teaching in Washington schools.
         a.   For full details about the new portfolio of evidence requirements, go to www.pesb.wa.gov
   C.   Existing professional certificates will remain valid until the expiration date stated on the certificate.
      1.   Renewal requires 150 clock hours every 5 years.

Administrator Certificates

I. Residency Administrator Certificate—Principal and Program Administrator (valid until completion of 2 consecutive years of successful service in the role in Washington)
   A. Master's degree from regionally accredited institution
   B. Completion of an administrator preparation program in the administrative role, or, if no state-approved program, completion of 3 years of successful experience in another state in the administrative role while holding a regular certificate issued by another state
   C. For Principal: Hold or have held a regular teaching certificate or ESA certificate
   D. For Principal: Verification of successful school-based instructional experience in an educational setting

II. Professional Administrator Certificate—Principal and Program Administrator
   A. Completion of a ProCert. Program for administration through a Washington college or university

III. Initial Administrator Certificate—Superintendent Only (valid 7 years)
   A. Master's degree from regionally accredited institution
   B. Completion of an administrator preparation program for superintendent or, if no state-approved college/university program, 3 years of successful experience as a superintendent, deputy superintendent, or assistant superintendent while holding a regular certificate issued by another state
   C. Must hold a valid regular teaching certificate, ESA, principal, or program administrator certificate

IV. Continuing Administrator Certificate—Superintendent Only (valid for 5-year periods; renewed upon completion of 150 clock hours professional development)
   A. Completed all requirements for the Initial Superintendent's Certificate
   B. Master's degree, plus 60 quarter hours (40 semester hours) of graduate-level course work in education completed after the baccalaureate degree, or a doctorate in education
   C. Completed 180 days of service as a superintendent, deputy superintendent, or assistant superintendent, 30 days of which must have been in the same school district

Educational Staff Associate Certification

I. Residency Educational Staff Associate (ESA) Certificate for school counselor, school psychologist (valid minimum of 7 years)
   A. Completion of master's degree with major in the appropriate specialization
   B. Completion of state-approved program for certification in the appropriate ESA role, *or*
      If no program, must have completed 3 years of experience under that certificate, *or*
      For school psychologist only: must hold NCSP Certificate issued after December 31, 1991, by the National School Psychology Certification Board; if the other state didn't require a certificate, must have 3 years of experience in that role.

C.   Completion of a comprehensive examination required in the master's degree program. If a candidate has been awarded a master's degree without a comprehensive examination, the candidate, as a condition for certification, must arrange to take such an examination with any accredited college or university and provide the superintendent of public instruction with an affidavit from the chair of the department of the academic field that he or she has successfully completed this comprehensive examination.

1.   School Counselor

a.   Successful completion of a proctored, comprehensive examination of the knowledge included in the course work for the required master's degree, given by a regionally accredited institution of higher education, *or*

b.   The candidate may meet this requirement by receiving a passing score on the Praxis II guidance and counseling examination administered by Educational Testing Service (ETS).

2.   School Psychologist

a.   Successful completion of a proctored, comprehensive examination of the knowledge included in the course work for the required master's degree, given by a regionally accredited institution of higher education, *or*

b.   The candidate may meet this requirement by receiving a passing score on the Praxis II school psychology examination administered by ETS.

II.   Professional ESA Certificate for school counselor and school psychologist (valid minimum of 5 years). Requirements:

A.   Hold a certificate from the National Board for Professional Teaching Standards (NBPTS) if a school counselor;

or

Successfully complete an approved professional ESA certificate program, including course on the issue of abuse; see III, A, 5, immediately below for full description of required course content;

or

Hold a valid certificate from the National Association of School Psychologists (NASP) if a school psychologist.

B.   Professional ESA school counselor certificate issued on the basis of holding a valid NBPTS school counselor certificate will have a validity of 5 years or the validity of the NBPTS certificate, whichever is greater.

III.   Continuing Educational Staff Associate (ESA)

A.   For school counselor and school psychologist (candidates must hold a valid initial certificate at time of application). Requirements:

1.   Candidate must have completed 180 days of experience in the role (or the equivalent of 180 days of full-time service), of which 30 days must be in the same district.

2.   Candidate must have completed role-specific academic requirements. (It is not, however, necessary for a candidate holding a master's degree or doctorate in

another field to obtain the specified master's degree if he or she has completed all course work requirements relevant to the required master's degree.)

   a.   School counselor: hold a master's degree with a major in counseling

   b.   School psychologist: Hold a master's degree with a major or specialization in school psychology

3.   Candidate must have completed a college-level course that includes peer review at a college/university in Washington while employed in the role.

4.   Candidate must have completed a comprehensive exam relevant to the field of specialization.

5.   Candidate must have taken course work in issues of abuse, which must include information related to identification of physical, emotional, sexual, and substance abuse; the impact on learning and behavior; the responsibilities of an ESA to report abuse or to provide assistance to victimized children; and methods of teaching about abuse and its prevention.

B.   For school nurse, school occupational therapist, school physical therapist, school social worker and school speech language pathologist or audiologist

1.   Continuing ESA is the advanced level regular certificate available for these positions. For full details, go to www.k12.wa.us/certification/ESA

IV.   Initial Educational Staff Associate (ESA) for school counselor, school psychologist, school social worker, school nurse, school occupational therapist, school physical therapist, and school speech language pathologist or audiologist

A.   Initial ESA is the first-level regular certificate for these positions. For full details, go to www.k12.wa.us/certification/ESA

West Virginia

General Information and Requirements

I. West Virginia licenses include:
   A. Professional Certificate
   B. Alternative Teaching Certificate
   C. Temporary Certificate
   D. Career/Technical Education Certificate
   E. Temporary Career/Technical Education Certificate
   F. Permit
   G. Adult Permit
   H. Authorization
   I. Paraprofessional Certificate (granted to service personnel)
   J. Special Education Content Endorsement
   K. Advanced Credential

II. Valid grade levels
   A. Preschool Education (PreK)
   B. Preschool to Adult (PreK–Adult)
   C. Kindergarten to Grade 12 (K–12)
   D. Early Education (PreK–K)
   E. Early Childhood (K–4)
   F. Elementary Education (K–6)
   G. Middle Childhood (5–9)
   H. Adolescent (9–12)
   I. Adult (Adult)

Licenses for Professional Educators

I. General requirements for all applicants for certificates detailed in this section:
   A. Applicant must be a U.S. citizen, unless otherwise noted; of good moral character; physically, mentally, and emotionally qualified to perform the duties of a teacher; and 18 years old.
   B. FBI background check for initial certificates
   C. State background check for initial certificates

II. Temporary Teaching Certificate (valid 1 year). For applicants who have met all requirements except West Virginia tests. Requirements:
   A. Bachelor's degree or master's degree from an accredited institution of higher education (IHE) or an equivalent degree from an IHE in a foreign country
   B. Out-of-State applicants must submit proof of:
      1. Successful completion of an out-of-state approved teacher education program from an accredited IHE.

or

C. Foreign academic credentials,
    or

D. Valid Out-of-State Certificate (for Administrative Certificate).

III. Initial Professional Certificate (valid 3 years) requirements:

A. Minimum proficiency levels in state board–approved tests

1. Basic skills: Praxis I—Pre-Professional Skills in Reading, Writing, and Mathematics

2. Content specialization(s): appropriate Praxis II test(s)

3. Professional knowledge: Praxis II that includes at least a portion of the grade levels indicated on license sought
    and either

B. Successful completion of a regionally accredited IHE's state-approved program and the recommendation of the designated official at the college or university through which the program was completed,
    or

C. A valid out-of-state professional certificate
    or

D. Successful completion of a state-approved alternative delivery program that incorporates the preprofessional skills, content, and professional education standards approved by the state board, including a student teaching experience or documentation of an "in lieu" experience.

E. Requirements for renewal of any Professional Teaching Certificate:

1. Six semester hours of appropriate college/university course work, with a minimum 3.0 GPA, related to the public school program,

a. The 6 semester hours must meet 1 of the following criteria:

i. Courses relevant to a master's degree in a curriculum related to the public school program,
    or

ii. Courses related to improvement of instruction and the applicant's current endorsement area,
    or

iii. Courses needed to qualify for an additional endorsement,
    or

iv. Credit prescribed by the county as a result of an applicant's evaluation,
    or

Master's degree plus 30 Salary Classification,
    or

Has reached 60 years of age and presents a photocopy of the birth certificate
    and

v. In addition, 3 of the 6 semester hours must be a course related to the improvement of instruction through the use of instructional technologies.

2. Recommendation of the employing county's superintendent.

IV. Professional Five-Year Teaching Certificate (valid 5 years; nonrenewable) requirements:
   A. Successful completion of the Beginning Educator Internship for classroom, unless the applicant holds a valid out-of-state certificate and has 5 years of teaching experience in another state
   B. Six semester hours of appropriate college/university course work reflecting a 3.0 GPA and related to the public school program, unless the applicant holds a minimum of a master's degree plus 30 Salary Classification based on the awarding of a master's degree
   C. Two years of experience, 1 of which must be completed in West Virginia, within 1 endorsement or a combination of the endorsements, on the Initial Professional Teaching Certificate
   D. Recommendation of superintendent in the county in which the educator teaches or last taught
V. Permanent Professional Teaching Certificate (valid unless surrendered, suspended or revoked) requirements:
   A. Hold or be eligible for the Professional Teaching Certificate (valid 5 years);
   and
   Master's degree related to the public school;
   and
   Five years of educational experience, including 2 within the specialization(s) for which the permanent certificate is requested.
   or
   B. Hold a valid Professional Five-Year Teaching Certificate,
   and
   Two Renewals of the Professional Five-Year Teaching Certificate based on:
   1. Six semester hours of appropriate renewal credit reflecting a 3.0 GPA,
   2. Minimum of a master's degree plus 30 Salary Classification based on the awarding of a master's degree,
      or
   3. Age 60,
      or
      Hold certification through the National Board for Professional Teaching Standards (NBPTS),
      or
      Valid out-of-state certificate.
VI. Individuals who hold a valid out-of-state teaching certificate, have completed a state-approved educator preparation program, and hold a bachelor's degree from a regionally accredited IHE should visit http://wvde.state.wv.us/certification for specific information.

Specializations

I. Recognized Programmatic Level
   A. Preschool Education (PreK–PreK), Early Education (PreK–K), Early Childhood (K–4), Middle Childhood (5–9), Adolescent (9–12), Adult (Adult)

II. Grade-Level Options for General Education Specializations Current Programs:
   A. Agriculture (5–Adult); American Sign Language (PreK–Adult, 5–Adult), any Modern Foreign Language (PreK–Adult, 5–Adult); Art (PreK–Adult, 5–Adult, 5–9); Biology (9–Adult); Business Education (5–Adult, 9–Adult); Chemistry (9–Adult); Chemistry/Physics (9–Adult); Chinese (PreK–Adult, 5–Adult); Computer Science Education (PreK–Adult); Dance (PreK–Adult, 5–Adult); Driver Education (9–Adult); Early Childhood Education (K–4); Early Education (PreK–K); Elementary Education (K–6); English (5–Adult, 5–9); English as a Second Language (PreK–Adult); Family & Consumer Science (5–Adult); French (PreK–Adult, 5–Adult); General Math through Algebra I (5–Adult, 5–9); General Science (5–Adult, 5–9); German (PreK–Adult, 5–Adult); Health (PreK–Adult, 5–Adult); Instructional Technology (PreK–Adult); Intermediate (Elementary Education Grades 3–5); Japanese (PreK–Adult, 5–Adult); Journalism (5–Adult, 9–Adult); Latin (PreK–Adult, 5–Adult); Marketing (9–Adult); Mathematics (5–Adult, 5–9); Middle Childhood Education (MCE) (5–9); Music (PreK–Adult); Oral Communications (5–Adult, 9–Adult); Physical Education (PreK–Adult, 5–Adult, 5–9); Physics (9–Adult); Preschool Education (PreK–PreK); Reading (PreK–K, K–6, 5–Adult); Reading Specialist* (PreK–Adult); Russian (PreK–Adult, 5–Adult); School Library/Media (PreK–Adult); Social Studies (5–Adult, 5–9); Spanish (PreK–Adult, 5–Adult); Technology Education (5–Adult); Theater (PreK–Adult); Wellness (Health–Physical Education) (PreK–Adult)

III. Grade-Level Options for Special Education Specializations:
   Autism (K–6, 5–Adult); Emotional/Behavior Disorders (K–6, 5–Adult); Gifted (1–12); Deaf and Hard of Hearing (PreK–Adult); Mentally Impaired Mild/Moderate (K–6, 5–Adult); Multi-Categorical (E/BD, MI, SLD) (K–, 5–Adult); Preschool Special Needs (PreK–K); Severe Disabilities (K–Adult); Specific Learning Disabilities (K–6, 5–Adult); Visually Impaired (PreK–Adult)

IV. Grade-Level Options for Student Support Specializations (all are PreK–Adult): Athetic Trainer, Counselor,* School Nurse, School Psychologist,* Social Services and Attendance, Speech Language Pathologist,* Speech Assistant

V. Grade-Level Options for Administrative Specializations (all are PreK–Adult): General Supervisor,* Principal,* Superintendent*

* Master's degree required

Administrative Certificates

I. Initial Professional Administrative Certificate (valid for 5 years)
   A. The Initial Professional Administrative Certificate shall be endorsed for Superintendent, Principal, and/or Supervisor of Instruction and shall indicate the specialization(s) and grade levels in which the holder can be legally assigned within the public schools.
   B. General Requirements:
      1. Successful completion of an IHE's state approved program and the recommendation of the designated official at the college or university through which the program was completed,

or

2. Applicants holding a valid out-of-state Administrative Certificate need only present the official transcripts evidencing graduation from a state-approved teacher education program at a regionally accredited college or university and a copy of his/her valid out-of-state Administrative Certificate.

3. Minimum GPA 3.0

4. Three years teaching/management experience

5. Complete Evaluation Leadership Institute (ELI)

6. Passing scores on Praxis II

7. Master's Degree Required

C. See Licenses for Professional Educators, III, E, 1 and 2, above

II. Permanent Professional Administrative Certificate (remains valid unless surrendered, suspended or revoked for just cause)

A. Requirements for converting the Initial Professional Administrative Certificate to the Permanent Professional Administrative Certificate:

1. Six semester hours of appropriate renewal credit related to the public school program,

or

Master's degree plus 30 Salary Classification,

and

2. Five years of educational experience

a. Two years of experience must be in any, or a combination of, the specializations reflected on the Professional Administration Certificate

b. One year of experience must be completed in West Virginia

3. Recommendation of Superintendent

III. Temporary Administrative Certificate

A. Endorsed for Superintendent, Principal, and/or Supervisor of Instruction and shall indicate the specialization(s) and grade levels in which the holder may be assigned within the public schools

B. Issued to administrators who graduate from an out-of-state IHE or who are transferring credential from another state or country to complete the requirements for testing, if applicable, and to complete the Evaluation Leadership Institute.

C. Issued for one year valid until June 30 of the expiring year.

D. Three years of teaching/management experience

E. Master's Degree required

Student Support Certificates

I. School Counselor

A. Temporary Professional Student Support Certificate (valid 1 year, nonrenewable)

1. Issued to applicant who meets requirements for a Temporary Teaching Certificate (see Licenses for Professional Educators, II, above) and the following criteria:

a. Master's degree in Counseling from a regionally accredited IHE in a state other than West Virginia,

        b.   Successful completion of an accredited School Counseling Program, *and*

        c.   3.0 GPA.

B.   Initial Professional Student Support Certificate (valid 3 years)

    1.   Issued to applicant who meets the following criteria:

        a.   Master's degree in Counseling from an accredited IHE

        b.   Successful completion of an accredited School Counseling Program

        c.   West Virginia required Praxis exam

C.   Professional Student Support Certificate (valid 5 years).

    1.   Issued to applicant who meets the requirements for a Professional Five-Year Student Support Certificate

        a.   Two years of work experience (one of which must be completed within West Virginia) as a school counselor, *and*

        b.   Master's degree plus 30 Salary Classification *or*

            Six semester hours of college course work relating to public education, *or*

            Has reached 60 years of age.

D.   Permanent Professional Student Support Certificate

    1.   Issued to an applicant who meets the requirements for a Permanent Professional Teaching Certificate

        a.   Five years of educational work experience in the area/s for which certification is held, including 2 years work as a school counselor (1 year must be completed within West Virginia) *and*

        b.   Master's degree plus 30 Salary Classification, *or*

            Six semester hours of college course work relating to public education, *or*

            Has reached 60 years of age.

II. School Psychologist

A.   Temporary Professional Student Support Certificate

    1.   Issued to applicant who meets requirements for a Temporary Student Support Certificate

    2.   See School Counselor, I, A, directly above

B.   Initial Professional Student Support Certificate (valid 3 years)

    1.   Issued to applicant who completes master's degree in a field related to education from an accredited institution of higher education

    2.   See School Counselor I, B, directly above

C.   Professional Student Support Certificate (valid 5 years)

    1.   See School Counselor I, C, directly above

D.   Permanent Professional Student Support Certificate

    1.   See School Counselor I, D, directly above

III. Speech-Language Pathologist
    A. Temporary Student Support Certificate
        1. Issued to applicant who meets requirements for a Temporary Student Support Certificate
        2. See School Counselor, I, A, directly above
    B. Initial Professional Student Support Certificate
        1. Issued to applicant who earns a master's degree in an approved program in Speech-Language Pathology from a regionally accredited IHE
    C. See I, C and D, directly above
IV. Renewal of the Professional Student Support Certificate
    A. Application for renewal of the Professional Student Support Certificate for School Counselor, School Psychologist, and Speech-Language Pathologist must be submitted after January 1 of the year in which the license expires.
    B. The applicant for licensure must submit evidence of satisfying the following:
        1. Completed 6 semester hours of appropriate college/university course work related to the public school program with a minimum 3.0 GPA
        2. See Licenses For Professional Educators, V, B, above, except that requirements must be met in the 5-year period immediately preceding the date of application
V. Professional Five-Year Student Support Certificate
    A. Six semester hours of appropriate college/university course work reflecting a 3.0 GPA and related to the public school program,
        or
        Minimum of a master's plus 30 Salary Classification,
        and
    B. Two years of experience within 1 endorsement or a combination of endorsements, on the Initial Professional Student Support Certificate,
        and
    C. Recommendation of superintendent.
VI. Permanent Professional Student Support Certificate
    A. Five years of educational experience in areas for which certification is held; 1 year. must be completed in West Virginia
        and
    B. Master's degree related to the public school program,
        or
        Professional Five-Year Student Support Certificate,
        and
    C. Six semester hours of appropriate renewal credit reflecting a 3.0 GPA,
        or
        Minimum of a master's degree plus 30 Salary Classification,
        or
        Has reached 60 years of age,
        or
    D. NBPTS certification.

Wisconsin

Educator Standards

I. Teacher Standards: To receive a license to teach in Wisconsin, an applicant shall complete an approved program and demonstrate proficient performance in the knowledge, skills, and dispositions under all of the following standards:

A. The teacher understands the central concepts, tools of inquiry, and structures of the disciplines he or she teaches and can create learning experiences that make these aspects of subject matter meaningful for pupils.

B. The teacher understands how children with broad ranges of ability learn and provides instruction that supports their intellectual, social, and personal development.

C. The teacher understands how pupils differ in their approaches to learning and the barriers that impede learning and can adapt instruction to meet the diverse needs of pupils, including those with disabilities and exceptionalities.

D. The teacher understands and uses a variety of instructional strategies, including the use of technology, to encourage children's development of critical thinking, problem solving, and performance skills.

E. The teacher uses an understanding of individual and group motivation and behavior to create a learning environment that encourages positive social interaction, active engagement in learning, and self-motivation.

F. The teacher uses effective verbal and nonverbal communication techniques as well as instructional media and technology to foster active inquiry, collaboration, and supportive interaction in the classroom.

G. The teacher organizes and plans systematic instruction based upon knowledge of subject matter, pupils, the community, and curriculum goals.

H. The teacher understands and uses formal and informal assessment strategies to evaluate and ensure the continuous intellectual, social, and physical development of the pupil.

I. The teacher is a reflective practitioner who continually evaluates the effect of his or her choices and actions on pupils, parents, professionals in the learning community, and others, and who actively seeks out opportunities to grow professionally.

J. The teacher fosters relationships with school colleagues, parents, and agencies in the larger community to support pupil learning and well-being and acts with integrity, fairness, and in an ethical manner.

II. Administrator standards: To receive a license in a school administrator category, an applicant shall complete an approved program in school administration and demonstrate proficient performance in the knowledge, skills, and dispositions under all of the following standards:

A. The administrator has an understanding of and demonstrates competence in the teacher standards.

B.   The administrator leads by facilitating the development, articulation, implementation, and stewardship of a vision of learning that is shared by the school community.

C.   The administrator manages by advocating, nurturing, and sustaining a school culture and instructional program conducive to pupil learning and staff professional growth.

D.   The administrator ensures management of the organization, operations, finances, and resources for a safe, efficient, and effective learning environment.

E.   The administrator models collaborating with families and community members, responding to diverse community interests and needs, and mobilizing community resources.

F.   The administrator acts with integrity, fairness, and in an ethical manner.

G.   The administrator understands, responds to, and interacts with the larger political, social, economic, legal, and cultural context that affects schooling.

III.   Pupil Services Standards: To receive a license in a pupil services category (school counselors, school social workers, school psychologists, and school nurses), an applicant shall complete an approved program and demonstrate proficient performance in the knowledge, skills, and dispositions under all of the following standards:

A.   The pupil services professional understands the 10 Teacher Standards (see I, directly above).

B.   The pupil services professional understands the complexities of learning and has knowledge of comprehensive, coordinated practice strategies that support pupil learning, health, safety, and development.

C.   The pupil services professional has the ability to use research, research methods, and knowledge about issues and trends to improve practice in schools and classrooms.

D.   The pupil services professional understands and represents professional ethics and social behaviors appropriate for school and community.

E.   The pupil services professional understands the organization, development, management, and content of collaborative and mutually supportive pupil services programs within educational settings.

F.   The pupil services professional is able to address comprehensively the wide range of social, emotional, behavioral, and physical issues and circumstances which may limit pupils' abilities to achieve positive learning outcomes through development, implementation, and evaluation of system-wide interventions and strategies.

G.   The pupil services professional interacts successfully with pupils, parents, professional educators, employers, and community support systems such as juvenile justice, public health, human services, and adult education.

License Stages

I.   Initial Educator License (valid 5 years; nonrenewable)

A.   Prerequisites

1.   Bachelor's degree and completion of state-approved educator preparation program at a regionally accredited institution

        a.   Officer of the institution's state-approved educator preparation program must endorse applicant

        b.   Additional requirements/experience may be required for specific license areas.

   2.   Graduates of professional educator programs in a state or U.S. territory other than Wisconsin who have never held a Wisconsin educator license must submit an "out-of-state" application even if they currently reside in Wisconsin.

   3.   See "Testing Requirements," below, for full details

  B. Professional Development Plan (PDP) addressing 2 or more standards required for advancement

   1.   Pre-service portfolio may be used to inform Initial Educator PDP development

   2.   PDP goal is approved by a majority of 3-member Initial Educator PDP team, including an administrator, an institution of higher education (IHE) representative, and a peer (not a mentor). PDP team also verifies completion of the PDP.

   3.   Support to educator is provided by mentor, and feedback is provided from initial educator team.

   4.   School district must provide:

        a.   Collaboratively developed ongoing orientation to Initial Educator

        b.   Support seminars reflecting the standards and district goals

        c.   A trained mentor holding an appropriate license. The mentor is an educator and colleague trained to provide support, assistance, and feedback to initial educators and is not part of the formal employment evaluation process.

II. Professional Educator License (valid 5 years; renewable)

  A. Educators licensed before August 31, 2004, have been grandparented as Professional Educators

   1.   Grandparenting choice for license renewal: 6 credits or PDP

  B. Professional Development Plan shows proficiency in Wisconsin standards; used for license renewal by post-8/31/04 program completers.

   1.   Professional Development Team verifies PDP completion to the Wisconsin Department of Public Instruction (DPI).

        a.   PDP Review Team is composed of at least 3 licensed teachers, pupil service professionals, and/or administrators selected by their peers.

        b.   Convened at the discretion of the educator

   2.   Required components of PDP

        a.   Reflection

        b.   Describe school and assignment

        c.   Rationale for and goals addressing standards

        d.   Plan to assess achievement of goals

        e.   Plan to meet the goals, including objectives, activities, timelines, and collaboration

   3.   Required evidence of successful completion of PDP

        a.   Annual review of PDP by educator

        b.   Summary and reflection statement

      c.   Demonstrated increase in proficiency in standards

      d.   Growth indicators

      e.   How professional knowledge was improved by meeting goals

      f.   How student learning was improved by meeting goals

III.   Master Educator License Optional (valid 10 years; renewable): Optional

    A.   Mastery of Wisconsin standards in high-stakes portfolio assessment through the Wisconsin Master Educator Assessment Process (WMEAP) requiring:

      1.   Related master's degree

      2.   Demonstrated improvement in pupil learning

      3.   Assessment by DPI-trained WMEAP Team

      4.   Professional contributions

        or

    B.   National Board of Professional Teaching Standards Certification

IV.   Administrative License (valid 5 years)

    A.   Required of superintendents, directors of instruction, principals, directors of special education and pupil services, instructional library media supervisors, career and technical education coordinators, school business managers, instructional technology coordinators and reading specialists.

    B.   Prerequisites

      1.   Completion of approved graduate education program leading to licensure in specific administrative category

      2.   Except for school business manager and career and technical education coordinator license, all applicants must hold, or be eligible to hold, a Wisconsin:

        a.   Professional educator teaching license and have 3 years of successful teaching experience,

          or

        b.   Professional educator license in a pupil services category (school counselor, psychologist, or social worker), have 3 years successful experience in that category, and 540 hours of classroom instruction experience.

      3.   Satisfactory background check is required of all applicants.

Testing Requirements

Note: Effective September 1, 2013, Wisconsin's Educator Preparation Programs (EPP) may use one of the three college entrance tests (ACT, SAT, and GRE) as the standardized test of communication skills required for admission to EPPs. Only test scores that are less than 5 years old are allowable.

    I.   Praxis I: Pre-Professional Skills Tests (PPST)

      A.   Required for admission to all professional education programs and usually taken during first or second year of undergraduate work

      B.   Teachers applying for licenses in Wisconsin who complete professional education programs after August 31, 1992, at colleges and universities located in other states must submit passing scores on this or equivalent basic skills tests.

    C.   Qualifying scores for PPST or Computerized PPST tests are: reading—175; writing—174; and mathematics—173.

II.   Subject Assessments

    A.   All students who complete professional education programs after August 31, 2004, must take the Praxis II subject assessment specified for their license area(s) or the Language Testing International (LTI) American Council on the Teaching of Foreign Languages (ACTFL) tests.

        1.   All state-approved professional education programs in Wisconsin require student assessments of content knowledge that are determined by passing scores on the Praxis II or LTI ACTFL tests.

        2.   This requirement may not be waived for any reason, including but not limited to these:

            a.   Educators licensed prior to September 2004 returning to complete a license program in a new subject,

            b.   Educators licensed prior to September 2004 returning to complete programs to add on age levels that were not covered by their previous licenses,

            c.   All educators who complete initial licensing programs after August 31, 2004, and all subsequent programs (requiring a content test) that they complete,
and

            d.   Students completing licensing programs at the undergraduate and graduate levels.

        3.   Educators who complete state-approved professional education programs after August 31, 2004, in other states must document passing grades on the specific content test(s) required to obtain an Initial or Professional Educator License in their area.

    B.   Foundations of Reading Test

        1.   Effective for applicants who apply for licensure after January 31, 2014

        2.   Elementary, special education, reading teacher, and reading specialist licenses

    C.   Contact the team at the Wisconsin Department of Public Instruction (see Appendix 1) or http://tepdl.dpi.wi.gov/licensing/wisconsin-educator-testing -requirements for qualifying scores for specific licenses.

Wyoming

General Licensure Information

I. All teachers and administrators employed in a Wyoming school district must be licensed in accordance with state law. The Wyoming Professional Teaching Standards Board (PTSB) requires all Wyoming educators to have completed an approved teacher preparation program from an accredited institution of higher education (IHE) in order to become licensed to teach in a Wyoming school district.

II. There are 2 routes to teacher licensure in Wyoming.
   A. Traditional Route to Teacher Licensure requires the completion of a teacher preparation program from a regionally or nationally accredited IHE.
   B. Alternative Route to Teacher Licensure offers an alternative program for secondary licensure through the Northern Plains Transition to Teaching (NPTT) program located at Montana State University-Bozeman. The NPTT allows applicants to obtain work in a Wyoming school district while completing the teacher preparation course work necessary to become fully licensed.

Requirements for Initial Licensure

I. To obtain initial, first-time licensure, applicants must meet all the following requirements:
   A. Complete an approved teacher preparation program at a regionally or nationally accredited college or university. The program must:
      1. Include student teaching
      2. Lead to an institutional recommendation for licensure
   B. Submit an institutional recommendation for licensure, signed by an authorized official, recommending the applicant for licensure in the applicable endorsement area(s)
   C. Submit official college transcripts documenting completion of teacher preparation program
   D. Undergo fingerprinting and complete a background check
   E. Demonstrate knowledge of the U.S. and Wyoming constitutions either through course work or by successfully passing an exam
   F. Pass approved Praxis II exams in 2 teaching areas:
      1. Elementary Education—A passing score of 160 or better on Praxis II exam 5011/0011 "Elementary Education: Curriculum, Instruction, and Assessment"
      2. Social Studies Composite—A passing score of 158 or better on Praxis II exam 5081/0081 "Social Studies: Content Knowledge" for grades 6–12, and 5089/0089 "Middle School Social Studies" for grades 5–8
   G. Submit a complete application packet and pay appropriate fees

II.   To obtain licensure through the NPTT program prior to program completion:
  A.   Applicant must currently hold a bachelor's degree in a secondary teaching area, *and*

  Be employed by a Wyoming school district.
  B.   The applicant must meet all the requirements for an Exception Authorization.
III. Troops to Teachers
  A.   Wyoming also participates in the Troops-to-Teachers (TTT) program through the regional office located in Montana. Visit the TTT site (http://www.montana.edu/ttt) for more information.
IV.   Out-of-State Applicants
  A.   All out-of-state applicants are required to submit the documentation listed below in addition to their complete application packet, fingerprint cards, institutional recommendation (if applicable), and U.S. and Wyoming constitution requirements.
    1.   Verification of work history for the past 6 years, signed by each of the applicant's school administrators or board chairs during that time period
    2.   Copy of the applicant's current, valid teaching certificate or license from the state in which he or she taught
    3.   Copy of the applicant's test scores from Praxis II exam(s) or an equivalent exam from his or her state
    4.   In accordance with the NASDTEC Interstate Agreement, PTSB may require an out-of-state applicant to complete additional requirements to obtain a Wyoming teaching license.

Endorsements by Grade/Age Level

Endorsement(s) for which an applicant qualifies will appear on the Standard License. As determined by program approval standards, the endorsement(s) will allow teachers to provide instruction in the classroom or the school personnel to provide services in the areas identified on the license. Teaching endorsements are valid at the grade level for which they are issued.

  I.   Birth to Age 5: Early Childhood/Special Education
  II.   Birth to Age 8 (or Grade 3): Early Childhood
  III. Birth to Age 5: Preschool Early Childhood (excluding Kindergarten)
  IV.   Elementary Level K–6: art; elementary teacher; English as a second language; music; music instrumental; music vocal; reading; physical education; adapted physical education; institutional teacher, world languages
  V.   Middle Level 5–8: art; English as a second language; health; language arts; mathematics; music; music instrumental; music vocal; reading; physical education; adapted physical education; science; social studies; Spanish
  VI.   Secondary level 6–12: agriculture; anthropology; art; biology; business; chemistry; computer science; drama; driver's education; earth science; economics; English; English as a second language; family consumer science; geography; health; history; journalism; mathematics; music; music instrumental; music vocal; physical education; adapted physical education; physical science; physics; political science; psychology; reading;

social studies comprehensive; sociology; speech; trade and technical; at-risk/alternative teacher; institutional teacher; world language (Chinese, Japanese, French, Latin, German, Russian, Italian, Spanish)

VII.   K–12: art; audiology; educational diagnostician; English as a second language; health; gifted and talented; music; music instrumental; music vocal; physical education; adapted physical education; reading; institutional teacher; school nurse; world languages

VIII. Special Education K–6/ 5–8/ 6–12/ K–12: exceptional generalist; exceptional specialist—behavioral & emotional disabilities; exceptional specialist—cognitive disability; exceptional specialist—deaf and hard of hearing; exceptional specialist—learning disability; exceptional specialist—physical and health disability; exceptional specialist—visual disability

Additional School Personnel

I.   School Administrator (valid 5 years)
   A. An individual who holds a standard Wyoming educator license may apply to add a school administrator endorsement to his or her license.
   B. This endorsement allows individuals to serve as an administrator or superintendent in any Wyoming school in accordance with his or her grade level of preparation.
   C. The following school administrator endorsements are offered by PTSB:
      1. District superintendent
      2. School principal
      3. Program director
   D. Requirements:
      1. Hold Wyoming licensure in a teaching or related services field
      2. Have completed an educational leadership program, from a nationally or regionally accredited college/university, that leads to an institutional recommendation in educational leadership, school principal, educational administrator, or other equivalent endorsement areas
   E. Educators who are applying concurrently for initial licensure and a school administrator endorsement must submit a complete application for Initial, First-Time Licensure.

II.   School Librarian (valid 5 years)
   A. An individual with this endorsement is eligible to serve as a school librarian in a Wyoming K–12 school.
   B. Endorsement requires completion of a bachelor's degree in school library science, K–12.

III. School Counselor (valid 5 years)
   A. Endorsement requires an institutional recommendation indicating completion of a master's degree in school counseling

IV.   School Psychologist (valid 5 years)
   A. Endorsement requires an institutional recommendation indicating completion of a master's degree in school psychology

V.   School Social Worker (valid 5 years)
    A.   Endorsement requires an institutional recommendation indicating completion of a master's degree in school social work
VI. Speech Pathologist (valid 5 years)
    A.   Endorsement requires an institutional recommendation indicating completion of a master's degree in speech pathology

Appendix 1

How to Contact State Offices of Certification

Alabama
Teacher Certification Section
  Office of Teaching and Leading
State Department of Education
5215 Gordon Persons Building
P.O. Box 302101
Montgomery, AL 36130-2101
334-353-8567
334-242-9998 (fax)
www.alsde.edu
tcert@alsde.edu

Alaska
Alaska Dept. of Education & Early
  Development
Attn: Teacher Certification
801 West 10th Street, Suite 200, P.O.
  Box 110500
Juneau, AK 99811-0500
907-465-2831
907-465-2800 (TTY/TTD)
907-465-2441 (fax)
http://www.eed.state.ak.us/teacher
  certification
tcwebmail@alaska.gov

Arizona
Arizona Dept. of Education
Educator Certification
http://www.azed.gov/educator-
  certification

Phoenix Office
P.O. Box 6490
Phoenix, AZ 85005-6490 (mail)
1535 W. Jefferson St.
Phoenix, AZ 85007 (walk-in)
602-542-4367 (8:30-4:30)
Certification@azed.gov

Arkansas
Office of Educator Licensure
State Dept. of Education
Four Capitol Mall, Room 106B
Little Rock, AR 72201-1071
501-682-4342 (8–4:30)
501-682-4898 (fax)
http://ArkansasEd.org

California
Commission on Teacher
  Credentialing
1900 Capitol Avenue
Sacramento, CA 95811-4213
916-322-4974 (12:30–4:30)
916-327-3166 (fax)
www.ctc.ca.gov
credentials@ctc.ca.gov

Colorado
Department of Education
Professional Services & Educator
  Licensure
6000 E Evans Ave
Building #2. Suite 100
Denver, CO 80222
303-866-6628
303-866-6866 (fax)
http://www.cde.state.co.us/cdeprof
educator.licensing@cde.state.co.us

Connecticut
Bureau of Educator Standards &
  Certification
State Department of Education
P.O. Box 150471, Room 243
Hartford, CT 06115-0471
860-713-6969 (12–4, M, T, Th, F)
860-713-7017 (fax)
www.sde.ct.gov/sde/cert
teacher.cert@ct.gov

Delaware
Educator Licensure and
  Certification
Department of Education
Collette Education Resource Center
35 Commerce Way, Suite 1
Dover, DE 19904
302-857-3388 (8–4:30, M–F)
888-759-9133 (toll free)
http://www.doe.k12.de.us
deeds@doe.k12.de.us

District of Columbia
Office of the State Superintendent of
  Education
Educator Licensure & Accreditation
810 First St., NE, 8th Floor
Washington, DC 20002
202-741-5881
http://osse.dc.gov/service/educator
  -licensure-services
educator.licensurehelp@dc.gov

Florida
Bureau of Educator
  Certification
Department of Education
325 W. Gaines Street
Turlington Bldg., Suite 201
Tallahassee, FL 32399-0400
800-445-6739 (in U.S.)
850-245-5049 (outside U.S.)
http://www.fldoe.org/edcert
Submit e-mail on website

Georgia
Professional Standards Commission
Educator Certification Division
200 Piedmont Ave., Suite 1702
Atlanta, GA 30334-9032
800-869-7775 (7–4:30 M, W, F)
404-232-2500
404-232-2560 (fax)
http://www.gapsc.com
mail@gapsc.com

Hawaii
Hawaii Teacher Standards Board
650 Iwilei Road, Suite 201
Honolulu, HI 96817
808-586-2600 (7:45 – 4:30)
808-586-2606 (fax)
http://www.htsb.org
licensingsection@htsb.org

Idaho
Certification/Professional Standards
    Commission
State Department of Education
650 W. State St., P.O. Box 83720
Boise, ID 83720-0027
208-332-6881/2
800-432-4601 (toll-free)
208-334-2228 (fax)
http://www.sde.idaho.gov/site/
    teacher_certification
jbjensen@sde.idaho.gov

Illinois
Illinois State Board of Education
Educator Licensure Division
100 North First Street
Springfield, IL 62777-0001
217-557-6763
http://www.isbe.net/certification/
    default.htm
Submit on website

Indiana
Educator Licensing and
    Development
Indiana Department of Education
115 W. Washington Street
South Tower, Suite 600
Indianapolis, IN 46204
317-232-9010
866-542-3672
317-232-9023 (fax)
http://www.doe.in.gov/licensing
licensinghelp@doe.in.gov

Iowa
Board of Educational Examiners
Grimes State Office Building
400 East 14th Street
Des Moines, IA 50319-0147
515-281-3245
515-281-7669 (fax)
http://www.boee.iowa.gov

Kansas
Teacher Licensure and Accreditation
Kansas State Department of
    Education
Landon State Office Building
900 SW Jackson Ave. Ste 106
Topeka, KS 66612-1182
785-291-3678
785-296-2288 (automated syst)
785-296-7933 (fax)
http://www.ksde.org

Kentucky
Education Professional Standards
    Board
Division of Certification
100 Airport Road, 3rd Floor
Frankfort, KY 40601
502-564-4606
888-598-7667
502-564-7080 (fax)
502-564-5845 Help Desk
http://www.epsb.ky.gov
dcert@ky.gov

Louisiana
Louisiana Department of Education
Certification, Preparation &
    Recruitment
P.O. Box 94064
Baton Rouge, LA 70804-9064
877-453-2721 (toll-free)
www. teachlouisiana.net
www.louisianabelieves.com/
    resources/ask-ldoe

Maine
Certification Office
Department of Education
23 State House Station
Augusta, ME 04333-0023
207-624-6603
207-624-6604 (fax)
www.maine.gov/doe/cert
cert.doe@maine.gov

Maryland
Certification Branch
Maryland State Department of
    Education
200 West Baltimore Street
Baltimore, MD 21201-2595
410-767-0412
866-772-8922 (toll-free)
410-333-6442 (TTY-TDD)
http://www.mdcert.org

Massachusetts
Department of Elementary and
    Secondary Education (ESE)
Office of Educator Licensure
75 Pleasant Street
Malden, MA 02148-4906
781-338-6600 (2–5 pm)
781-338-3391 (fax)
781-338-3000 (24/7 automated)
http://www.doe.mass.edu/educators

Michigan
Office of Professional Preparation
    Services
Michigan Department of Education
608 West Allegan Street
P.O. Box 30008
Lansing, MI 48909
517-373-3310
517-373-0542 (fax)
http://www.michigan.gov/
    teachercert

Minnesota
Educator Licensing
State Department of Education
1500 Highway 36 West
Roseville, MN 55113-4266
651-582-8691
651-582-8201 (TTY)
651-582-8809 (fax)
http://education.state.mn.us/MDE/
    EdExc/Licen/index.html
mde.educator-licensing@state.mn.us

Mississippi
Office of Educator Licensure
Mississippi Department of
    Education
359 North West Street, P.O. Box 771
Jackson, MS 39205-0771
601-359-3483
601-359-2778 (fax)
http://www.mde.k12.ms.us/
    educator–licensure
teachersupport@mde.k12.ms.us

Missouri
Educator Certification
Dept. of Elementary & Secondary
  Education
P.O. Box 480
Jefferson City, MO 65102-0480
573-751-0051
573-526-3580 (fax)
http://dese.mo.gov/eq/cert/index
  .html
certification@dese.mo.gov

Montana
Educator Licensure
Office of Public Instruction
P.O. Box 202501
Helena, MT 59620-2501
406-444-3150
406-444-0743 (fax)
http://www.opi.mt.gov/cert
cert@mt.gov

Nebraska
Teacher Certification
Nebraska Department of Education
301 Centennial Mall South
P.O. Box 94987
Lincoln, NE 68509-4987
402-471-0739
402-471-2496 (elec voice mail)
402-742-2359 (fax)
http://www.education.ne.gov/tcert
nde.tcertweb@nebraska.gov

Nevada
Teacher Licensure, Southern Nevada
Nevada Department of Education
9890 South Maryland Parkway,
  Suite 221, Room 234
Las Vegas, NV 89183
702-486-6458 (1–4:30 pm)
702-486-6450 (fax)
http://nvteachers.doe.nv.gov
license@doe.nv.gov

Teacher Licensure, Northern Nevada
700 East Fifth Street
Carson City, NV 89701-5906
775-687-9115
775-687-9101 (fax)

New Hampshire
Bureau of Credentialing
State Department of Education
Division of Program Support
101 Pleasant Street
Concord, NH 03301-3860
603-271-2408
603-271-4134 (fax)
http://www.education.nh.gov
Judith.Fillion@doe.nh.gov

New Jersey
New Jersey Department of
  Education
Office of Licensure and Credentials
P.O. Box 500
Trenton, NJ 08625-0500
609-292-2070 (8 am–3:30 pm M–F)
609-292-3768 (fax)
http://www.state.nj.us/education/
  educators/license

New Mexico
Professional Licensure Bureau
New Mexico Public Education
  Department
300 Don Gaspar
Santa Fe, NM 87501-2786
505-827-6587 (for app status)
505-827-5821 (help desk)
505-827-4148 (fax)
http://www.ped.state.nm.us/licensure
LicensureUnit@state.nm.us

New York
Office of Teaching Initiatives
New York State Education
  Department
89 Washington Avenue, 5N EB
Albany, NY 12234
518-474-3901 (M–F 9–4:30)
518-486-6041 (TEACH Online
  System Help Line)
http://www.highered.nysed.gov/tcert

North Carolina
Department of Public Instruction
Licensure Section
6365 Mail Service Center
Raleigh, NC 27699-6365
919-807-3310 (out of state)
800-577-7994 (in-state only)
http://www.NCPublicSchools.org/
  licensure/
asklicensure@dpi.nc.gov

North Dakota
Education Standards & Practices
  Board
Teacher Licensure
2718 Gateway Ave., Suite 303
Bismarck, ND 58503-0585
701-328-9641
701-328-9647 (fax)
www.ND.gov/espb
espbinfo@nd.gov

North Dakota Dept. of Public
  Instruction
School Approval & Accreditation
Teacher Credentials
600 E. Boulevard Ave., Dept. 201
Bismarck, ND 58505-0440
701-328-2260
701-328-2461 (fax)
http://www.dpi.state.nd.us

Ohio
Office of Educator Licensure
Ohio Department of Education
25 South Front St., Mail Stop 105
Columbus, OH 43215-4183
614-466-3593
877-644-6338 (toll-free)
www.education.ohio.gov
Educator.Licensure@education
  .ohio.gov

Oklahoma
Teacher Certification
State Department of Education
2500 N. Lincoln Blvd., Rm. 212
Oklahoma City, OK 73105-4599
405-521-3337
405-522-1520 (fax)
http://www.ok.gov/sde
jeff.smith@sde.ok.gov

Oregon
Teacher Standards and Practices
  Commission
250 Division St. NE
Salem, OR 97301-1012
503-378-3586
503-378-6961 (TDD)
503-378-4448 (fax)
http://www.oregon.gov/tspc
contact.tspc@state.or.us

Pennsylvania
PA Department of Education
Bureau of School Leadership and
  Teacher Quality
333 Market Street
Harrisburg, PA 17126-0333
717-728-3224, 717-787-3356
  (8–4:30, M, W, F)
http://www.education.state.pa.us
Submit e-mail on website

Rhode Island
Office of Educator Quality and
  Certification
State Department of Education
255 Westminster St.
Providence, RI 02903-3400
401-222-8892
http://www.ride.ri.gov/
  TeachersAdministrators/
  EducatorCertification.aspx
Submit e-mail on website

South Carolina
Office of Educator Services
Department of Education
8301 Parklane Road
Columbia, SC 29223
803-896-0325 (1–4:30pm)
877-885-5280 (toll-free)
803-896-0368 (fax)
http://ed.sc.gov/agency/se/
  educator-services/Licensure
licensure@ed.sc.gov

South Dakota
Department of Education
Certification Office
800 Governors Drive
Pierre, SD 57501-2291
605-773-3426
605-773-6139 (fax)
http://doe.sd.gov/oatq/teachercert
  .aspx
certification@state.sd.us

Tennessee
Tennessee Department of Education
Office of Educator Licensing
12th Floor, Andrew Johnson Tower
710 James Robertson Parkway
Nashville, TN 37243-0377
615-532-4885
615-532-1448 (fax)
http://www.tennessee.gov/
  education/lic
education.licensing@tn.gov

Texas
Texas Education Agency
Educator Certification
1701 N. Congress Ave., Suite 5-100
Austin, TX 78701-1494
512-936-8400
512-936-8277 (fax)
http://www.tea.state.tx.us
Submit e-mail on website

Utah
Teaching and Learning Licensing
State Office of Education
250 East 500 South
P.O. Box 144200
Salt Lake City, UT 84114-4200
801-538-7740
801-538-7973 (fax)
http://www.schools.utah.gov/cert
travis.rawlings@schools.utah.gov

Vermont
Educator Licensing Office
Vermont Agency of Education
1311 U.S. Route 302
Berlin, VT 05641
802-828-2445 (7:45 am–4:30 pm)
802-828-5107 (fax)
http://education.vermont.gov/
  licensing
AOE.LicensingInfo@state.vt.us

Virginia
Virginia Department of Education
Division of Teacher Education and
  Licensure
P.O. Box 2120
Richmond, VA 23218-2120
804-225-2022
804-530-4510 (fax)
http://www.doe.virginia.gov/
  teaching/licensure/index.shtml
licensure@doe.virginia.gov

Washington
Professional Certification Office
Old Capitol Building
600 Washington Street, S.E.
P.O. Box 47200
Olympia, WA 98504-7200
360-725-6400
360-664-3631 (TTY)
360-586-0145 (fax)
http://www.k12.wa.us/certification/
  TeacherMain.aspx
cert@k12.wa.us

West Virginia
Office of Professional Preparation
Building 6, Room 722
1900 Kanawha Blvd., East
Charleston, WV 25305-0330
304-558-7010
800-982-2378
304-558-7843 (fax)
http://wvde.state.wv.us/certification
mfmiller@access.k12.wv.us

Wisconsin
Teacher Education, Professional
  Development & Licensing
Department of Public Instruction
125 S. Webster St., P.O. Box 7841
Madison, WI 53707-7841
608-266-1027
800-266-1027
608-264-9558 (fax)
http://tepdl.dpi.wi.gov
licensing@dpi.wi.gov

Wyoming
Professional Teaching Standards
  Board
State of Wyoming
1920 Thomes Avenue, Suite 400
Cheyenne, WY 82002
307-777-7291
800-675-6893
307-777-8718 (fax)
http://ptsb.state.wy.us
ptsbtemp@wyo.gov

Appendix 2

Addresses for Certification Information for U.S. Possessions and Territories

American Samoa
American Samoa Department of
  Education (Utulei)
Pago Pago, AS 96799
Phone: (684) 633-5237
Fax: (684) 633-4240
http://www.doe.as

**Commonwealth of Northern
  Mariana Islands**
CNMI Public School System
P.O. Box 501370
Commonwealth of Northern
  Mariana Islands
  Bwughos Street, Susupe
Saipan, MP 96950
Board of Education phone: (670)
  237-3027
Board of Education fax: (670) 664-
  3711
http://www.cnmipss.org

Federated States of Micronesia
FSM Department of Education
P.O. Box PS 87
Palikir, Pohupei, FM 96941
Phone: (691) 320-2609
Fax: (691) 320-5500
http://www.fsmed.fm

Guam
Guam Commission for Educator
  Certification
Office: University of Guam School
  of Education, Room 105 (1st Flr)
Mail: UOG Station-SOE Bldg,
  Room 105, Mangilao, Guam
  96923
Phone: 671-735-2554
Fax: 671-735-2569
http://gcec.guam.gov/

Marshall Islands
Ministry of Education
P.O. Box 3
Majuro, Marshall Islands 96960
(692) 625-5261/5262
www.gooverseas.com/teach-abroad/
  marshall-islands

Palau
Palau does not currently have a
  teacher certification system.
Bureau of Education
Emery Wenty, Director
Ministry of Education
P.O. Box 189
Koror, Palau 96940
Tel. (680) 488–2489/2567/4220
Fax. (680) 488–8465
http://palaugov.org/bureau-of
  -education/
Email: ewenty@palaumoe.net

Puerto Rico
Board of Education of Puerto Rico
  (CEPR)
P.O. Box 19900
San Juan PR 00910-1900
Phone: (787) 641-7100
Fax: (787) 641-2573
http://www.de.gobierno.pr/tags/
  certificacion-de-maestros
http://www.ce.pr.gov/

Virgin Islands
http://www.teachusvi.net/
  certification.htm
Virgin Islands Board of Education
  (St. Thomas)
P.O. Box 11900 Dronningens Gade
  Nos. 60B, 61 and 62
St. Thomas, VI 00801
Phone: (340) 774-4546
Fax: (340) 774-3384

Virgin Islands Board of Education
  (St. Croix)
Sunny Isles Professional Building,
  Suite #5 & 6
St. Croix, VI 00820
Phone: (340) 772-4144
Fax: (340) 772-2895

**United States Department of
  Defense Education Activity**
DoDEA Headquarters
4800 Mark Center Drive
Alexandria, VA 22350-1400
Human Resources Recruitment and
  Staffing: (571) 372-0576
http://www.dodea.edu/offices/hr/
  employment/categories/index.cfm